The Complete Guide
to Becoming
a U.S. Citizen

The Complete Guide
to Becoming
a U.S. Citizen

Eve P. Steinberg, M.A.

Macmillan • USA

*Dedicated to Gabriella,
who served as the inspiration for Curla*

First Edition

Macmillan General Reference
A Prentice Hall Macmillan Company
15 Columbus Circle
New York, NY 10023

Copyright © 1994 by Arco Publishing, a division
of Simon & Schuster, Inc.
All rights reserved
including the right of reproduction
in whole or in part in any form

An Arco Book

MACMILLAN is a registered trademark of Macmillan, Inc.
ARCO is a registered trademark of Prentice-Hall, Inc.

Library of Congress Cataloging-in-Publication Data

Steinberg, Eve P.
  The complete guide to becoming a U.S. citizen / Eve P. Steinberg.
    p. cm.
  At head of title: ARCO
  "An Arco book"—T.p. verso.
  ISBN 0-671-89291-6
  1. Americanization. 2. Citizenship. 3. Civics. 4. United States—
Politics and government. I. Arco Publishing. II. Title. III. Title:
Complete guide to becoming a United States citizen.
JK1758.S83 1994   94-32804
323.6'0973—dc20   CIP

Manufactured in the United States of America

10 9 8 7 6 5 4 3 2 1

Contents

Introduction

Here you are in the United States, and you think it is a great country. In fact, you like it so well that you would like to stay forever and become a citizen. Just wanting to become a citizen is not sufficient. You must fulfill certain requirements, complete many forms, and follow detailed procedures. The process may be a complicated and lengthy one, but the goal of citizenship is worth the effort. This book will help you work your way step-by-step from the status of legal visitor or legal resident to that of citizen of the United States of America.

You will notice the use of the word "legal." There are a few special instances in which a person who is in the United States without legal status can become a citizen, but these are very few and are not addressed in this book. This book is intended to serve as a handbook for people who are already in the United States and who have entered by legal means and have maintained legal status.

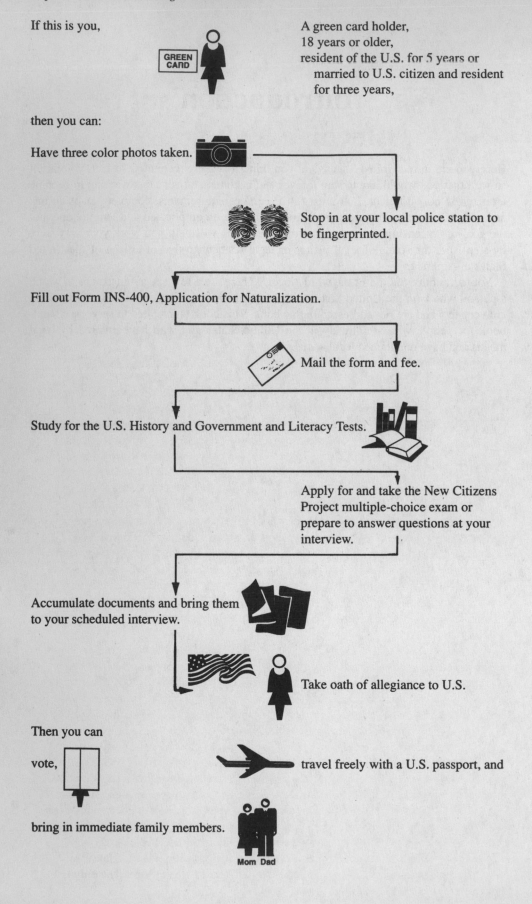

If this is you,

A green card holder,
18 years or older,
resident of the U.S. for 5 years or
    married to U.S. citizen and resident
    for three years,

then you can:

Have three color photos taken.

Stop in at your local police station to
be fingerprinted.

Fill out Form INS-400, Application for Naturalization.

Mail the form and fee.

Study for the U.S. History and Government and Literacy Tests.

Apply for and take the New Citizens
Project multiple-choice exam or
prepare to answer questions at your
interview.

Accumulate documents and bring them
to your scheduled interview.

Take oath of allegiance to U.S.

Then you can

vote,

travel freely with a U.S. passport, and

bring in immediate family members.

Why You Should Want to Become a Citizen

If asked why you wish to remain in the United States, you could quickly respond with a large number of reasons. You might say that this a beautiful country or that much of your family is here and that you would like to remain with these close family members. You might mention the economic opportunities open to you and your hopes for a better quality of life than that which was possible for you in the country from which you came. You might speak of war or famine or political oppression in your previous home country. It is easy to think of really good reasons for wanting to stay here. Can you just as easily state your reasons for wanting to become a citizen?

- A citizen has the privilege of participating in the government of his or her school district, locality, state, and nation. This participation includes nominating candidates, voting for candidates, and even holding office. (A naturalized citizen may hold any elected office except those of President and Vice-President.)
- A U.S. citizen is entitled to carry a U.S. passport. Many countries will admit the holder of a U.S. passport for purposes of tourism or business without requiring a visa. A resident of the United States who has maintained foreign citizenship must regularly renew the foreign passport and must apply for visas for visits to many foreign countries. Applying for visas is usually inconvenient, time-consuming, and costly. U.S. citizenship simplifies travel.
- A U.S. citizen is free to live outside of the United States for an unlimited period of time for purposes of business or pleasure. A legal permanent resident, that is, a "Green Card" holder, may not remain outside of the United States for more than one year except under special circumstances and with special permission. In other words, life is less complicated and less restricted for the United States citizen.
- A U.S. citizen can enjoy the services of U.S. Embassies and Consulates abroad. Emergencies can occur, and it is reassuring to come under the protection of U.S. officials.
- Most jobs in the U.S. Civil Service are reserved for U.S. citizens. Civil Service employment offers security, good wages, excellent growth opportunities, and many other benefits. You might think of your U.S. citizenship as a passport to economic success. Citizenship is also required for employment in state and local law enforcement positions. This means that if you would like to serve as a police officer or correction officer, for example, you must first become a citizen.
- A U.S citizen is entitled to bring members of his or her immediate family into the United States as permanent "Green Card" residents without regard to any quota or preference requirements. Immediate family members include parents of a citizen who is over 21 years of age, spouse of a citizen, and children under the age of 21 with at least one U.S. citizen parent. Noncitizen permanent residents must wait for a number in a preference category to bring in these same family members.
- A final benefit of citizenship is immunity from deportation. We sincerely hope that you will be a law-abiding citizen in every way, but should you commit a crime as a naturalized citizen, your penalty will not be deportation. The only U.S.

citizen who is subject to deportation is the individual who achieved citizenship through fraudulent statements.

Along with the rights and privileges of citizenship come certain responsibilities. Citizens have a duty to inform themselves about issues and candidates. They should read, listen, and involve themselves, speaking up and voting regularly. All Americans should obey the laws, pay their taxes, and behave responsibly with respect to the environment. When called upon to sit on juries, citizens should serve willingly and thoughtfully; and, in times of national emergency, citizens should be willing to serve in the armed forces or some appropriate alternative.

An immigration examiner or judge may ask you about the duties that accompany American citizenship and may ask you if you willingly accept these duties. The examiner may also ask you why you want to be a citizen. Reread this chapter before you go for your final hearing. Think about what citizenship means to you so that you will be prepared to answer these questions.

What to Do if You Are Currently a Nonimmigrant

STAY LEGAL

Whatever your current status is, do not let it expire. The person who has allowed his or her legal permission to lapse is at a disadvantage as an applicant for permanent status and later for citizenship. Be careful to fulfill all the conditions of your current visa and do not violate any of its restrictions.

WATCH DATES

Until you become a citizen of the United States, you are the citizen of some other country. Your passport is the passport of the country of your citizenship. Your passport must remain up-to-date. This means that you must take note of its expiration date and take steps to renew regularly. Since you are not physically in the country that issued the passport, you must deal with that country's consulate in the United States for purposes of passport renewal. The process may take considerably longer than you expect. As you approach a date six months from your passport's expiration date, you should contact your country's consulate, make inquiries, and begin the renewal application process.

The I-94 card that you received at your port of entry to the United States is stamped with the date of arrival and with the date by which you must leave. Keep track of that date and do not let it pass. You will lose your legal status if you overstay the date on your I-94. If you extend your visa or change your nonimmigrant status to a visa that permits you to remain for a longer period of time, you will have to turn in your I-94 card to the Immigration and Naturalization Service (INS) for updating. When you get your I-94 card back from INS, check to make certain that the new date has been entered accurately. Follow-through is your responsibility. Be alert and insistent.

If you are in the United States on a temporary visa of any kind, you must be careful not to let that visa expire. Visitors' visas — B-1 visas for business purposes and B-2 visas for tourists only — which are valid for six months can be renewed for another six-month period. The holder of a B-2 visa who finds the perfect college or technical school and decides to remain to complete his or her education can, if accepted to the school, convert the B-2 visa to a student visa — F-1 for an academic or language program, M-1 for a vocational or technical program. A student visa is valid until the program of study is fully completed. You maintain your status as long as you remain in school.

There are a number of other temporary visas, among them J-1 visas for exchange students, E-1 visas for treaty traders, E-2 visas for treaty investors, L-1 visas for intracompany transfers, H-1A visas for registered nurses as temporary workers, H-1B visas for temporary workers in other professions, H-2B visas for temporary nonagricultural workers, H-3 visas for trainees, K-1 visas for fiancés of U.S. citizens coming for the purpose of getting married, and O, P, Q, and R visas for temporary workers in selected occupations. Each of these visas, as well as those not listed here, is defined by certain requirements and limitations.

DO NOT VIOLATE THE TERMS
OF YOUR VISA

Some of these visas are designed for the purpose of permitting their holders to work in the United States. Others specifically prohibit the holder from working. In fact, some temporary visas will be issued only to applicants who submit proof that they have access to adequate funds to support themselves while in this country so that they will not need to work. Most student visas and tourist visas fall into this category.

If your visa restricts you from working but you manage to find and accept a job, you are violating the terms of your visa. In effect, you are endangering your legal status. Don't do it! You may be seriously endangering your chances for citizenship. If circumstances have changed and you must earn money for, let's say, living expenses while in school, you may make special application for permission to work. Your school can help you by filing form I-538, Certification by Designated School Official. If you are in the United States legally, find that you must work, and are not a student, you may file form I-765, Application for Employment Authorization. (You will find copies of both these forms in the forms appendix.) Once permission is granted, you may work despite the restrictions originally attached to your visa.

DO NOT HURRY TO MAKE CHANGES

Even though it is relatively easy to extend the effective period of a visa or to convert from, let us say, a tourist visa to a student visa, you should not apply to make any changes in the first three months of your stay in the United States. Regardless of your total honesty in originally applying for a six-month visitor's visa, if you attempt to extend the term or change the visa too quickly, the Immigration and Naturalization Service (INS) may misinterpret your intentions. The INS is likely to assume that you really intended to stay in this country for a much longer period. If the INS suspects that you misstated your intentions, it may not believe other statements you make when you apply for immigrant status and may make the whole process more difficult for you.

After you have been in the United States for three months, you can apply for a visa extension or change without arousing suspicion. It is assumed that three months is a long enough period in which you might reasonably change your mind or discover legitimate reasons to remain in another capacity.

You may find the whole process easier to understand by following the story of a case illustration. Your own situation will be different, of course, but Carla's story is not an unusual one.

Carla Rojas at the age of 15 was an Argentine citizen with an Argentine passport. Carla's mother received a grant from the Argentine government to come to the United States as an exchange student for special training to make her a more effective English teacher in Argentina. As an exchange student, Carla's mother was issued a J-1 visa which would be valid for the two-year duration of her course. The terms of the grant included both tuition and living expenses, so there was no need for her to seek permission to work. As a dependent child, Carla accompanied her mother. Carla was issued a J-2 visa. While her mother attended college classes as provided in her grant, Carla attended the local public high school in the same town in which the university was located and earned a high school diploma.

At the end of the two-year period, Carla's mother prepared to return to Argentina, but Carla wanted to stay in the United States. Carla applied to another local university that offered a cooperative work-study program in her field of interest, pre-school education, and was accepted into the freshman class. The work-study program would cover Carla's college costs but not her living expenses. Carla then arranged with Dr. and Mrs. Turner to live in their home and care for their children in exchange for room and board. Dr. and Mrs. Turner had come to know and respect Carla and her mother over the previous two years and were delighted at the prospect of having Carla with them and their children.

There was no INS office in the town in which Carla was living, so she wrote to the nearest INS office, which happened to be located in a not-too-distant city. Carla asked for the following forms:

I-539 Application to Extend/Change Nonimmigrant Status
I-134 Affidavit of Support

Carla's completed Form I-539 begins on page 8.

Carla then made photocopies of the completed forms I-539 and I-134 and a copy of the I-94 card she had received from INS officers at the airport when she first arrived in the United States. The I-94 card, stamped with date of entry, date of intended departure, and nonimmigrant status category, would serve as proof that Carla had entered and remained in the United States legally. Carla hated to let that card out of her possession, but she had to send it along with her request for change of status so that it could be updated by the INS. The INS would change the date on the card to reflect her new status as holder of an F-1 visa and would stamp it with a new date showing that an extension of her stay had been granted. The I-94 card would be returned to her with the mailing label she prepared to enclose with her application packet. She also photocopied her passport, including its expiration date, her birth certificate, and her high school diploma. Carla mailed the originals of forms I-539 and I-134 and her I-94 card, photocopies of the supporting documents and of her form I-20, and the required filing fee by certified mail, return receipt requested, to the INS Regional Service Center nearest the town in which she was living.

You will note that Carla mailed photocopies of documents which might prove impossible or very difficult to replace while mailing originals of the forms which she and Dr. Turner had completed. INS always wants originals with "live" handwritten signatures on its own forms; all other documents should be submitted as photocopies unless the original is specifically requested, as is the case with the I-94 card. Carla filed a photocopy of her student copy of I-20 for purposes of submitting a complete package. The college should have filed an original document directly with INS. Carla also went to the expense of mailing the package by certified mail with return receipt requested. Mail sometimes does go astray. The mailing receipt proves the fact and date of mailing. The delivery receipt proves the fact and date that the packet was received by INS. Establishing these dates can save your application in situations governed by a time deadline. Papers do get lost in transit and in government offices. Keep copies of every paper that passes through your hands and staple to each packet of copies official proofs of mailing and receipt.

U.S. Department of Justice
Immigration and Naturalization Service

OMB #1115-0093
Application to Extend/ChangeNonimmigrant Status

START HERE - Please Type or Print

Part 1. Information about you.

Family Name ROJAS	Given Name CARLA	Middle Initial A.

Address - In Care of:

Street # and Name **1504 High Street** Apt. # **4-D**

City **Madison** State **New Jersey**

Zip Code **07941**

Date of Birth (month/day/year) June 6, 1966	Country of Birth Argentina
Social Security # (if any) none	A# (if any) none
Date of Last Arrival Into the U.S. Aug. 20, 1981	I-94# 133-56210988
Current Nonimmigrant Status J-2	Expires on (month/day/year) Sept. 1, 1983

Part 2. Application Type.   (See instructions for fee.)

1. **I am applying for:** (check one)
   a. ☐ an extension of stay in my current status
   b. ☒ a change of status. The new status I am requesting is: **F-1**
2. **Number of people included in this application:** (check one)
   a. ☒ I am the only applicant
   b. ☐ Members of my family are filing this application with me. The Total number of people included in this application is (complete the supplement for each co-applicant) _____

Part 3. Processing Information.

1. I/We request that my/our current or requested status be extended until (month/day/year) **Sept. 1, 1987**
2. Is this application based on an extension or change of status already granted to your spouse, child or parent?
   ☒ No   ☐ Yes (receipt # _____)
3. Is this application being filed based on a separate petition or application to give your spouse, child or parent an extension or change of status?
   ☒ No   ☐ Yes, filed with this application   ☐ Yes, filed previously and pending with INS
4. If you answered yes to question 3, give the petitioner or applicant name:

If the application is pending with INS, also give the following information.

Office filed at _____ Filed on _____ (date)

Part 4. Additional information.

1. For applicant #1, provide passport information:

Country of issuance Argentina	Valid to: (month/day/year) Oct. 30, 1990

2. Foreign address:

Street # and Name **1160 Camino Cruz Blanca** Apt# **1**

City or Town Buenos Aires	State or Province Pampas
Country Argentina	Zip or Postal Code n/a

Form I-539 (Rev. 12-2-91)   ***Continued on back.***

FOR INS USE ONLY

Returned	Receipt
Date _____ _____	

Resubmitted

Date _____ _____

Reloc Sent

Date _____ _____

Reloc Rec'd

Date _____

Date _____

☐ Applicant Interviewed

☐ *Extension Granted* to (date): _____

☐ *Change of Status/Extension Granted*
New Class: _____   To (date): _____

If denied:
☐ Still within period of stay
☐ V/D to: _____
☐ S/D to: _____
☐ Place under docket control

Remarks

Action Block

To Be Completed by *Attorney or Representative*, if any
☐ Fill in box if G-28 is attached to represent the applicant

VOLAG# _____

ATTY State License # _____

Part 4.   Additional Information. *(continued)*

3. Answer the following questions. If you answer yes to any question, explain on separate paper.	Yes	No
a. Are you, or any other person included in this application, an applicant for an immigrant visa or adjustment of status to permanent residence?		X
b. Has an immigrant petition ever been filed for you, or for any other person included in this application?		X
c. Have you, or any other person included in this application ever been arrested or convicted of any criminal offense since last entering the U.S.?		X
d. Have you, or any other person included in this application done anything which violated the terms of the nonimmigrant status you now hold?		X
e. Are you, or any other person included in this application, now in exclusion or deportation proceedings?		X
f. Have you, or any other person included in this application, been employed in the U.S. since last admitted or granted an extension or change of status?		X

If you answered YES to question 3f, give the following information on a separate paper: Name of person, name of employer, address of employer, weekly income, and whether specifically authorized by INS.

If you answered NO to question 3f, fully describe how you are supporting yourself on a separate paper. Include the source and the amount and basis for any income.

Part 5.   Signature. *Read the information on penalties in the instructions before completing this section. You must file this application while in the United States.*

I certify under penalty of perjury under the laws of the United States of America that this application, and the evidence submitted with it, is all true and correct. I authorize the release of any information from my records which the Immigration and Naturalization Service needs to determine eligibility for the benefit I am seeking.

Signature *Carla A. Rojas*	Print your name Carla A. Rojas	Date June 12, 1983

Please Note: *If you do not completely fill out this form, or fail to submit required documents listed in the instructions, you cannot be found eligible for the requested document and this application will have to be denied.*

Part 6.   Signature of person preparing form if other than above. *(Sign below)*

I declare that I prepared this application at the request of the above person and it is based on all information of which I have knowledge.

Signature n/a	Print Your Name	Date

| Firm Name and Address | |

(Please remember to enclose the mailing label with your application)

Forrm I-539 (Rev. 12-2-91)

Where To File.

File this application at your local INS office if you are filing:

- for an extension as a B-1 or B-2, or change to such status;
- for reinstatement as an F-1 or M-1 or filing for change to F or M status; or
- for an extension as a J, or change to such status.

In all other instances, file your application at an INS Service Center, as follows:

If you live in Connecticut, Delaware, District of Columbia, Maine, Maryland, Massachusetts, New Hampshire, New Jersey, New York, Pennsylvania, Puerto Rico, Rhode Island, Vermont, Virgin Islands, Virginia, or West Virginia, mail your application to: USINS Eastern Service Center, 75 Lower Welden Street, St. Albans, VT 05479-0001.

If you live in Alabama, Arkansas, Florida, Georgia, Kentucky, Louisiana, Mississippi, New Mexico, North Carolina, Oklahoma, South Carolina, Tennessee, or Texas, mail your application to: USINS Southern Service Center, P.O. Box 152122, Dept. A, Irving, TX 75015-2122.

If you live in Arizona, California, Guam, Hawaii, or Nevada, mail your application to: USINS Western Service Center, P.O. Box 30040, Laguna Niguel, CA 92607-0040.

If you live elsewhere in the United States, mail your application to: USINS Northern Service Center, 100 Centennial Mall North, Room, B-26, Lincoln, NE 68508.

Fee.

The fee for this application is $70.00 for the first person included in the application, and $10.00 for each additional person. The fee must be submitted in the exact amount. It cannot be refunded. DO NOT MAIL CASH.

All checks and money orders must be drawn on a bank or other institution located in the United States and must be payable in United States currency. The check or money order should be made payable to the Immigration and Naturalization Service, except that:

- If you live in Guam, and are filing this application in Guam, make your check or money order payable to the "Treasurer, Guam."
- If you live in the Virgin Islands, and are filing this application in the Virgin Islands, make your check or money order payable to the "Commissioner of Finance of the Virgin Islands."

Checks are accepted subject to collection. An uncollected check will render the application and any document issued invalid. A charge of $5.00 will be imposed if a check in payment of a fee is not honored by the bank on which it is drawn.

Processing Information.

Acceptance. Any application that is not signed or is not accompanied by the correct fee will be rejected with a notice that the application is deficient. You may correct the deficiency and resubmit the application. An application is not considered properly filed until accepted by the Service.

Initial processing. Once the application has been accepted, it will be checked for completeness. If you do not completely fill out the form, or file it without required initial evidence, you will not establish a basis for eligibility, and we may deny your application.

Requests for more information or interview. We may request more information or evidence or we may request that you appear at an INS office for an interview. We may also request that you submit the originals of any copy. We will return these originals when they are no longer required.

Decision. An application for extension of stay, change of status, or reinstatement may be approved in the discretion of the Service. You will be notified in writing of the decision on your application.

Penalties.

If you knowingly and willfully falsify or conceal a material fact or submit a false document with this request, we will deny the benefit you are filing for, and may deny any other immigration benefit. In addition, you will face severe penalties provided by law, and may be subject to criminal prosecution.

Privacy Act Notice.

We ask for the information on this form, and associated evidence, to determine if you have established eligibility for the immigration benefit you are filing for. Our legal right to ask for this information is in 8 USC 1184, and 1258. We may provide this information to other government agencies. Failure to provide this information, and any requested evidence, may delay a final decision or result in denial of your request.

Paperwork Reduction Act Notice.

We try to create forms and instructions that are accurate, can be easily understood, and which impose the least possible burden on you to provide us with information. Often this is difficult because some immigration laws are very complex. The estimated average time to complete and file this application is as follows: (1) 10 minutes to learn about the law and form; (2) 10 minutes to complete the form; and (3) 25 minutes to assemble and file the application; for a total estimated average of 45 per application. If you have comments regarding the accuracy of this estimate, or suggestions for making this form simpler, you can write to both the Immigration and Naturalization Service, 425 I Street, N.W., Room 5304, Washington, D.C. 20536; and the Office of Management and Budget, Paperwork Reduction Project, OMB No. 1115-0093, Washington, D.C. 20503.

Mailing Label--Complete the following mailing label and submit this page with your application if you are required to submit your original Form I-94.

- -

Name and address of applicant

Name   Carla A. Rojas

Street   1504 High Street, Apt. 4-D

City, State, & Zip Code   Madison, NJ 07941

Your I-94 Arrival-Departure Record is attached. It has been amended to show the extension of stay/change of status granted.

This how Dr. Turner completed form I-134:

OMB No. 1115-0062

U. S. Department of Justice
Immigration and Naturalization Service

Affidavit of Support

(ANSWER ALL ITEMS: FILL IN WITH TYPEWRITER OR PRINT IN BLOCK LETTERS IN INK.)

I, _____Robert L. Turner, M.D._____ , *residing at* _____19 Maple Lane_____

(Name)   (Street and Number)

_____Madison_____   _____New Jersey_____   _____07941_____

(City)   (State)   (ZIP Code if in U.S.)   (Country)

BEING DULY SWORN DEPOSE AND SAY:

1. I was born on _____January 24, 1950_____ at _____Trenton_____ _____New Jersey_____   _____U.S.A._____

(Date)   (City)   (Country)

If you are *not* a native born United States citizen, answer the following as appropriate:

   a. If a United States citizen through naturalization, give certificate of naturalization number _____

   b. If a United States citizen through parent(s) or marriage, give citizenship certificate number _____

   c. If United States citizenship was derived by some other method, attach a statement of explanation.

   d. If a lawfully admitted permanent resident of the United States, give "A" number _____

2. That I am ___33___ years of age and have resided in the United States since (date) _____January 24, 1950_____

3. That this affidavit is executed in behalf of the following person:

Name			Sex	Age
Carla A. Rojas			F	17

Citizen of—(Country)	Marital Status	Relationship to Deponent
Argentina	single	none

Presently resides at—(Street and Number)	(City)	(State)	(Country)
1504 High Street	Madison	New Jersey	U.S.A.

Name of spouse and children accompanying or following to join person: none

Spouse	Sex	Age	Child		Sex	Age
Child	Sex	Age	Child		Sex	Age
Child	Sex	Age	Child		Sex	Age

4. That this affidavit is made by me for the purpose of assuring the United States Government that the person(s) named in item 3 will not become a public charge in the United States.

5. That I am willing and able to receive, maintain and support the person(s) named in item 3. That I am ready and willing to deposit a bond, if necessary, to guarantee that such person(s) will not become a public charge during his or her stay in the United States, or to guarantee that the above named will maintain his or her nonimmigrant status if admitted temporarily and will depart prior to the expiration of his or her authorized stay in the United States.

6. That I understand this affidavit will be binding upon me for a period of three (3) years after entry of the person(s) named in item 3 and that the information and documentation provided by me may be made available to the Secretary of Health and Human Services and the Secretary of Agriculture, who may make it available to a public assistance agency.

7. That I am employed as, or engaged in the business of _____medical practice_____ with _____self-employed_____

(Type of Business)   (Name of concern)

at _____210 Main Street_____   _____Madison_____   _____NJ_____   _____07941_____

(Street and Number)   (City)   (State)   (Zip Code)

I derive an annual income of *(if self-employed, I have attached a copy of my last income tax return or report of commercial rating concern which I certify to be true and correct to the best of my knowledge and belief. See instruction for nature of evidence of net worth to be submitted.)* $ ___130,000.00___

I have on deposit in savings banks in the United States $ ___14,000.00___

I have other personal property, the reasonable value of which is $ ___10,000.00___

Form I-134 (Rev. 12-1-84) Y   **OVER**

I have stocks and bonds with the following market value, as indicated on the attached list
which I certify to be true and correct to the best of my knowledge and belief. $ 85,000.00

I have life insurance in the sum of $ 200,000.00

With a cash surrender value of $ none

I own real estate valued at $ 140,000.00

With mortgages or other encumbrances thereon amounting to $ 102,000.00

Which is located at   19 Maple Lane   Madison   New Jersey   07941

          (Street and Number)   (City)   (State)   (Zip Code)

8. That the following persons are dependent upon me for support: *(Place an "X" in the appropriate column to indicate whether the person named is **wholly** or **partially** dependent upon you for support.)*

Name of Person	Wholly Dependent	Partially Dependent	Age	Relationship to Me
Barbara Turner		x	31	spouse
Stacy Turner	x		5	child
Michael Turner	x		3	child

9. That I have previously submitted affidavit(s) of support for the following person(s). If none, state *"None"*

Name	Date submitted
none	

10. That I have submitted visa petition(s) to the Immigration and Naturalization Service on behalf of the following person(s). If none, state none.

Name	Relationship	Date submitted
none		

11. *(Complete this block only if the person named in item 3 will be in the United States temporarily.)*

That I ☒ do intend ☐ do not intend, to make specific contributions to the support of the person named in item 3. (*If you check "do intend", indicate the exact nature and duration of the contributions. For example, if you intend to furnish room and board, state for how long and, if money, state the amount in United States dollars and state whether it is to be given in a lump sum, weekly, or monthly, or for how long.)*

room, board, and $40 per week for four years

OATH OR AFFIRMATION OF DEPONENT

I acknowledge at that I have read Part III of the Instructions, Sponsor and Alien Liability, and am aware of my responsibilities as an immigrant sponsor under the Social Security Act, as amended, and the Food Stamp Act, as amended.

I swear (affirm) that I know the contents of this affidavit signed by me and the statements are true and correct.

Signature of deponent   *Robert L. Turner*

Subscribed and sworn to (affirmed) before me this 17th day of   June   19 83

at   Madison, New Jersey   .My commission expires on   March 31, 1985

Signature of Officer Administering Oath   *Stephen Lau*   Title   Notary Public

If affidavit prepared by other than deponent, please complete the following: I declare that this document was prepared by me at the request of the deponent and is based on all information of which I have knowledge.

(Signature)	*(Address)*	*(Date)*

Carla also requested that the college file form I-20 with the INS on her behalf.
The college sent Carla the Student copy of form I-20. It looked like this:

I-20-ID (STUDENT) COPY

U.S. Department of Justice Immigration and Naturalization Service Please Read Instructions on Page 2	**Certificate of Eligibility for Nonimmigrant (F-1) Student Status - For Academic and Language Students**

OMB No. 1115-0051

Page 3

This page must be completed and signed in the U.S. by a designated school official.

1. Family Name (surname)

ROJAS

First (given) name (do not enter middle name)

Carla

Country of birth Argentina

Date of birth (mo./day/year) 6/6/66

Country of citizenship Argentina

Admission number (Complete if known) 9-386-83

For Immigration Official Use

Visa issuing post

Date Visa issued

Reinstated, extension granted to:

2. School (school district) name

Friendly Town University

School official to be notified of student's arrival in U.S. (Name and Title)

John Doe, Dean of Freshmen

School address (include zip code)

852 Madison Ave., Madison, NJ 07940

School code (including 3-digit suffix, if any) and approval date

1234 214F 557 approved on Jan. 2, 1976

3. This certificate is issued to the student named above for:
(Check and fill out as appropriate)
   - a. ☒ Initial attendance at this school.
   - b. ☐ Continued attendance at this school.
   - c. ☐ School transfer.
     Transferred from _____
   - d. ☐ Use by dependents for entering the United States.
   - e. ☐ Other _____

4. Level of education the student is pursuing or will pursue in the United States:
(Check only one)
   - a. ☐ Primary
   - b. ☐ Secondary
   - c. ☐ Associate
   - d. ☒ Bachelor's
   - e. ☐ Master's
   - f. ☐ Doctorate
   - g. ☐ Language training
   - h. ☐ Other

5. The student named above has been accepted for a full course of study at this school, majoring in pre-school education
The student is expected to report to the school not later than (date) 9/5/83 and complete studies not later than (date) 5/30/87
The normal length of study is 4 years

6. ☒ English proficiency is required:
   - ☒ The student has the required English proficiency.
   - ☐ The student is not yet proficient, English instructions will be given at the school.
   - ☐ English proficiency is not required because _____

7. This school estimates the student's average costs for an academic term of 9 (up to 12) months to be:
   - a. Tuition and fees $ 10,000
   - b. Living expenses $ 5,000
   - c. Expenses of dependents $ none
   - d. Other (specify): books $ 500
   - Total $ 15,500

8. This school has information showing the following as the student's means of support, estimated for an academic term of 9 months (Use the same number of months given in item 7).
   - a. Student's personal funds $ _____
   - b. Funds from this school (specify type) $ 10,000 see remarks
   - c. Funds from another source (specify type and source) $ 5,500 Dr. Turner
   - d. On-campus employment (if any) $ _____
   - Total $ 15,500

9. Remarks: College cooperative work-study program in which student works and learns in supervised setting of campus day-care center covers entire tuition.

10. School Certification: I certify under penalty of perjury that all information provided above in items 1 through 8 was completed before I signed this form and is true and correct; I executed this form in the United States after review and evaluation by me or other officials of the school of the student's application, transcripts or other records of courses taken and proof of financial responsibility, which were received at the school prior to the execution of this form; the school has determined that the above named student's qualifications meet all standards for admission to the school; the student will be required to pursue a full course of study as defined by 8 CFR 214.2(f)(6); I am a designated official of the above named school and I am authorized to issue this form.

John Doe
Signature of designated school official

John Doe, Dean of Freshmen
Name of school official (print or type) / Title

4/15/83
Date issued

Madison, NJ
Place issued (city and state)

11. Student Certification: I have read and agreed to comply with the terms and conditions of my admission and those of any extension of stay as specified on page 2. I certify that all information provided on this form refers specifically to me and is true and correct to the best of my knowledge. I certify that I seek to enter or remain in the United States temporarily, and solely for the purpose of pursuing a full course of study at the school named on Page 1 of this form. I also authorize the named school to release any information from my records which is needed by the INS pursuant to 8 CFR 214.3(g) to determine my nonimmigrant status.

Carla A. Rojas
Signature of student

Carla A. Rojas
Name of student

4/15/83
Date

Martina del Campo
Signature of parent or guardian if student is under 18

Martina delCampo, 1504 High St.Madison, NJ USA 4/15/83
Name of parent/guardian (Print or type) / Address(city) / (State or province) / (Country) / (Date)

Form I-20 A-B/I-20ID (Rev 04-27-88)N

For official use only
Microfilm Index Number

Changing Your Status From Nonimmigrant to Immigrant

The most common entry to the United States for purposes of immigration and citizenship is as an immigrant—as a Green Card applicant. ["Green Card" is the term commonly used to refer to an Alien Registration Receipt Card. Many years ago, Green Cards were green. Over the years, their color has been changed a number of times. Alien Registration Receipt Cards being issued at the present time are pink, but they are still called "Green Cards." The number that appears on the Alien Registration Receipt Card is called an "Alien Registration Number," or "A number" for short. The "A number" is a very important identification number from the time of its issuance until the permanent resident alien finally achieves U. S. citizenship.]

Immediate family members of U.S. citizens may be admitted as immigrants. Other family members of U.S. citizens and immediate family members of permanent residents (Green Card holders) may be admitted as immigrants according to preference categories and quota numbers. There are also a number of employment preference categories under which immigrants may be admitted. In addition, some immigrants are winners in a green card lottery, and some have been admitted under a number of special programs. People who have been admitted as immigrants and who already have green cards may wish to skip over this chapter and go directly to the chapters concerning naturalization procedures and passing the tests.

Only an immigrant can apply for citizenship, so, if you are in the United States legally as a nonimmigrant, you must take steps to change your status to that of immigrant.

APPLY IN A PREFERENCE CATEGORY

You do not need to be outside the country to apply for immigrant status. The holder of a visitor visa, a student visa, or almost any of the nonimmigrant visas discussed earlier may decide to remain in the United States and apply for change to immigrant status. Of course there are qualifications. The first of these we have already mentioned. We refer to the caution that you do not attempt to make any changes until you have been in the states for at least three months. This caution applies most strongly in the case of change from nonimmigrant to immigrant status. If you apply within less than three months of arrival, the INS will assume that you came under false pretenses—that you really intended all along to immigrate but entered more quickly by falsely claiming that you were only a temporary visitor. The INS will simply deny your immigrant application. Having this denial in your file will not make immigration easier should you apply at a later time.

The other restriction on conversion from nonimmigrant to immigrant status has to do with the temporary visa with which you were admitted. Most J-1 visas have a home residency requirement. These J-1 visas are issued with the understanding that their recipients must return to the home country for two years before returning to the United States as immigrants. J-1 visas with the home residency requirement include those for foreign medical graduates coming to the United States for specialized training, those designed for teaching certain skills that are in short supply in the home country, and those for exchange students whose expenses were paid by their own government or by the United States government. Exceptions are sometimes made under extraordinary circumstances, but they are truly exceptional. If you hold a J-1 visa with a home residency requirement, plan to return to your home country for two years and research the best category under which to apply for immigration from your home country.

Under almost any other circumstances, you may apply for a change to immigrant status provided that you can fit into any of the preference categories. Only immediate relatives of U.S. citizens are not bound by the preference categories. These immediate relatives are: spouses of U.S. citizens, including recent widows and widowers; unmarried people under the age of 21 who have at least one U.S. citizen parent; and parents of U.S. citizens, provided that the U.S. citizen child is over the age of 21. Stepchildren and stepparents are considered immediate relatives provided that the marriage creating the stepchild or step-parent relationship occurred before the child's eighteenth birthday. Adoptive relationships apply if the adoption took place before the child's sixteenth birthday.

There is no limit to the number of green cards that can be issued to the immediate relatives of U.S. citizens as listed above. If you qualify, you are practically assured of prompt immigrant status. [You may be denied if the U.S government considers you undesirable and therefore excludable. Grounds for excludability include: health problems, that is certain diseases like tuberculosis or AIDS; criminal violations and prostitution; terrorism and other national security violations; a Nazi past; likelihood of becoming dependent on public welfare; previous immigration violation; document violation; and a few miscellaneous violations.] The grounds for excludability apply equally to immediate relatives and to those in the various preference categories. The possibility of waivers of excludability applies equally as well. You will find a sample form I-690, Application for Waiver of Grounds of Excludability, in the forms appendix at the back of this book.

If you cannot qualify as an immediate family member, then you must apply through a preference category or one of the special immigrant categories. Various quotas govern the issuance of all green cards other than those issued to immediate family members. There are a number of quotas, some based on category, some based on birthplace, some overlapping. There are also absolute total numbers for any given year.

THE PREFERENCE CATEGORIES

Family-Sponsored Green Cards

- **Family First Preference.** Unmarried people of any age with at least one U.S. citizen parent. (Remember that in the immediate relative category the unmarried child was required to be under the age of 21.)
- **Family Second Preference.** Spouses of green card holders and any age unmarried children of green card holders.
- **Family Third Preference.** Married people of any age with at least one U.S. citizen parent.
- **Family Fourth Preference.** Sisters and brothers of U.S. citizens.

Employment-based Green Cards

- **Employment First Preference**

1. Persons of extraordinary ability in the arts, sciences, education, business, or athletics.
2. Outstanding professors and researchers.

3. Managers and executives of multinational companies.

- **Employment Second Preference.** Professionals with advanced degrees or exceptional ability.
- **Employment Third Preference.** Professionals and skilled or unskilled workers.

Ethnic Diversity: Green Card Lottery

A pool of green cards has been set aside to be issued to applicants from countries with low immigration in recent years. In the first year of the program, green cards were issued on a first-come, first-served basis. Now the process more closely resembles a true lottery. The list of lottery eligible countries changes every year. The list is based on immigration over the previous five years and is prepared according to a rather complicated formula. There is a short period each year in which lottery applications may be filed, and the filing period is likely to change from year to year. (In 1993, for instance, the filing period was from March 2 to March 31.) The lottery is administered by the Department of State rather than by the INS. For information about eligible countries and filing dates, call the Department of State at (202) 647-4000. If the recorded message does not answer your questions, call again and ask to speak to a staff member who can help you. If you are eligible to enter the green card lottery, follow the instructions and do so. If you are not selected, try again the next year that your country of birth is on the list. Remember, though, that this is a lottery. You are competing with many other entrants; winning a green card is by no means guaranteed. Still, if your country is on the list, there is no harm in trying. A special advantage of a lottery green card is that it erases the two-year home residency requirement of a J-1 visa.

Investor green cards

As a spur to the American economy, the government offers a green card to a prospective immigrant who is eager and able to invest one million dollars in a new business that will hire at least ten full-time American workers. If the business will be located in a rural or economically depressed area, an investment of only $500,000 will gain a green card for the investor.

Many of the employment-based visas require labor certification. This means that the labor department must certify that no qualified American citizen is available to fill the position. Other of these visas require lengthy documentation proving that the applicant truly is a "superstar" in his or her field. Needless to say, some of these certifications and proofs are not easy to obtain or to produce. Still other employment-based visas require the firm offer of a job, in writing. It is not easy to find an employer who will make a firm offer of a permanent job to a person who is unable to accept that job until he or she obtains assurance of that green card. An employer may be reluctant to fill a vacancy with a temporary worker while waiting for the preferred applicant to obtain a green card. The lucky applicant finds an employer who is creating a new position to be filled by a person with precisely the qualifications of the prospective employee.

If you are ineligible for an employment-based green card; if you do not have any family members who can apply for your immigration in a family-preference category; if you do not come from a lottery country; and if you are not a millionaire, you may find that there is indeed no way for you to immigrate to the United States and become a citizen. If you are single, there is one more possibility open to you—marry an American citizen or marry a green card holder. The spouse of an American citizen is an immediate family member. The spouse of a green card holder falls into the Family Second Preference group. This person may have to wait for a quota number in order to immigrate, but the wait should be shorter than the wait in most other categories.

Because of the benefits immediately available to the spouse of a citizen, a great many people take advantage of the marriage option. And many of these people have indeed fallen in love with a person they met during their stay in the U.S. or, perhaps, with an American they met while the American was travelling abroad. For these lovers, the marriage option is a dream come true.

Unfortunately, the marriage option also appeals to people who intend to use it to enter or to remain in the United States fraudulently. Marriage fraud involves two people's entering into a marriage with no intention of creating a life together. The sole purpose of such a marriage of convenience is to obtain a green card for the alien partner. Often marriage fraud is committed for money. The alien who wishes to remain pays a sizeable sum to an individual who will go through a ceremony, sign papers, and assist in creating the necessary proofs. Sometimes marriage fraud is committed out of kindness. A sympathetic American will offer to marry just to help a friend. Marriage fraud is marriage fraud whether or not money changes hands. The legal penalty for marriage fraud may include a long jail sentence. The alien party to marriage fraud risks certain deportation and will never be able to obtain a green card even through the proper legal channels. You may have seen the movie "Green Card." This comedy depicts a serious problem in a humorous way. The movie is fun. However, the fact that marriage fraud occurs, and occurs often, makes it difficult for legitimate marriages to be taken seriously. Green card by marriage involves more questioning and more proofs than green card by way of preference categories.

If you are truly in love and there are no other factors to stop you, do not hesitate to marry because of the extra burden of proof required. Save invitations, guest lists, caterer's receipts, photographs, and any other records of the event. Clip your marriage notice from the newspaper. Open a joint bank account, get both your names on the apartment lease, and keep a paper and photographic record of your life together.

By whatever route you feel that you can qualify for permanent status—immediate relative of a U.S. citizen or any of the preference categories—you must now begin filing papers. The paperwork varies according to the prospective immigrant's current status and location and according to the category under which the person hopes to qualify. You will have to make telephone calls, write letters, and, if your case is unusual, perhaps even consult an immigration attorney to start the process. Do not rely on the advice and experiences of a friend or relative who may have become a permanent resident some years ago, or even last year. Forms change often. Procedures change often. Fees change often. You do not want to take a wrong step that will delay your application by many months.

While each case is slightly different, following one person's story can help you to sort out the steps. Let us return now to Carla.

With the permission granted by her F-1 visa, Carla entered college and proceeded through her course of study. She kept track of the expiration date of her Argentine passport and renewed it months before it expired so as to maintain her legal status. Then, as she began her last year of schooling, she met David. Carla and David dated through most of the year, deepening their love. They announced their engagement and made themselves a big party to celebrate. Friends had alerted them to the INS requirement for documentation, so they had their engagement announced in the newspaper and took lots of photos at the party. As their wedding date approached, they hired a hall and contracted for all the services that go with a wedding. They labeled a folder "our wedding" and kept copies of contracts and receipts in it. The folder also held a copy of the invitation list and, eventually, a photocopy of marriage license and marriage certificate as well. A friend videotaped the wedding as his wedding gift.

Carla was moving from the Turner residence, and David's apartment was tiny, so they rented a new apartment and had both their names entered upon the lease as husband and wife. Then they began filling out forms.

David completed form I-130, Petition for Alien Relative. Here is how the completed form looked:

U.S. Department of Justice
Immigration and Naturalization Service (INS)

OMB #1115-0054
Petition for Alien Relative

DO NOT WRITE IN THIS BLOCK – FOR EXAMINING OFFICE ONLY		
Case ID#	Action Stamp	Fee Stamp
A#		
G-28 or Volag #		

Section of Law:
☐ 201 (b) spouse ☐ 203 (a)(1)
☐ 201 (b) child   ☐ 203 (a)(2)
☐ 201 (b) parent ☐ 203 (a)(4)
                  ☐ 203 (a)(5)
AM CON: _____

Petition was filed on: _____ (priority date)
☐ Personal Interview   ☐ Previously Forwarded
☐ Pet. ☐ Ben. "A" File Reviewed   ☐ Stateside Criteria
☐ Field Investigations   ☐ I-485 Simultaneously
☐ 204 (a)(2)(A) Resolved   ☐ 204 (h) Resolved

Remarks:

A. Relationship

1. The alien relative is my
☒ Husband/Wife ☐ Parent ☐ Brother/Sister ☐ Child

2. Are you related by adoption?
☐ Yes ☒ No

3. Did you gain permanent residence through adoption?
☐ Yes ☒ No

B. Information about you

1. Name (Family name in CAPS) (First) (Middle)
STONE   David   B.

2. Address (Number and Street) (Apartment Number)
46 Chester Street   3-L

(Town or City) (State/Country) (ZIP/Postal Code)
Madison   NJ   07941

3. Place of Birth (Town or City) (State/Country)
Philadelphia   Pennsylvania

4. Date of Birth (Mo/Day/Yr)
3/2/63

5. Sex
☒ Male ☐ Female

6. Marital Status
☒ Married ☐ Single ☐ Widowed ☐ Divorced

7. Other Names Used (including maiden name)
none

8. Date and Place of Present Marriage (if married)
August 2, 1987   Madison, NJ

9. Social Security Number
083-22-1111

10. Alien Registration Number (if any)
none

11. Names of Prior Husbands/Wives
none

12. Date(s) Marriage(s) Ended
n/a

13. If you are a U.S. citizen, complete the following:
My citizenship was acquired through (check one)
☒ Birth in the U.S.
☐ Naturalization (Give number of certificate, date and place it was issued)

☐ Parents
Have you obtained a certificate of citizenship in your own name?
☐ Yes ☐ No
If "Yes", give number of certificate, date and place it was issued.

14a. If you are a lawful permanent resident alien, complete the following:
Date and place of admission for, or adjustment to, lawful permanent residence, and class of admission:

14b. Did you gain permanent resident status through marriage to a United States citizen or lawful permanent resident? ☐ Yes ☐ No

C. Information about your alien relative

1. Name (Family name in CAPS) (First) (Middle)
STONE   Carla   Rojas

2. Address (Number and Street) (Apartment Number)
46 Chester Street   3-L

(Town or City) (State/Country) (ZIP/Postal Code)
Madison   NJ   07941

3. Place of Birth (Town or City) (State/Country)
Buenos Aires   Argentina

4. Date of Birth (Mo/Day/Yr)
6/6/66

5. Sex
☐ Male ☒ Female

6. Marital Status
☒ Married ☐ Single ☐ Widowed ☐ Divorced

7. Other Names Used (including maiden name)
Carla A. Rojas

8. Date and Place of Present Marriage (if married)
August 2, 1987   Madison, NJ

9. Social Security Number
246-80-1234

10. Alien Registration Number (if any)
none

11. Names of Prior Husbands/Wives
none

12. Date(s) Marriage(s) Ended
n/a

13. Has your relative ever been in the U.S.?
☒ Yes ☐ No

14. If your relative is currently in the U.S., complete the following: He or she last arrived as a (visitor, student, stowaway, without inspection, etc.)
accompanying minor/exchange/student

Arrival/Departure Record (I-94) Number
133 5 621 0 988

Date arrived (Month/Day/Year)
8/10/81

Date authorized stay expired, or will expire, as shown on Form I-94 or I-95
Sept. 1, 1987

15. Name and address of present employer (if any)
none

Date this employment began (Month/Day/Year)
n/a

16. Has your relative ever been under immigration proceedings?
☐ Yes ☒ No Where _____ When _____
☐ Exclusion ☐ Deportation ☐ Recission ☐ Judicial Proceedings

INITIAL RECEIPT	RESUBMITTED	RELOCATED		COMPLETED		
		Rec'd	Sent	Approved	Denied	Returned

Form I-130 (Rev. 10/01/89) Y

C. (continued) Information about your alien relative

16. List husband/wife and all children of your relative (if your relative is your husband/wife, list only his or her children).

(Name)	(Relationship)	(Date of Birth)	(Country of Birth)
n/a			

17. Address in the United States where your relative intends to live

(Number and Street)	(Town or City)	(State)
46 Chester Street	Madison	NJ

18. Your relative's address abroad

(Number and Street)	(Town or City)	(Province)	(Country)	(Phone Number)
n/a				

19. If your relative's native alphabet is other than Roman letters, write his or her name and address abroad in the native alphabet: n/a

(Name)	(Number and Street)	(Town or City)	(Province)	(Country)

20. If filing for your husband/wife, give last address at which you both lived together:

(Name) (Number and Street) (Town or City) (Province) (Country)	From (Month) (Year)	To (Month) (Year)
46 Chester Street, Madison, NJ U.S.A.	8/2/87	8/11/87

21. Check the appropriate box below and give the information required for the box you checked:

☐ Your relative will apply for a visa abroad at the American Consulate in _____

(City)　　　　　(Country)

☒ Your relative is in the United States and will apply for adjustment of status to that of a lawful permanent resident in the office of the Immigration and

Naturalization Service at ___Newark___　___New Jersey___ . If your relative is not eligible for adjustment of status, he or she will

(City)　　　　　(State)

apply for a visa abroad at the American Consulate in _____ ,

(City)　　　　　(Country)

(Designation of a consulate outside the country of your relative's last residence does not guarantee acceptance for processing by that consulate. Acceptance is at the discretion of the designated consulate.)

D. Other Information

1. If separate petitions are also being submitted for other relatives, give names of each and relationship.　　n/a

2. Have you ever filed a petition for this or any other alien before?　☐ Yes　☒ No
If "Yes," give name, place and date of filing, and result.

Warning: The INS investigates claimed relationships and verifies the validity of documents. The INS seeks criminal prosecutions when family relationships are falsified to obtain visas.

Penalties: You may, by law be imprisoned for not more than five years, or fined $250,000, or both, for entering into a marriage contract for the purpose of evading any provision of the immigration laws and you may be fined up to $10,000 or imprisoned up to five years or both, for knowingly and willfully falsifying or concealing a material fact or using any false document in submitting this petition.

Your Certification: I certify, under penalty of perjury under the laws of the United States of America, that the foregoing is true and correct. Furthermore, I authorize the release of any information from my records which the Immigration and Naturalization Service needs to determine eligibility for the benefit that I am seeking.

Signature _David B. Stone_　　　Date _8/11/87_　　Phone Number _(201)123-4567_

Signature of Person Preparing Form if Other than Above

I declare that I prepared this document at the request of the person above and that it is based on all information of which I have any knowledge.

Print Name _____ (Address) _____ (Signature) _____ (Date) _____

G–28 ID Number _____

Volag Number _____

NOTICE TO PERSONS FILING FOR SPOUSES IF MARRIED LESS THAN TWO YEARS

Pursuant to section 216 of the Immigration and Nationality Act, your alien spouse may be granted conditional permanent resident status in the United States as of the date he or she is admitted or adjusted to conditional status by an officer of the Immigration and Naturalization Service. Both you and your conditional permanent resident spouse are required to file a petition, Form I-751, Joint Petition to Remove Conditional Basis of Alien's Permanent Resident Status, during the ninety day period immediately before the second anniversary of the date your alien spouse was granted conditional permanent residence.

Otherwise, the rights, privileges, responsibilities and duties which apply to all other permanent residents apply equally to a conditional permanent resident. A conditional permanent resident is not limited to the right to apply for naturalization, to file petitions in behalf of qualifying relatives, or to reside permanently in the United States as an immigrant in accordance with the immigration laws.

> **Failure to file Form I-751, Joint Petition to Remove the Conditional Basis of Alien's Permanent Resident Status, will result in termination of permanent residence status and initiation of deportation proceedings.**

NOTE: You must complete Items 1 through 6 to assure that petition approval is recorded. Do not write in the section below item 6.

---

1. **Name of relative** (Family name in CAPS)   (First)   (Middle)
   STONE   Carla   Rojas

2. **Other names used by relative** (including maiden name)
   Carla A. Rojas

3. **Country of relative's birth**   4. **Date of relative's birth** (Month/Day/Year)
   Argentina   June 6, 1966

5. **Your name** (Last name in CAPS) (First)   (Middle)   6. **Your phone number**
   STONE   David   B.   (201) 123-4567

Action Stamp

SECTION	DATE PETITION FILED
☐ 201 (b)(spouse)	
☐ 201 (b)(child)	
☐ 201 (b)(parent)	
☐ 203 (a)(1)	☐ STATESIDE
☐ 203 (a)(2)	CRITERIA GRANTED
☐ 203 (a)(4)	
☐ 203 (a)(5)	SENT TO CONSUL AT;

CHECKLIST

Have you answered each question?
Have you signed the petition?
Have you enclosed:

☑ The filing fee for each petition?
☑ Proof of your citizenship or lawful permanent residence?
☑ All required supporting documents for each petition?

If you are filing for your husband or wife have you included:

☑ Your picture?
☑ His or her picture?
☑ Your G-325A?
☑ His or her G-325A?

Relative Petition Card
Form I-130A (Rev. 10/01/89) Y

Carla completed this form I-485, Application for Permanent Residence:

U.S. Department of Justice
Immigration and Naturalization Service

OMB No. 1115-0053

Application to Register Permanent Residence or Adjust Status

START HERE - Please Type or Print

Part 1. Information about you.

Family Name	STONE	Given Name	Carla	Middle Initial	R.

Address - C/O

Street Number and Name	46 Chester Street	Apt. #	3-L

City	Madison

State	New Jersey	Zip Code	07941

Date of Birth (month/day/year)	June 6, 1966	Country of Birth	Argentina

Social Security #	246-80-1234	A # (if any)	none

Date of Last Arrival (month/day/year)	August 10, 1981	I-94 #	133-56210988

Current INS Status	F-1	Expires on (month/day/year)	Sept. 1, 1987

Part 2. Application Type. *(check one)*

I am applying for adjustment to permanent resident status because:

a. ☒ an immigrant petition giving me an immediately available immigrant visa number has been approved (attach a copy of the approval notice), or a relative, special immigrant juvenile, or special immigrant military visa petition filed with this application will give me an immediately available visa number if approved.

b. ☐ My spouse or parent applied for adjustment of status or was granted lawful permanent residence in an immigrant visa category which allows derivative status for spouses and children.

c. ☐ I entered as a K-1 fiance(e) of a U.S. citizen whom I married within 90 days of entry, or I am the K-2 child of such a fiance(e) (attach a copy of the fiance(e) petition approval notice and the marriage certificate).

d. ☐ I was granted asylum or derivative asylum status as the spouse or child of a person granted asylum and am eligible for adjustment.

e. ☐ I am a native or citizen of Cuba admitted or paroled into the U.S. after January 1, 1959, and thereafter have been physically present in the U.S. for at least 1 year.

f. ☐ I am the husband, wife, or minor unmarried child of a Cuban described in (e) and am residing with that person, and was admitted or paroled into the U.S. after January 1, 1959, and thereafter have been physically present in the U.S. for at least 1 year.

g. ☐ I have continuously resided in the U.S. since before January 1, 1972.

h. ☐ Other-explain _____

I am already a permanent resident and am applying to have the date I was granted permanent residence adjusted to the date I originally arrived in the U.S. as a nonimmigrant or parolee, or as of May 2, 1964, whichever is later, and: *(Check one)*

i. ☐ I am a native or citizen of Cuba and meet the description in (e), above.

j. ☐ I am the husband, wife or minor unmarried child of a Cuban, and meet the description in (f), above.

Form I-485 (09-09-92)N   **Continued on back.**

FOR INS USE ONLY

Returned	Receipt

Resubmitted	

Reloc Sent	

Reloc Rec'd	

☐ Applicant Interviewed

Section of Law
☐ Sec. 209(b), INA
☐ Sec. 13, Act of 9/11/57
☐ Sec. 245, INA
☐ Sec. 249, INA
☐ Sec. 1 Act of 11/2/66
☐ Sec. 2 Act of 11/2/66
☐ Other_____

Country Chargeable

Eligibility Under Sec. 245
☐ Approved Visa Petition
☐ Dependent of Principal Alien
☐ Special Immigrant
☐ Other_____

Preference

Action Block

To Be Completed by Attorney or Representative, if any
☐ Fill in box if G-28 is attached to represent the applicant

VOLAG#

ATTY State License #

Part 3. Processing Information.

A. City/Town/Village of birth

Buenos Aires, Argentina

Current occupation
none

Your mother's first name
Martina

Your father's first name
Simon

Give your name exactly how it appears on your Arrival /Departure Record (Form I-94)

Carla A. Rojas

Place of last entry into the U.S. (City/State)
Newark, New Jersey

In what status did you last enter? *(Visitor, Student, exchange alien, crewman, temporary worker, without inspection, etc.)*

Were you inspected by a U.S. Immigration Officer? ☒ Yes ☐ No

accompanying minor/exchange/student

Nonimmigrant Visa Number   98765

Consulate where Visa was issued
Buenos Aires, Argentina

Date Visa was Issued (month/day/year)   7/7/81

Sex: ☐ Male ☒ Female

Marital Status: ☒ Married ☐ Single ☐ Divorced ☐ Widowed

Have you ever before applied for permanent resident status in the U.S.? ☒ No ☐ Yes (give date and place of filing and final disposition):

B. List your present husband/wife, all of your sons and daughters (if you have none, write "none". If additional space is needed, use separate paper).

Family Name	Given Name	Middle Initial	Date of Birth (month/day/year)
STONE	David	B.	3/2/63
Country of birth	Relationship	A #	Applying with you?
United States	husband	none	☐ Yes ☒ No
none			
Country of birth	Relationship	A #	Applying with you? ☐ Yes ☐ No
Family Name	Given Name	Middle Initial	Date of Birth (month/day/year)
Country of birth	Relationship	A #	Applying with you? ☐ Yes ☐ No
Family Name	Given Name	Middle Initial	Date of Birth (month/day/year)
Country of birth	Relationship	A #	Applying with you? ☐ Yes ☐ No
Family Name	Given Name	Middle Initial	Date of Birth (month/day/year)
Country of birth	Relationship	A #	Applying with you? ☐ Yes ☐ No

C. List your present and past membership in or affiliation with every political organization, association, fund, foundation, party, club, society, or similar group in the United States or in any other place since your 16th birthday. Include any foreign military service in this part. If none, write "none". Include the name of organization, location, dates of membership from and to, and the nature of the organization. If additional space is needed, use separate paper.

Form I-485 (Rev. 09-09-92) N   Continued On Next Page

Part 3. Processing Information. *(Continued)*

Please answer the following questions. (If your answer is **"Yes"** on any one of these questions, explain on a separate piece of paper. Answering **"Yes"** does not necessarily mean that you are not entitled to register for permanent residence or adjust status).

1. Have you ever, in or outside the U. S.:
    a. knowingly committed any crime of moral turpitude or a drug-related offense for which you have not been arrested?
    b. been arrested, cited, charged, indicted, fined, or imprisoned for breaking or violating any law or ordinance, excluding traffic violations?
    c. been the beneficiary of a pardon, amnesty, rehabilitation decree, other act of clemency or similar action?
    d. exercised diplomatic immunity to avoid prosecution for a criminal offense in the U. S.? ☐ Yes ☒ No

2. Have you received public assistance in the U.S. from any source, including the U.S. government or any state, county, city, or municipality (other than emergency medical treatment) , or are you likely to receive public assistance in the future? ☐ Yes ☒ No

3. Have you ever:
    a. within the past 10 years been a prostitute or procured anyone for prostitution, or intend to engage in such activities in the future?
    b. engaged in any unlawful commercialized vice, including, but not limited to, illegal gambling?
    c. knowingly encouraged, induced, assisted, abetted or aided any alien to try to enter the U.S. illegally?
    d. illicitly trafficked in any controlled substance, or knowingly assisted, abetted or colluded in the illicit trafficking of any controlled substance? ☐ Yes ☒ No

4. Have you ever engaged in, conspired to engage in, or do you intend to engage in, or have you ever solicited membership or funds for, or have you through any means ever assisted or provided any type of material support to, any person or organization that has ever engaged or conspired to engage, in sabotage, kidnapping, political assassination, hijacking, or any other form of terrorist activity? ☐ Yes ☒ No

5. Do you intend to engage in the U.S. in:
    a. espionage?
    b. any activity a purpose of which is opposition to, or the control or overthrow of, the Government of the United States, by force, violence or other unlawful means?
    c. any activity to violate or evade any law prohibiting the export from the United States of goods, technology or sensitive information? ☐ Yes ☒ No

6. Have you ever been a member of, or in any way affiliated with, the Communist Party or any other totalitarian party? ☐ Yes ☒ No

7. Did you, during the period March 23, 1933 to May 8, 1945, in association with either the Nazi Government of Germany or any organization or government associated or allied with the Nazi Government of Germany, ever order, incite, assist or otherwise participate in the persecution of any person because of race, religion, national origin or political opinion? ☐ Yes ☒ No

8. Have you ever engaged in genocide, or otherwise ordered, incited, assisted or otherwise participated in the killing of any person because of race, religion, nationality, ethnic origin, or political opinion? ☐ Yes ☒ No

9. Have you ever been deported from the U.S., or removed from the U.S. at government expense, excluded within the past year, or are you now in exclusion or deportation proceedings? ☐ Yes ☒ No

10. Are you under a final order of civil penalty for violating section 274C of the Immigration Act for use of fraudulent documents, or have you, by fraud or willful misrepresentation of a material fact, ever sought to procure, or procured, a visa, other documentation, entry into the U.S., or any other immigration benefit? ☐ Yes ☒ No

11. Have you ever left the U.S. to avoid being drafted into the U.S. Armed Forces? ☐ Yes ☒ No

12. Have you ever been a J nonimmigrant exchange visitor who was subject to the 2 year foreign residence requirement and not yet complied with that requirement or obtained a waiver? ☐ Yes ☒ No

13. Are you now withholding custody of a U.S. Citizen child outside the U.S. from a person granted custody of the child? ☐ Yes ☒ No

14. Do you plan to practice polygamy in the U.S.? ☐ Yes ☒ No

Form I-485 (Rev. 09-09-92)N **Continued on back**

Part 4. **Signature.** *(Read the information on penalties in the instructions before completing this section. You must file this application while in the United States.)*

I certify under penalty of perjury under the laws of the United States of America that this application, and the evidence submitted with it, is all true and correct. I authorize the release of any information from my records which the Immigration and Naturalization Service needs to determine eligibility for the benefit I am seeking.

Signature	Print Your Name	Date	Daytime Phone Number
Carla R. Stone	Carla R. Stone	8/11/87	(201) 123-4567

Please Note: *If you do not completely fill out this form, or fail to submit required documents listed in the instructions, you may not be found eligible for the requested document and this application may be denied.*

Part 5. **Signature of person preparing form if other than above.** *(Sign Below)*

I declare that I prepared this application at the request of the above person and it is based on all information of which I have knowledge.

Signature	Print Your Name	Date	Day time Phone Number

Firm Name
and Address

Both David and Carla filled out form G-325A:

INSTRUCTIONS: USE TYPEWRITER. BE SURE ALL COPIES ARE LEGIBLE. Failure to answer fully all questions delays action.
Do Not Remove Carbons: If typewriter is not available, print heavily in block letters with ball-point pen.

U.S. Department of Justice	FORM G-325A	OMB No. 1115-0066
Immigration and Naturalization Service	**BIOGRAPHIC INFORMATION**	

(Family name) STONE	(First name) Carla	(Middle name) Rojas	☐ MALE ☒ FEMALE	BIRTHDATE(Mo.-Day-Yr.) 6/6/66	NATIONALITY Argentine	FILE NUMBER A none

ALL OTHER NAMES USED (Including names by previous marriages) Carla A. Rojas	CITY AND COUNTRY OF BIRTH Buenos Aires, Argentina	SOCIAL SECURITY NO. (If any) 246-80-1234

	FAMILY NAME	FIRST NAME	DATE, CITY AND COUNTRY OF BIRTH(If known)	CITY AND COUNTRY OF RESIDENCE
FATHER	Rojas, Simon		2/8/32 Argentina	Rosario, Argentina
MOTHER(Maiden name)	delCampo, Martina		9/21/37 Argentina	Buenos Aires, Argentina

HUSBAND(If none, so state) OR WIFE	FAMILY NAME (For wife, give maiden name) STONE	FIRST NAME David	BIRTHDATE 3/2/63	CITY & COUNTRY OF BIRTH Philadelphia USA	DATE OF MARRIAGE 8/2/87	PLACE OF MARRIAGE Madison,NJ

FORMER HUSBANDS OR WIVES(if none, so state) FAMILY NAME (For wife, give maiden name) none	FIRST NAME	BIRTHDATE	DATE & PLACE OF MARRIAGE	DATE AND PLACE OF TERMINATION OF MARRIAGE

APPLICANT'S RESIDENCE LAST FIVE YEARS. LIST PRESENT ADDRESS FIRST.

STREET AND NUMBER	CITY	PROVINCE OR STATE	COUNTRY	FROM MONTH	YEAR	TO MONTH	YEAR
46 Chester Street	Madison	New Jersey	USA	8	87	PRESENT TIME	
19 Maple Lane	Madison	New Jersey	USA	9	83	8	87
1504 High Street	Madison	New Jersey	USA	8	81	9	83

APPLICANT'S LAST ADDRESS OUTSIDE THE UNITED STATES OF MORE THAN ONE YEAR

STREET AND NUMBER	CITY	PROVINCE OR STATE	COUNTRY	FROM MONTH	YEAR	TO MONTH	YEAR
1160 Camino Cruz Blanca	Buenos Aires	Pampas	Argentina	10	72	8	81

APPLICANT'S EMPLOYMENT LAST FIVE YEARS. (IF NONE, SO STATE.) LIST PRESENT EMPLOYMENT FIRST

FULL NAME AND ADDRESS OF EMPLOYER	OCCUPATION(SPECIFY)	FROM MONTH	YEAR	TO MONTH	YEAR
none except cooperative work-	pre-school			PRESENT TIME	
study program arranged through	teacher asst	9	83	5	87
Fairleigh-Dickinson University					
at campus day care center					

Show below last occupation abroad if not shown above. (Include all information requested above.)

none					

THIS FORM IS SUBMITTED IN CONNECTION WITH APPLICATION FOR: ☐ NATURALIZATION ☒ STATUS AS PERMANENT RESIDENT ☐ OTHER (SPECIFY)	SIGNATURE OF APPLICANT *Carla R. Stone*	DATE 8/11/87
Are all copies legible? ☒ Yes	IF YOUR NATIVE ALPHABET IS IN OTHER THAN ROMAN LETTERS, WRITE YOUR NAME IN YOUR NATIVE ALPHABET IN THIS SPACE: N/A	

PENALTIES: SEVERE PENALTIES ARE PROVIDED BY LAW FOR KNOWINGLY AND WILLFULLY FALSIFYING OR CONCEALING A MATERIAL FACT.

APPLICANT: BE SURE TO PUT YOUR NAME AND ALIEN REGISTRATION NUMBER IN THE BOX OUTLINED BY HEAVY BORDER BELOW.

COMPLETE THIS BOX (Family name) STONE	(Given name) Carla	(Middle name) Rojas	(Alien registration number) none

★ U.S. GOVERNMENT PRINTING OFFICE: 1992 – 335-614

INSTRUCTIONS: USE TYPEWRITER. BE SURE ALL COPIES ARE LEGIBLE. Failure to answer fully all questions delays action.
Do Not Remove Carbons: If typewriter is not available, print heavily in block letters with ball-point pen.

U.S. Department of Justice

Immigration and Naturalization Service

FORM G-325A

BIOGRAPHIC INFORMATION

OMB No. 1115-0066

(Family name) STONE	(First name) David	(Middle name) B.	☒ MALE ☐ FEMALE	BIRTHDATE(Mo.-Day-Yr.) 3/2/63	NATIONALITY USA	FILE NUMBER A none

ALL OTHER NAMES USED (Including names by previous marriages) none	CITY AND COUNTRY OF BIRTH Philadelphia, PA USA	SOCIAL SECURITY NO. (If any) 083-22-1111

	FAMILY NAME	FIRST NAME	DATE, CITY AND COUNTRY OF BIRTH(If known)	CITY AND COUNTRY OF RESIDENCE
FATHER	Stone,	Howard	7/30/30 Miami, FL USA	Philadelphia, PA USA
MOTHER(Maiden name)	Lee,	Linda	1/22/37 Canton, OH USA	Philadelphia, PA USA

HUSBAND(If none, so state) OR WIFE	FAMILY NAME (For wife, give maiden name) ROJAS	FIRST NAME Carla	BIRTHDATE 6/6/66	CITY & COUNTRY OF BIRTH Buenos Aires Argentina	DATE OF MARRIAGE 8/2/87	PLACE OF MARRIAGE Madison, NJ

FORMER HUSBANDS OR WIVES(if none, so state) none FAMILY NAME (For wife, give maiden name)	FIRST NAME	BIRTHDATE	DATE & PLACE OF MARRIAGE	DATE AND PLACE OF TERMINATION OF MARRIAGE

APPLICANT'S RESIDENCE LAST FIVE YEARS. LIST PRESENT ADDRESS FIRST.

				FROM		TO	
STREET AND NUMBER	CITY	PROVINCE OR STATE	COUNTRY	MONTH	YEAR	MONTH	YEAR
46 Chester Street	Madison	New Jersey	USA	8	87	PRESENT TIME	
71 Third Avenue	Madison	New Jersey	USA	3	86	8	87
276 Market Street	Madison	New Jersey	USA	11	85	3	86
13860 Lancaster Pike	Philadelphia	PA	USA	5	75	11	85

APPLICANT'S LAST ADDRESS OUTSIDE THE UNITED STATES OF MORE THAN ONE YEAR

				FROM		TO	
STREET AND NUMBER	CITY	PROVINCE OR STATE	COUNTRY	MONTH	YEAR	MONTH	YEAR
none							

APPLICANT'S EMPLOYMENT LAST FIVE YEARS. (IF NONE, SO STATE.) LIST PRESENT EMPLOYMENT FIRST

		FROM		TO	
FULL NAME AND ADDRESS OF EMPLOYER	OCCUPATION(SPECIFY)	MONTH	YEAR	MONTH	YEAR
Barton Mfg. Co., 410 Front St. Madison, NJ	engineer	11	85	PRESENT TIME	
Manpower, Inc., 1313 Race St. Phila. PA	temporary	6	85	10	85
	computer	also	summers	of	
	programmer	83	and	84	

Show below last occupation abroad if not shown above. (Include all information requested above.)

none						

THIS FORM IS SUBMITTED IN CONNECTION WITH APPLICATION FOR: ☐ NATURALIZATION ☐ STATUS AS PERMANENT RESIDENT ☒ OTHER (SPECIFY) permanent status for spouse	SIGNATURE OF APPLICANT *David B. Stone*	DATE 8/11/87

Are all copies legible? ☒ Yes

IF YOUR NATIVE ALPHABET IS IN OTHER THAN ROMAN LETTERS, WRITE YOUR NAME IN YOUR NATIVE ALPHABET IN THIS SPACE:

N/A

PENALTIES: SEVERE PENALTIES ARE PROVIDED BY LAW FOR KNOWINGLY AND WILLFULLY FALSIFYING OR CONCEALING A MATERIAL FACT.

APPLICANT: BE SURE TO PUT YOUR NAME AND ALIEN REGISTRATION NUMBER IN
THE BOX OUTLINED BY HEAVY BORDER BELOW.

COMPLETE THIS BOX (Family name)	(Given name)	(Middle name)	(Alien registration number)

Carla went to a doctor on the INS list and had a complete physical examination. The doctor filled out a form I-693, Medical Exam of Aliens Seeking Adjustment of Status (see Forms Appendix for sample), and she submitted it with the other forms and papers.

David completed an I-134, Affidavit of Support, similar to that completed by Dr. Turner when Carla first went to live in his household. David also enclosed a letter from his employer stating his current salary, copies of his most recent bank statements, and photocopies of all his stock certificates and U.S. Savings Bonds. Carla also filled out Form 9003, Additional Questions to be Completed by All Applicants for Permanent Residence in the United States. Even though she had not held a real job in the United States and had earned only pocket money in the Turner household, Dr. Turner had recommended that Carla apply for a Social Security Number and Carla had done so. Completion of the form was very simple. Carla's looked like this:

Form **9003** (January 1992)	Department of the Treasury—Internal Revenue Service **Additional Questions to be Completed by All Applicants for Permanent Residence in the United States**	OMB Clearance No. 1545-1065 Expires 8-31-94

This form must accompany your application for permanent residence in the United States

Privacy Act Notice: Your responses to the following questions will be provided to the Internal Revenue Service pursuant to Section 6039E of the Internal Revenue Code of 1986. Use of this information is limited to that needed for tax administration purposes. Failure to provide this information may result in a $500 penalty unless failure is due to reasonable cause.

On the date of issuance of the Alien Registration Receipt Card, the Immigration and Naturalization Service will send the following information to the Internal Revenue Service: your name, social security number, address, date of birth, alien identification number, occupation, class of admission, and answers to IRS Form 9003.

Name *(Last—Surname—Family)*   *(First—Given)*   *(Middle Initial)*

    STONE   Carla   R.

Taxpayer Identification Number .... 2 4 6 | 8 0 | 1 2 3 4

Enter your Social Security Number (SSN) if you have one. If you do not have an SSN but have used a Taxpayer Identification Number issued to you by the Internal Revenue Service, enter that number. Otherwise, write "NONE" in the space provided; i.e., "⌴⌴⌴ N,O,N,E ".

	Yes	No
1. Are you self-employed? Mark "yes" if you own and actively operate a business in which you share in the profits other than as an investor.		X
2. Have you been in the United States for 183 days or more during any one of the three calendar years immediately preceding the current calendar year? Mark "yes" if you spent 183 days or more (not necessarily consecutive) in the United States during any **one of the three prior** calendar years **whether or not you worked** in the United States.	X	
3. During the last three years did you receive income from sources in the United States? Mark "yes" if you received income paid by individuals or institutions located in the United States. Income includes, but is not limited to, compensation for services provided by you, interest, dividends, rents, and royalties.	X	
4. Did you file a United States Individual Income Tax Return (Forms 1040, 1040A, 1040EZ or 1040NR) in any of the last three years?		X

If you answered yes to question 4, for which tax year was the last return filed? .... 19 __ __

Paperwork Reduction Act Notice—We ask for the information on this form to carry out the Internal Revenue laws of the United States. You are required to give us the information. We need it to ensure that you are complying with these laws and to allow us to figure and collect the right amount of tax.

The time needed to complete and file this form will vary depending on individual circumstances. The estimated average time is 5 minutes. If you have comments concerning the accuracy of this time estimate or suggestions for making this form more simple, we would be happy to hear from you. You can write to both the **Internal Revenue Service**, Washington, DC 20224. Attention: IRS Reports Clearance Officer, T:FP, and **Office of Management and Budget**. Paperwork Reduction Project (1545-1065) Washington, DC 20503. **DO NOT send this form to either of these offices. Instead, return it to the appropriate office of the Department of State or the Immigration and Naturalization Service.**

Remarks

    My cash income was less than $2100 per year so I did not file a tax return.

Carla and David worked together to complete the application package. They included: two sets of Carla's fingerprints taken on FD-258 (see forms appendix) by the desk sergeant at the local police station; a photocopy of Carla's I-94 card (the green card would supersede the I-94 card as authorization to remain in the United States, so Carla did not need to return the original I-94 for updating); a photocopy of Carla's passport; a photocopy of her current visa; a photocopy of her birth certificate and a translation of her birth certificate prepared by a friend fluent in both Spanish and English. At the end of the translation, Carla's friend wrote and signed the following statement: *I hereby certify that I translated this document from Spanish to English. This translation is accurate and complete. I further certify that I am fully competent to translate from Spanish to English.* They also enclosed three photographs of Carla and three photographs of David, all complying with the following specifications:

Color Photograph Specifications

◄ Sample Photograph

Head Size (Including Hair) Must fit inside oval. ►

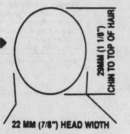

29MM (1 1/8") CHIN TO TOP OF HAIR

22 MM (7/8") HEAD WIDTH

Color films of the integral type, non-peel-apart, are unacceptable. These are easily recognized as the back of the films are black. The acceptable instant color film has a white backing.

- Photograph must show the subject in a 3/4 frontal portrait as shown above.
- Right ear must be exposed in photograph for all applicants, hats must not be worn.
- Photograph outer dimension *must* be larger than 1 1/4" X 1 3/8", but head size, (including hair) *must* fit within the illustrated oval (outer dimension does not include border if one is used).
- Photograph must be color with a white background equal in reflectance to bond typing paper.
- Surface of the photograph *must be glossy.*
- Photograph must not be stained, cracked, or mutilated, and must lie flat.
- Photographic image must be sharp and correctly exposed, photograph must be un-retouched.

- Photograph must not be pasted on card or mounted in any way.
- *Three (3)* photographs of every applicant, regardless of age, must be submitted.
- Photographs must be taken within thirty (30) days of application date.
- Snapshots, group pictures, or full length portraits *will not* be accepted.
- Using crayon or felt pen, to avoid mutilation of the photographs, *lightly* print your name (and Alien Registration Receipt Number, if known) on the back of all photographs.
- **Important Note:** Failure to submit photographs in compliance with these specifications will delay the processing of your application.

In addition, they included a photocopy of their marriage certificate, a photocopy of David's birth certificate, and all the proofs required to be attached to David's Affidavit of Support (I-134).

Carla and David made photocopies of all the original forms that they were submitting. They also photocopied the photocopies they were including in the packet so as to have a complete record of everything they were submitting in the same mailing. Carla's visa and I-94 were close to their expiration date, so she and David would have liked to file all the papers in person to be certain that they were accurately recorded. However, the instructions accompanying I-495, Application to Register Permanent Residence or Adjust Status, specify that the form must be filed by mail only. So, they enclosed the required fees and sent off the entire packet via certified mail, return receipt requested.

David had a good job, but Carla was eager to go to work and did not know how long she would have to wait for her green card, so she completed this form I-765, Application for Employment Authorization:

U. S. Department of Justice
Immigration and Naturalization Service

OMB # 1115-0163
Application for Employment Authorization

Do Not Write In This Block

Please Complete Both Sides of Form

Case ID#	Action Stamp	Fee Stamp
A#		
Applicant is filing under 274a.12 _____		Remarks

☐ Application Approved. Employment Authorized / Extended (Circle One) _____ (Date).
   Subject to the following conditions: _____ until _____ (Date).
☐ Application Denied.
   ☐ Failed to establish eligibility under 8 CFR 274a.12 (a) or (c).
   ☐ Failed to establish economic necessity as required in 8 CFR 274a.12(c), (10), (13), (14).

I am applying for:
☒ Permission to accept employment
☐ Replacement (of lost employment authorization document).
☐ Extension of my permission to accept employment (attach previous employment authorization document).

1. Name (Family Name in CAPS)   (First)   (Middle)
   STONE   Carla Rojas

2. Other Names Used (Include Maiden Name)
   Carla A. Rojas

3. Address in the United States (Number and Street)   (Apt. Number)
   46 Chester Street   3-L
   (Town or City)   (State/Country)   (ZIP Code)
   Madison, NJ   07941

4. Country of Citizenship
   Argentina

5. Place of Birth (Town or City)   (State/Province)   (Country)
   Buenos Aires   Pampas   Argentina

6. Date of Birth (Month/Day/Year)   7. Sex
   June 6, 1966   ☐ Male ☒ Female

8. Marital Status   ☒ Married   ☐ Single
                     ☐ Widowed   ☐ Divorced

9. Social Security Number (Include all Numbers you have ever used)
   246-80-1234

10. Alien Registration Number (A-Number) or I-94 Number (if any)
    I-94 133-56210988

11. Have you ever before applied for employment authorization from INS?
    ☐ Yes (If yes, complete below)   ☒ No
    Which INS Office?   Date(s)

    Results (Granted or Denied - attach all documentation)

12. Date of Last Entry into the U.S. (Month/Day/Year)
    August 10, 1981

13. Place of Last Entry into the U.S.
    Newark, New Jersey

14. Manner of Last Entry (Visitor, Student, etc.)
    accompanying minor/exchange/student

15. Current Immigration Status (Visitor, Student, etc.)
    F-1 student

16. Go to the Eligibility Section on the reverse of this form and check the box which applies to you. In the space below, place the number of the box you selected on the reverse side:

    Eligibility under 8 CFR 274a.12

    (c) (9) (   )

Complete the reverse of this form before signature.

Your Certification: I certify, under penalty of perjury under the laws of the United States of America, that the foregoing is true and correct. Furthermore, I authorize the release of any information which the Immigration and Naturalization Service needs to determine eligibility for the benefit I am seeking. I have read the reverse of this form and have checked the appropriate block, which is identified in item #16, above.

Signature   Telephone Number   Date
Carla R. Stone   (201) 123-4567   8/11/87

Signature of Person Preparing Form If Other Than Above: I declare that this document was prepared by me at the request of the applicant and is based on all information of which I have any knowledge.

Print Name   Address   Signature   Date

Initial Receipt	Resubmitted	Relocated		Completed		
		Rec'd	Sent	Approved	Denied	Returned

Form I-765 (08/24/89) Page 2

Eligibility

GROUP A

The current immigration laws and regulations permit certain classes of aliens to work in the United States. If you are an alien described within one of the classes below, you do not need to request that employment authorization be granted to you, but you do need to request a document to show that you are able to work in the United States. **NO FEE will be required for your original card. If you need a replacement employment authorization document the fee will be required to process your request.**

Place an **X** in the box next to the number which applies to you.

☐ (a) (3) - I have been admitted to the United States as a refugee.

☐ (a) (4) - I have been paroled into the United States as a refugee.

☐ (a) (5) - My application for asylum has been granted.

☐ (a) (6) - I am the fiancé(e) of a United States citizen and I have K-1 nonimmigrant status; **OR** I am the dependent of a fiancé(e) of a United States citizen and I have K-2 nonimmigrant status.

☐ (a) (7) - I have N-8 or N-9 nonimmigrant status in the United States.

☐ (a) (8) - I am a citizen of the Federated States of Micronesia or of the Marshall Islands.

☐ (a) (9) - I have been granted suspension of deportation and I have not yet been granted lawful permanent resident status in the United States.

☐ (a) (10) - I have been granted withholding of deportation.

☐ (a) (11) - I have been granted extended voluntary departure by the Attorney General.

GROUP C

The immigration law and regulations allow certain aliens to apply for employment authorization. If you are an alien described in one of the classes below you may request employment authorization from the INS and, if granted, you will receive an employment authorization document.

Place an **X** in the box next to the number which applies to you.

☐ (c) (1) - I am the dependent of a foreign government official (A-1 or A-2). I have attached certification from the Department of State recommending employment. **NO FEE.**

☐ (c) (2) - I am the dependent of an employee of the Coordination Council of North American Affairs and I have E-1 nonimmigrant status. I have attached certification of my status from the American Institute of Taiwan. **FEE REQUIRED.**

☐ (c) (3) (i) - I am a foreign student (F-1). I have attached certification from the designated school official recommending employment for economic necessity. I have also attached my INS Form I-20 ID copy. **FEE REQUIRED.**

☐ (c) (3) (ii) - I am a foreign student (F-1). I have attached certification from the designated school official recommending employment for practical training. I have also attached my INS Form I-20 ID copy. **FEE REQUIRED.**

☐ (c) (3) (iii) - I am a foreign student (F-1). I have attached certification from my designated school official and I have been offered employment under the sponsorship of an international organization within the meaning of the International Organization Immunities Act. I have certification from this sponsor and I have also attached my INS Form I-20 ID copy. **FEE REQUIRED.**

☐ (c) (4) - I am the dependent of an officer or employee of an international organization (G-1 or G-4). I have attached certification from the Department of State recommending employment. **NO FEE.**

☐ (c) (5) - I am the dependent of an exchange visitor and I have J-2 nonimmigrant status. **FEE REQUIRED.**

☐ (c) (6) - I am a vocational foreign student (M-1). I have attached certification from the designated school official recommending employment for practical training. I have also attached my INS Form I-20ID Copy. **FEE REQUIRED.**

☐ (c) (7) - I am the dependent of an individual classified as NATO-1 through NATO-7. **FEE REQUIRED.**

☐ (c) (8) - I have filed an application for asylum in the United States and the application is pending. **FEE REQUIRED FOR REPLACEMENT ONLY.**

☒ (c) (9) - I have filed an application for adjustment of status to lawful permanent resident status and the application is pending. **FEE REQUIRED.**

☐ (c) (10) - I have filed an application for suspension of deportation and the application is still pending. **I understand that I must show economic necessity and I will refer to the instructions concerning "Basic Criteria to Establish Economic Necessity." FEE REQUIRED.**

☐ (c) (11) - I have been paroled into the United States for emergent reasons or for reasons in the public interest. **FEE REQUIRED.**

☐ (c) (12) - I am a deportable alien and I have been granted voluntary departure either prior to or after my hearing before the immigration judge. **FEE REQUIRED.**

☐ (c) (13) - I have been placed in exclusion or deportation proceedings. I have not received a final order of deportation or exclusion and I have not been detained. **I understand that I must show economic necessity and I will refer to the instructions concerning "Basic Criteria to Establish Economic Necessity." FEE REQUIRED.**

☐ (c) (14) - I have been granted deferred action by INS as an act of administrative convenience to the government. **I understand that I must show economic necessity and I will refer to the instructions concerning "Basic Criteria to Establish Economic Necessity." FEE REQUIRED.**

☐ (c) (15) (i) - I am a nonimmigrant temporary worker (H-1, H-2, H-3) and I have filed a timely application for extension of my stay. My application for extension has not been adjudicated within 120 days. **FEE REQUIRED.**

☐ (c) (15) (ii) - I am a nonimmigrant exchange visitor (J-1) and I have filed a timely application for extension of my stay. My application for extension has not been adjudicated within 120 days. **FEE REQURIED.**

☐ (c) (15) (iii) - I am a nonimmigrant intracompany transferee (L-1) and I have filed a timely application for extension of my stay. My application has not been adjudicated within 120 days. **FEE REQUIRED.**

☐ (c) (15) (iv) - I am a nonimmigrant E-1, E-2, I, A-3, or G-5 and I have filed a timely application for extension of my stay. My application has not been adjudicated within 120 days. **FEE REQUIRED.**

She kept a photocopy of this form, then filed it with the required fee in person at the nearest INS office. When she went to file the form I-765, Carla carried with her the folder of copies that accompanied her I-485 application and her original I-94 card.

Some months after filing the I-485 application, Carla and David were summoned to appear for an interview. They brought to the interview originals of all documents of which they had filed photocopies. In addition, they brought along their entire copies envelope, their wedding folder, their wedding album and videotape, David's birth certificate, and snapshots taken of them together since their wedding day. At the interview, an examiner checked all of the forms and documentation that Carla and David had submitted. Then the interviewer questioned David and Carla separately. The questions concerned daily living habits, what they had eaten for dinner the previous Saturday, the brand of toothpaste each used, and the color of the sheets on the bed. David and Carla are married and are living together so should have had no trouble answering the questions, but it is easy to get confused under this type of questioning. Fortunately they had been warned by friends that they would have to submit to this type of questioning, called a "Stokes interview," so they did their best to answer politely. The process may be unpleasant and even insulting, but the end result, the green card, is worth it. So smile, as they did.

At the conclusion of the interview, Carla received assurances and a receipt showing that she was green-card eligible. However, since Carla and David had been married for less than two years before applying for the green card, Carla was not eligible for a permanent green card. Most green cards are permanent except for the requirement that they be renewed every ten years. In general, green cards are permanently valid unless their holder commits a deportable offense or abandons U.S. residency by remaining outside of the country for an excessive period of time. However, green cards issued on the basis of a marriage of less than two years to an American citizen are valid for only two years. These are called "conditional green cards," and the condition must be removed precisely at the end of the two-year conditional period. If the condition is not removed at the proper time, INS assumes that the marriage was not valid, the green card is cancelled, and the now unauthorized alien is deported.

To remove the condition and obtain a permanent green card, wait two years and then file form I-751, Petition to Remove the Conditions on Residence. This form should be filed 90 days before the second anniversary of the conditional green card. With this form you must submit a photocopy of your conditional green card and documents proving that the marriage has continued. Documents which might support your claim of legitimate marriage could include birth certificates of children born within the two-year period, joint tax returns, insurance policies naming each other as beneficiaries, joint loan agreements, and such. I-751 and its fee are filed with the nearest regional service center.

Ninety days before expiration of Carla's conditional green card, Carla and David together prepared the following I-751.

U.S. Department of Justice
Immigration and Naturalization Service

OMB No. 1115-0145
Petition to Remove the Conditions on Residence

START HERE - Please Type or Print

Part 1.   Information about you.

Family Name STONE	Given Name Carla	Middle Initial R.

Address - C/O:

Street Number and Name 46 Chester Street	Apt. # 3-L

City Madison	State or Province New Jersey

Country U.S.A.	ZIP/Postal Code 07941

Date of Birth (month/day/year) June 6, 1966	Country of Birth Argentina

Social Security # 246-80-1234	A # A066987002

Conditional residence expires on (month/day/year)   November 30, 1989

Mailing address if different from residence in C/O:

Street Number and Name	Apt #

City	State or Province

Country	ZIP/Postal Code

FOR INS USE ONLY

Returned

Receipt

Resubmitted

Reloc Sent

Reloc Rec'd

☐ Applicant Interviewed

Remarks

Action

Part 2.   Basis for petition *(check one).*

a. ☒ My conditional residence is based on my marriage to a U.S. citizen or permanent resident, and we are filing this petition together.

b. ☐ I am a child who entered as a conditional permanent resident and I am unable to be included in a Joint Petition to Remove the Conditional Basis of Alien's Permanent Residence (Form I-751) filed by my parent(s).

My conditional residence is based on my marriage to a U.S. citizen or permanent resident, but I am unable to file a joint petition and I request a waiver because: (check one)

c. ☐ My spouse is deceased.

d. ☐ I entered into the marriage in good faith, but the marriage was terminated though divorce/annulment.

e. ☐ I am a conditional resident spouse who entered in to the marriage in good faith, or I am a conditional resident child, who has been battered or subjected to extreme mental cruelty by my citizen or permanent resident spouse or parent.

f. ☐ The termination of my status and deportation from the United States would result in an extreme hardship.

Part 3.   Additional information about you.

Other names used (*including maiden name*): Carla A. Rojas	Telephone # (201) 123-4567

Date of Marriage August 2, 1987	Place of Marriage Madison, New Jersey

If your spouse is deceased, give the date of death (month/day/year)

Are you in deportation or exclusion proceedings?   ☐ Yes ☒ No

Was a fee paid to anyone other than an attorney in connection with this petition?   ☐ Yes ☒ No

To Be Completed by Attorney or Representative, if any

☐ Fill in box if G-28 is attached to represent the applicant

VOLAG#

ATTY State License #

Form I-751 (Rev. 12-4-91)   *Continued on back.*

Part 3. Additional Information about you. (con't)

Since becoming a conditional resident, have you ever been arrested, cited, charged, indicted, convicted, fined or imprisoned for breaking or violating any law or ordinace (excluding traffic regulations), or committed any crime for which you were not arrested?

☐ Yes ☒ No

If you are married, is this a different marriage than the one through which conditional residence status was obtained?

☐ Yes ☒ No

Have you resided at any other address since you became a permanent resident?

☐ Yes ☒ No *(If yes, attach a list of all addresses and dates.)*

Is your spouse currently serving employed by the U. S. government and serving outside the U.S.?

☐ Yes ☒ No

Part 4. Information about the spouse or parent through whom you gained your conditional residence

Family Name	Given Name	Middle Initial	Phone Number
STONE	David	B.	(201) 123-4567

Address: 46 Chester Street, Madison, NJ 07941

Date of Birth (month/day/year)	Social Security #	A#
March 2, 1963	083-22-1111	none

Part 5. Information about your children. *List all your children. Attach another sheet if necessary*

	Name	Date of Birth (month/day/year)	If in U S, give A#, current immigration status and U.S. Address	Living with you?
1	Adam Stone	6/17/89	born in the U.S.A.	☒ Yes ☐ No
2				☐ Yes ☐ No
3				☐ Yes ☐ No
4				☐ Yes ☐ No

Part 6. Complete if you are requesting a waiver of the joint filing petition requirement based on extreme mental cruelty.

Evaluator's ID Number: State: ☐ Number: ☐☐☐☐☐☐☐	Expires on (month/day/year)	Occupation

Last Name	First Name	Address

Part 7. Signature. *Read the information on penalties in the instructions before completing this section. If you checked block "a" in Part 2 your spouse must also sign below.*

I certify, under penalty of perjury under the laws of the United States of America, that this petition, and the evidence submitted with it, is all true and correct. If conditional residence was based on a marriage, I further certify that the marriage was entered into in accordance with the laws of the place where the marriage took place, and was not for the purpose of procuring an immigration benefit. I also authorize the release of any information from my records which the Immigration and Naturalization Service needs to determine eligibility for the benefit being sought.

Signature	Print Name	Date
Carla R. Stone	Carla Rojas Stone	August 8, 1989
Signature of Spouse *David B. Stone*	Print Name David B. Stone	August 8, 1989

Please note: If you do not completely fill out this form, or fail to submit any required documents listed in the instructions, then you cannot be found eligible for the requested benefit, and this petition may be denied.

Part 8. Signature of person preparing form if other than above.

I declare that I prepared this petition at the request of the above person and it is based on all information of which I have knowledge.

Signature	Print Name	Date

Firm Name and Address

Form I-751 (Rev. 12-4-91)   * GPO : 1992 0 - 316-463

Carla also completed another Form 9003 reflecting the fact that she had now worked for a period and that she and David had filed a joint income tax return each year since their marriage. This form served two purposes: it proved that Carla was a law abiding taxpaying citizen and it served as additional documentation of the legitimacy of her marriage to David. Here is how her new Form 9003 looked:

Form **9003** (January 1992)	Department of the Treasury—Internal Revenue Service **Additional Questions to be Completed by All Applicants for Permanent Residence in the United States**	OMB Clearance No. 1545-1065 Expires 8-31-94

This form must accompany your application for permanent residence in the United States
Privacy Act Notice: Your responses to the following questions will be provided to the Internal Revenue Service pursuant to Section 6039E of the Internal Revenue Code of 1986. Use of this information is limited to that needed for tax administration purposes. Failure to provide this information may result in a $500 penalty unless failure is due to reasonable cause.
On the date of issuance of the Alien Registration Receipt Card, the Immigration and Naturalization Service will send the following information to the Internal Revenue Service: your name, social security number, address, date of birth, alien identification number, occupation, class of admission, and answers to IRS Form 9003.

Name (*Last—Surname—Family*)	(*First—Given*)	(*Middle Initial*)
STONE	Carla	R.

Taxpayer Identification Number 2 4 6 8 0 1 2 3 4
Enter your Social Security Number (SSN) if you have one. If you do not have an SSN but have used a Taxpayer Identification Number issued to you by the Internal Revenue Service, enter that number. Otherwise, write "NONE" in the space provided; i.e., " _ _ _ _ N,O,N,E, ".

	Mark appropriate column	
	Yes	**No**
1. Are you self-employed? Mark "yes" if you own and actively operate a business in which you share in the profits other than as an investor.		x
2. Have you been in the United States for 183 days or more during any one of the three calendar years immediately preceding the current calendar year? Mark "yes" if you spent 183 days or more (not necessarily consecutive) in the United States during any one of the three prior calendar years whether or not you worked in the United States.	x	
3. During the last three years did you receive income from sources in the United States? Mark "yes" if you received income paid by individuals or institutions located in the United States. Income includes, but is not limited to, compensation for services provided by you, interest, dividends, rents, and royalties.	x	
4. Did you file a United States Individual Income Tax Return (Forms 1040, 1040A, 1040EZ or 1040NR) in any of the last three years?	x	

If you answered yes to question 4, for which tax year was the last return filed? 19 8 8

Paperwork Reduction Act Notice—We ask for the information on this form to carry out the Internal Revenue laws of the United States. You are required to give us the information. We need it to ensure that you are complying with these laws and to allow us to figure and collect the right amount of tax.
The time needed to complete and file this form will vary depending on individual circumstances. The estimated average time is 5 minutes. If you have comments concerning the accuracy of this time estimate or suggestions for making this form more simple, we would be happy to hear from you. You can write to both the **Internal Revenue Service**, Washington, DC 20224. Attention: IRS Reports Clearance Officer, T:FP, and **Office of Management and Budget.** Paperwork Reduction Project (1545-1065) Washington, DC 20503. **DO NOT send this form to either of these offices. Instead, return it to the appropriate office of the Department of State or the Immigration and Naturalization Service.**

Remarks
Joint return filed with husband David B. Stone, SS#083-22-1111

They photocopied the forms and all the accompanying documentation and sent the original form together with a set of photocopies by certified mail, return receipt requested. Then they waited.

About six weeks later, they were summoned to appear for an interview on September 17, 1989. Carla was instructed to undergo another physical examination by an INS physician and to submit the report on the physician's I-693. She went to the police station to make and certify another set of fingerprints and sat for more photographs conforming to the INS size and angle of view requirements. By now David and Carla had a suitcase full of documents to carry to the INS office. They brought all the materials they had brought to the original green card interview and copies of the materials sent with the petition requesting removal of the condition. In addition they brought an album of photographs of them together taken during the past two years. They also brought little Adam. Despite all this evidence, the INS inspector chose to conduct another Stokes interview. David and Carla were annoyed but were careful not to show their annoyance. They answered questions politely, and the interview was soon over. Three months later, Carla received this permanent alien registration card, this I-551, this GREEN CARD, in the mail:

GREEN CARD (front)

(back)

Applying for Naturalization

The permanent resident alien is authorized to remain in the United States indefinitely, to have a job and develop a career, and to sponsor certain family members for immigration under family preference categories. The permanent resident alien must pay taxes but cannot vote to affect the rate of taxation or to influence the use to which tax monies will be put. This right is reserved to citizens. You may become a citizen through the process of naturalization.

The first requirement for naturalization is the green card. Once you have obtained your green card, you must fulfill residency requirements. Most people are required to maintain residency within the physical boundaries of the United States for at least five years from the date of issuance of the green card before they are eligible for naturalization. Maintaining residency means actually living here. Of course, a permanent resident alien, a green card holder, may travel abroad and may live abroad temporarily for limited periods of time. The five-year requirement specifies that at least one-half of that period be spent in the U.S. and that absences from the United States be for periods of six months or less except under unusual circumstances.

A notable exemption from the five-year requirement applies to spouses of U.S. citizens. Persons married to U.S. citizens are eligible for naturalization one year after the condition has been removed from their green cards, that is, one year after they become permanent residents. The same rules concerning residency for at least half of the total waiting time and concerning length of absences applies to these spouses.

There are a few other exceptions to the residency requirements. These apply to persons married to American citizens who are employed by the U.S. government and are assigned abroad and to certain non-Americans who have served in the United States armed forces.

Any time after he or she has become a permanent resident of the United States, a green card holder over the age of 18 may file a form N-300, Application to File Declaration of Intention. Until 1952, filing this form was a necessary first step along the path towards naturalization. In fact, the Declaration of Intention was known as "First Papers." Since 1952, this form has no longer been required by the INS. However, if a permanent resident alien has taken out first papers, that person is interpreted as having made a positive statement, "I intend to become a U.S. citizen as soon as I am eligible." Where U.S. citizenship is required for issuance of certain certifications or professional licenses, filing of a Declaration of Intention may allow for temporary licensing and the opportunity to practice the profession before final issuance of citizenship papers. Sometimes, even where citizenship is not a legal requirement, a Declaration of Intention may serve to reassure a prospective employer of the applicant's enthusiasm and may open doors to employment.

Some people are naturally cautious and choose to file a Declaration of Intention just to be extra certain to maintain a full file and to leave no room for doubt of their sincerity in seeking citizenship. This filing is not necessary, but it is permissible. If you choose to file N-300 or if you are required to file for purposes of licensing or employment, you may study the copy in the forms appendix and may obtain your own copy by mail request from your nearest INS office.

Since a permanent green card does not expire, the holder of a green card is not under time pressure to file a Petition for Naturalization, N-400. It is possible to remain a permanent resident alien for an entire lifetime, but, since you have purchased this book, you obviously are planning on becoming a U.S. citizen. You may file form N-400 when you reach a date 90 days or closer to the date by which you will have fulfilled your residency requirement. You may also wait until after you have fulfilled or surpassed the required term of residency. There is no deadline to meet, but the sooner after reaching eligibility that you apply, the sooner you can begin enjoying all the privileges of citizenship.

Requirements for Naturalization

Filing of a form N-400 does not automatically confer citizenship. There are a number of requirements that every petitioner must meet.

- To apply for and become a citizen in your own right, you must be at least 18 years of age. Children under the age of 18 become naturalized automatically with the naturalization of both parents. These children attain "derivative" citizenship. They may petition the court and receive their own papers as well, but their citizenship becomes effective when their parents take the oath.
- You must have a valid green card and must have fulfilled the residency requirements that apply to you. At least one-half of your five-year or three-year period of residency must have been spent within the physical boundaries of the United States, and you must have been absent for not more than six months at a stretch except under exceptional circumstances.
- Along with fulfilling your residency in the United States, you must have lived for at least three months in the same state or the same INS district. The naturalization process may take a long time even after you have fulfilled all requirements. If you move while your application is being processed, your application may be transferred to your new district.
- You must have maintained good moral character throughout your residency. Part of maintaining good moral character involves paying your taxes and not committing crimes. If you are a young man between the ages of 18 and 26, good moral character involves registering in the Selective Service System. Any activity that might have made you excludable when you applied for permanent status will make you ineligible for citizenship now. Furthermore, if it is now discovered that you lied on any previous application forms, you will be denied citizenship.
- You must understand and be able to make yourself understood in simple English and must have some knowledge of American government and history. If you are over the age of 50 and have been in this country more than 20 years or over the age of 55 and have been in the U.S. for more than 15 years, you may be excused from the English language requirement. There is no exemption from the requirement that you know about and appreciate the significance of American government and history. [If you are excused from the English requirement by virtue of age and time in this country (known as the 50/20 waiver) you may answer questions in your own language. You may also sign your name in the alphabet of your own language if you do not know how to sign it in English. Of course special allowances are made for the applicant who is unable to speak because of deafness or physical inability or who is unable to read or write because of blindness or paralysis.]

Do not take the English requirement nor the history and government requirement lightly. People have been denied U.S. citizenship because they were unable to pass these tests. There are a number of ways to prepare yourself and a number of ways to prove your knowledge.

Prepare Yourself by Going to School

If you are of school age, enroll in public school and pursue secondary education to high school graduation. This course of action will serve two useful purposes. You will be well prepared for the citizenship examination, and you will earn the high school diploma which you will need to get a job and advance in a career. If you hope for a college education, you must earn that high school diploma to qualify for college admission. A high school graduate should have no trouble proving English ability and knowledge of American history and government either in an oral interview/examination or by means of written multiple-choice examination.

If you are over the age of 22 (the age may vary in different states), you are no longer eligible for daytime public education. However, many public school systems offer an opportunity to earn a high school diploma in a night high school program. You may also earn a high school equivalency diploma (a GED diploma) by enrolling in GED preparation courses and passing the GED examination. If you are able to prepare yourself individually, you may take the GED examination without ever enrolling in a course. If Spanish is your native language, you may earn your GED diploma by taking and passing a GED exam in Spanish. There are two ARCO publications which give valuable training and practice in the subjects and question styles of the GED exams. These books are: *GED* and *GED en Espanol*. These books are available at your bookstore. If you do not wish to prepare for a United States high school diploma at this time, you can enroll in a citizenship class. Many public school systems offer an evening citizenship class. You may also find citizenship education offered at a community college, in a union or company sponsored program, or in classes offered by an organization of people who immigrated from your homeland and who are now eager to help others from their former country. Some of these programs will give you excellent preparation for oral and written tests even if the programs themselves are not accredited. The accredited programs, usually those given in schools or community colleges, lead to an examination at the last class meeting. If you pass the final test of an accredited school program, the INS will be notified of your passing and you will receive a certificate of completion. You will not need to be tested again. The naturalization examiner will not ask you history or government questions and you will not have to prove your literacy in English by writing a sentence at the interview. You will still have to answer personal questions and questions based on your application when you appear for your interview.

Prepare Yourself by Individual Study

If you are able to read and understand printed English, you may choose to study on your own instead of attending formal classes.

You might go to your local public library and ask the librarian to assist you in choosing textbooks written at your level of English reading ability. If you complete a book on American history and another covering American government, you should find yourself well prepared for any INS examination. Individual study from textbooks will take longer than individual study from pamphlets, but it will give you a more complete education and understanding.

If your daily routine does not leave you a great deal of study time, some shorter study programs may prove adequate. The INS has prepared a series of booklets which it has published and made available through the Government Printing Office. The 100 standard questions from which examiners draw the questions they ask at the naturalization interview and the multiple-choice New Citizens Project/ETS English and Citizenship

Examination which we are about to describe to you are based on information in these booklets. These booklets and their prices at the time of publication of this book are:

United States History: 1600-1987 — $5.50

U.S. Government Structure — $3.00

Citizenship Education and Naturalization Information — $2.00

You may order these booklets by mail. Send a check or money order made out to the Superintendent of Documents:

Superintendent of Documents
P.O. Box 371954
Pittsburgh, PA 15250-7954

Or you may order by telephone and credit card by calling (202) 783-3238. There is no sales tax and no shipping charge for government publications.

If you feel that you already have a reasonable knowledge of American history and government, then you may find the chapter of this book entitled "Preparing for Your Exam" sufficient as a compact and handy review. Or you might start with this chapter and, if you find it puzzling, follow up with a textbook that can fill in the gaps in your knowledge.

Choose the Testing Method that is Best for You

If you attend an accredited citizenship program and pass the final exam, you do not have to worry about any further testing. In such a case, you must merely answer the interviewer's questions about your application and about you. However, if you have attended the classes offered by an unaccredited program or have studied on your own, you must prove to the INS that you have the knowledge and understanding that is expected of new citizens.

The most common way to prove your knowledge to the INS is to answer the questions of a naturalization examiner. The examiner asks questions about U.S. government and history, and the applicant answers. As a test of literacy in English, the examiner dictates a short sentence in English, and the applicant must write that sentence on a piece of paper. You may have heard frightening stories from people who were examined in the past. The examiner asked complicated questions based on facts that were not even covered or were not stressed in the textbooks and then became impatient and even unpleasant when the applicant was unable to answer. The questions and the manner of questioning were determined by the personality of the examiner, his or her mood of the day, and the first impression made by the applicant. The process has been made fairer and more "user friendly" in the past few years. Now the INS has prepared a standardized list of 100 questions. Examiners may choose as many or as few of the questions as they wish and may choose which questions to ask. They are limited, however, to asking only questions on the list. The topics covered by the questions are important topics, and the facts that the immigrant is expected to know are important facts. The most recent complaints about the examination process have been concerned with the long wait for the interview. The changes in immigration laws over the past years have permitted many previously unauthorized aliens to gain permanent status and to begin the naturalization process. Other provisions of the new laws have permitted greater numbers of immigrants to enter the country, to fulfill the requirements, and to petition for naturalization. At the same time, the government is trying to hold down operating costs and has reduced the number of personnel. What this means to people who want to become citizens is that they may have to wait up to a year, or even a bit longer, from the time they become eligible by virtue of residency and filing of N-400, Application to File Petition for Naturalization, and the time they are called for the interview.

The INS recognizes that people who are eager to become United States citizens would like to be naturalized as quickly as possible. Therefore, the INS has approved The New Citizens Project English and Citizenship Examination for United States Naturalization. The New Citizens Project administers a multiple choice type examination developed by the Naturalization Assistance Board in conjunction with the Educational Testing Service. The examination is offered all over the United States at least four times a year and, in many locations, once a month. An eager prospective citizen can now take and pass an exam as soon as he or she feels adequately prepared. The interview of an applicant who has already passed a citizenship exam takes a much shorter time. As more and more people appear for their interviews after passing the New Citizens Project examination, interviews will become shorter and more applicants can be scheduled for the same day. In this way the time delay from filing of the N-400 to interview will be shortened and the whole naturalization process will be speeded up. The New Citizens Project supplies INS with the names of all the people who have passed the exam. Those people do not have to pass an oral interview/examination. Aside from the $16 fee, there is nothing to be lost from taking the New Citizens Project exam. INS is given only the names of those who pass the exam. If you fail, you can retake the exam or can wait and submit to the oral exam instead.

You may be frightened at the very thought of a written exam. Do not be. Consider these good reasons to take the New Citizens Project exam:

1. The exam is given often. You can take the exam right after you complete your study. You also can have the satisfaction of feeling that you have taken an active part in speeding the process along. Unless you know of some questionable behavior in your past, you can go into the naturalization interview knowing that you have already met the knowledge requirements and that your application will be approved. The security of having this phase of the process behind you will give you peace of mind.

2. You will be asked more questions on the written exam than at an interview, but you do not need to know all of the answers. At an oral interview, you must answer whatever questions are asked and must answer almost immediately. The written exam allows you time to think about your answers. You are permitted 30 minutes to answer 20 questions. You are far more likely to make errors or to just not be able to think of the answer under the time pressure of an oral interview. A kind examiner may permit you to miss one or two, but you are supposed to be able to answer all of the questions you are asked. The New Citizens Project exam asks 20 questions of which you must answer 12 correctly to pass. You may take two exams at the same session for the same fee. This means that you have two chances to answer 12 questions correctly. If you know your American history and government and if you can read English well enough to answer the questions, you have a very good chance of passing.

3. If you are insecure about understanding English when you are spoken to by a stranger; if you have trouble finding the right words with which to express yourself; if persons unfamiliar with your accent often have difficulty understanding you, you may find a written examination much easier to handle. Obviously, you must feel secure about your ability to read English.

4. Being questioned by an authority figure can make anyone nervous. When your naturalization depends upon the answers you give under questioning, you are

bound to become even more nervous. If you are nervous, you are likely to be unable to answer questions even though you know the material very well.

5. Multiple-choice questions ask you a question and then offer you a number of possible answers. In answering New Citizens Project questions, you choose the one best answer from four possible choices. You do not have to think up the answer, only to choose it. Most people find this much easier than actually thinking of the answer.

There are also a number of very good reasons NOT to take the New Citizens Project exam. If any of these reasons applies to you, you will probably decide not to take the exam:

1. If you have taken an accredited citizenship course and have passed its written exam, you do not need to take another exam of any sort.

2. At the New Citizens Project exam, the examiner will read the questions aloud in English as you follow the printed question. The examiner will not read the four choices to you. You must read and understand the choices and choose the answer that seems best to you. If your reading comprehension in English is poor, you may find that the oral exam is the better choice for you.

3. The New Citizens Project exam concludes with the writing test, that is, with the examiner's dictating a sentence which you must write down. There is no 50/20 waiver for the New Citizens Project exam. If you are exempt from the English language requirement because of age and time in this country, and if you cannot write English, you must not take the New Citizens Project exam. If you are exempt from the English language requirement by virtue of the 50/20 waiver, you must still prove your knowledge of U.S. history and government, but you may be questioned and give your answers in your native language.

4. The immigration process from the first visa application to the filing of N-400 is expensive. The forms themselves are supplied free of charge, but each form requires a filing fee, and some of the filing fees are quite high. In light of all the required fees, the $16 charge for the exam is not too high. However, if the $16 is $16 too much, then wait to be called for the oral interview/examination which is free of charge.

5. If you belong to a recognized religious group that observes the Sabbath on Saturday, you may encounter some difficulty finding a testing center that will administer the exam on an alternate day of the week. All of the scheduled testing, with one exception, is for the second Saturday of the month. If you are a Saturday Sabbath observer and live in the Miami area, you may take the New Citizens Project exam on a Sunday at a testing center at 10003 87th Avenue, Hialeah Gardens, FL 33016. The telephone number of this center is (305) 558-4114. Call the center to inquire about date and time.

If you live in the New York City area, you can arrange an alternative day of the week individually by contacting either of two cooperative testing agencies. For Brooklyn testing, contact Project Ari at 3300 Coney Island Avenue, telephone (718) 934-3500. For Manhattan testing, special arrangements may be made through the Northern Manhattan Coalition for Immigration Rights located at JHS 143, 515 West 182nd Street, telephone (212) 781-0355.

If you think you would like to take the New Citizens Project exam, write to:

New Citizens Project/ETS
2 North Lake, Suite 540
Pasadena, CA 91101-1867

Or call: (800) 358-6230. Ask for registration materials. Along with the application form, you will receive a list of testing centers for your area of the United States. Choose a few centers that you can conveniently get to and call the person named on the list for that location. Explain your religious restriction and ask if the center would be willing to make an accommodation for you. The testing center can write to the same Pasadena, California, office from which you got your list or can telephone (818) 578-1971 to speak to the project supervisor about special arrangements. The day-of-the week adjustment should be possible, but if you are a Saturday Sabbath observer and cannot arrange for non-Saturday testing, then you cannot take advantage of the New Citizens Project exam.

Taking the New Citizens Project Exam

If you decide that passing the New Citizens Project exam is the best way for you to prove your knowledge of American history and government and of the English language, and if you feel that you are ready, you may take the exam before you apply for naturalization. However, you must apply for naturalization by filing N-400, within one year of the date on which you take the test. If you pass the test and file for naturalization within one year of the test date, your test score will be accepted no matter how long the naturalization process actually takes.

When you are ready for the exam, contact the New Citizens Project/ETS by writing to 2 North Lake, Suite 540, Pasadena, CA 91101-1867 or by calling (800) 358-6230. You will receive a registration form that looks like this:

Effective: December 1, 1992

The 1993 Registration Form for the New Citizens Project
English and Citizenship Examination for Naturalization

Eligibility: This test is for those individuals who have been a permanent U.S. resident for 4 years from the date they were given permanent residency. There is no charge to complete this form.

*Please print the information requested here. Print your name exactly as it appears on your green card. (Those with 9 digit numbers should omit the "0" in front.) It would be helpful to send a copy of your green card.

"A" Number: A ☐ ☐ ☐ ☐ ☐ ☐ ☐ ☐

Name: _____
            (First Name)   (Last Name)

Address: _____

City _____ State _____ ZIP _____

Phone _____

Your ticket to the examination session and examination results will be mailed to the address you indicate above.

*Please check all test dates acceptable to you. If your date is not available we will schedule you for the next date.

☐ January 9   ☐ February 13   ☐ March 13   ☐ April 10   ☐ May 8   ☐ June 12
☐ July 10   ☐ August 14   ☐ September 11   ☐ October 9   ☐ November 13   ☐ December 11

All Saturday tests begin at 10:30 a.m. You must check-in by 10:00 a.m. at the test center.

At which test center/s do you want to take the exam? Make your choice by selecting at least two test center numbers on the reverse side of this page. Note that centers marked with "†" are *only open* in March, June, September and December.

First Choice: Test Center Number ☐ ☐ ☐   City: _____

Second Choice: Test Center Number ☐ ☐ ☐   City: _____

Third Choice: Test Center Number ☐ ☐ ☐   City: _____

To register, ETS must **receive no later than 30 days before the test date** this completed form and a money order for $16 (SIXTEEN) dollars made out to **New Citizens Project/ETS** to:

New Citizens Project/ETS
2 North Lake, Suite 540
Pasadena, CA 91101-1867

Note: If ETS cannot schedule you on the dates you select, your money will be refunded. If you miss your scheduled date, simply register again at no cost using your ticket in place of a money order. No refunds are made to ticketed persons.

If you miss the registration deadline, you may come to any test center on the day of the test if you do the following:
- Bring with you a money order for TWENTY ($20.00) dollars made out to **New Citizens Project/ETS**
- Bring this form with you with your name, address, and "A" number written in above
- Please note that you cannot be guaranteed a place; you may check with the Test Center by phone on the Thursday or Friday before the test

---

Reminder: The INS will accept these examination results *only if you apply for naturalization within one year* of the date of the test. For example, if you take the test on December 10, 1992, you must apply by December 10, 1993. The test satisfies section 312, demonstrated knowledge of United States history and government and English proficiency in reading and writing. At the interview, you must be able to understand and respond in English to questions about the contents of your application. *Be sure to take your ticket, a photo ID and an INS document that shows your "A" number with you to the test center.* For many, the INS card will serve as the photo ID.

On the back of the registration form, you will find the test center list for the region of the country in which you plan to take the test. The list includes addresses, telephone numbers, and the names of individuals you may contact to ask further questions. If you need to make special arrangements for non-Saturday testing, or if you want information as to availability of seats for walk-in registration, you will know who to call. You will also receive a pamphlet entitled "A Guide to the New Citizens Project English and Citizenship Examination." So that you may know in advance just what to expect, we quote now, with permission, from this pamphlet.

These examinations for persons with lawful permanent residence seeking to become United States citizens have been officially approved by the Immigration and Naturalization Service (INS). A passing score obtained no more than one year before your application for citizenship will satisfy all requirements of the INS for knowledge of English (reading and writing proficiency), history and government for naturalization. If you pass this examination, you will not be asked questions about history, government, or your reading and writing abilities in English at your INS interview. However, at the interview you must be able to understand and respond in English to questions about the contents of your application. If you decide instead to be examined by INS during your interview and fail that examination, you can take this examination instead of a re-examination at the INS.

These examinations include:

• Twenty (20) questions in English on United States history and government based on the Federal Textbooks on Citizenship. (See the list of these textbooks on page 40.)
  You must mark the right answer from four possible answers given. The examiner will read aloud the questions (but not the possible answers) as you read them from your test booklet.
• One (1) short sentence read to you in English which you must write or print in English.

Other Information About These Examinations:

• When you sign up for an examination date you will take two equivalent examinations (Part A and Part B — each with different questions). You have two chances to pass. You need to pass only one of the two examinations.
• The examination costs only $16 for one date if you register by mail ahead of time.
• The examination costs $20 for one date if you do not register by mail ahead of time.
• Each examination takes only 1/2 hour (30 minutes); a complete examination session takes just over 1 hour.
• While you need not take both examinations, the one fee covers both examinations. Completing the full session can only help you to pass the examination. It is recommended that you take both examinations.
• These examinations are offered in all centers four times a year in March, June, September, and December, and in many test centers the examinations are offered on a monthly basis. Check current registration forms for exact dates and locations.
  To pass any test, you need to answer 12 out of 20 questions correctly on any one date. You also need to pass one of the writing exercises on the same date, even if you are exempt from the language requirement due to age or length of residence.

If you pass—INS is notified that you passed. You will not be tested again by INS. You also will receive an official notice that you passed. You should keep this notice and bring it to your naturalization interview with INS.

If you fail—NO information about your score is given to INS.

You can take the test again by signing up and paying the fee.

There are two ways to take the test—

• The best way is to sign up in advance by mail. To sign up for the test ahead of time, you should use the list of test centers on the registration form included here. Be sure to fill out the registration form completely (full address, etc.) and mail it to the address on the form. Enclose a money order for $16 (sixteen dollars) made out to New Citizens Project/ETS. Do not send cash. ETS must receive your registration form and money order 30 days before the test date or it will be returned to you.

You will receive a ticket for the test session in the mail no later than three days before the test. If you do not receive your ticket by then, please call (818) 578-1971.

Be sure to take your ticket, a photo ID and an INS card or other document that shows your "A" number with you to the test center. You may have a card issued by INS that can serve as the photo ID.

• A second way to take the examination is to come to the test center on the day of the test. You may call ahead to the center on the Thursday or Friday before the test to make sure the test session will be conducted as scheduled and to obtain directions to the test center. Test center managers may decide not to offer the test if no test-takers signed up ahead of time. The fee for taking the test without signing up is $20.

Registration Form Required

To take the examination, you must obtain a registration form (1-800-358-6230). This registration form will list locations of each test center in your region. You must complete this form to sign up for the examination.

Put It All Together

You are all prepared for naturalization. You have a valid, permanent green card; you have fulfilled your residency requirement, or will have fulfilled it within the next three months; you are prepared to prove your literacy in English and your knowledge of U.S. government and history, or you have passed the New Citizens Project English and Citizenship Examination within the past year, or you have passed the course at an accredited citizenship school. Your next task is to assemble one more packet of forms. You will need:

N-400 Application for Naturalization
G-325A Biographic Information
FD-258 Fingerprint Card
Two more photos conforming to size and view regulations
A check or money order for the proper fee; fees change so verify the current amount before filing
Photocopies of your I-551 Alien Registration Receipt Card and of your birth certificate

Except for the N-400 itself, you have completed all of these forms before. You should already be friendly with the police officer at the local police station who has been taking your fingerprints on a regular basis. Maintain your sense of humor. Keep copies of everything that you are submitting to your local INS office. N-400 must be filed by mail. Be sure to send this packet by certified mail with return receipt requested just as you have been doing throughout the process.

Now wait. INS may notify you that it requires additional documents such as copies of passport or marriage certificate. Send whatever is requested. Keep records. Eventually you will be called for your final interview. Arrive for this interview promptly and appropriately dressed for an interview. You want to impress this final examiner as exactly the kind of person he or she would like to see as a citizen of the United States. At this interview, the examiner will go over your application with you and will ask questions based upon statements on your application. The examiner may also ask questions to verify your residency, questions such as "Who is your Representative in Congress?" Or the examiner may ask you why you want to become a citizen. (Do you remember the duties and benefits of citizenship that we listed at the beginning of this book? Now this information will come in handy.) If you have chosen to permit the examiner to test your English literacy and knowledge of U.S. government and history, the examiner will ask you a number of questions and will dictate a sentence for you to write. If you pass the test and satisfy the examiner with your answers to all questions, the examiner will sign your application and will recommend you to an immigration judge for naturalization as a citizen of the United States.

The final step is the taking of the oath of citizenship. In taking this oath, the new citizen formally renounces, that is gives up, all ties to the government of his or her former country and declares total allegiance to the United States.

Here is the oath of citizenship:

I hereby declare, on oath, that I absolutely and entirely renounce and abjure all allegiance and fidelity to any foreign prince, potentate, state, or sovereignty of whom or which I have heretofore been a subject or citizen; that I will support and defend the Constitution and laws of the United States of America against all enemies, foreign and domestic; that I will bear true faith and allegiance to the same; that I will bear arms on behalf of the United States when required by law; that I will perform noncombatant service in the Armed Forces of the United States when required by the law; that I will perform work of national importance under civilian direction when required by the law; and that I take this obligation freely without any mental reservation or purpose of evasion; so help me God. In acknowledgment whereof I have hereunto affixed my signature.

A person who is prohibited by religious dictates from serving in the armed forces may take the oath without the following lines:

...that I will bear arms on behalf of the United States when required by law; that I will perform noncombatant service in the Armed Forces of the United States when required by law...

Of course, the new citizen may maintain ties of affection to the old country and its people. The oath refers to governments and governmental systems not to family loyalties. The oath may be taken privately or in a small group before a judge or it may be taken in a large public ceremony on a major patriotic holiday. (If the oath is taken with the armed services exception, it must be taken before a judge.) Once the oath has been taken, the immigrant is officially a U.S. citizen. An official certificate of naturalization serves as paper recognition. The new citizen's pride should show in a happy smile.

Let us return one more time to our friend Carla and follow her as she attains citizenship.

Life as a permanent resident alien presented no difficulties for Carla, but her mother, who had now been back in Argentina for more than the two years required by her having been in the United States on a J-1 visa, was eager to immigrate to be closer to her daughter and grandson. Carla was aware that it would be easiest to bring in her mother as an immediate family member of a U.S. citizen, so she began steps to attain her own citizenship as soon as possible. After she had held her permanent, unconditional green card for a full nine months, Carla filed this form N-400.

U.S. Department of Justice
Immigration and Naturalization Service

OMB #1115-0009
Application for Naturalization

START HERE - Please Type or Print

Part 1. Information about you.

Family Name	Given Name	Middle Initial
STONE	Carla	R.

U.S. Mailing Address - Care of

Street Number and Name	Apt. #
5 Allenby Drive	none

City	County
Madison	U.S.A.

State	ZIP Code
New Jersey	07941

Date of Birth (month/day/year)	Country of Birth
June 6, 1966	Argentina

Social Security #	A #
246-80-1234	A066987002

Part 2. Basis for Eligibility (check one).

a. ☐ I have been a permanent resident for at least five (5) years .

b. ☒ I have been a permanent resident for at least three (3) years and have been married to a United States Citizen for those three years.

c. ☐ I am a permanent resident child of United States citizen parent(s) .

d. ☐ I am applying on the basis of qualifying military service in the Armed Forces of the U.S. and have attached completed Forms N-426 and G-325B

e. ☐ Other. (Please specify section of law) _____

Part 3. Additional information about you.

Date you became a permanent resident (month/day/year)	Port admitted with an immmigrant visa or INS Office where granted adjustment of status.
December 20, 1989	Newark, New Jersey

Citizenship
Argentina

Name on alien registration card (if different than in Part 1)
same

Other names used since you became a permanent resident (including maiden name)
none

Sex	Height	Marital Status:
☐ Male ☒ Female	5ft. 4in.	☐ Single ☒ Married ☐ Divorced ☐ Widowed

Can you speak, read and write English ? ☐No ☒Yes.

Absences from the U.S.:

Have you been absent from the U.S. since becoming a permanent resident? ☐ No ☒Yes.

If you answered **"Yes"**, complete the following. Begin with your most recent absence. If you need more room to explain the reason for an absence or to list more trips, continue on separate paper.

Date left U.S.	Date returned	Did absence last 6 months or more?	Destination	Reason for trip
10/4/91	10/24/91	☐ Yes ☒ No	Argentina	visit
		☐ Yes ☐ No		
		☐ Yes ☐ No		
		☐ Yes ☐ No		
		☐ Yes ☐ No		
		☐ Yes ☐ No		

Form N-400 (Rev. 07/17/91)N

Continued on back.

FOR INS USE ONLY

Returned	Receipt

Resubmitted

Reloc Sent

Reloc Rec'd

☐ Applicant Interviewed

At interview
☐ request naturalization ceremony at court

Remarks

Action

To Be Completed by Attorney or Representative, if any
☐ Fill in box if G-28 is attached to represent the applicant

VOLAG#

ATTY State License #

Part 4. Information about your residences and employment.

A. List your addresses during the last five (5) years or since you became a permanent resident, whichever is less. Begin with your current address. If you need more space, continue on separate paper:

Street Number and Name, City, State, Country, and Zip Code	Dates (month/day/year)	
	From	To
5 Allenby Drive, Madison, NJ 07941 U.S.A.	7/1/90	present
46 Chester Street, 3-L, Madison, NJ 07941 U.S.A.	8/2/87	6/30/90

B. List your employers during the last five (5) years. List your present or most recent employer first. If none, write "None". If you need more space, continue on separate paper.

Employer's Name	Employer's Address	Dates Employed (month/day/year)		Occupation/position
	Street Name and Number - City, State and ZIP Code	From	To	
First Federal Bank	1 State St., Madison , NJ	10/2/87	4/20/89	teller

Part 5. Information about your marital history.

A. Total number of times you have been married __1__. If you are now married, complete the following regarding your husband or wife.

Family name STONE	Given name David	Middle initial B.

Address 5 Allenby Drive, Madison, NJ 07941

Date of birth (month/day/year) March 2, 1963	Country of birth U.S.A.	Citizenship U.S.A.
Social Security# 083-22-1111	A# (if applicable) N/A	Immigration status (If not a U.S. citizen) N/A

Naturalization (If applicable) (month/day/year) N/A   Place (City, State)

If you have ever previously been married or if your current spouse has been previously married, please provide the following on separate paper: Name of prior spouse, date of marriage, date marriage ended, how marriage ended and immigration status of prior spouse.

Part 6. Information about your children.

B. Total Number of Children __1__ Complete the following information for each of your children. If the child lives with you, state "with me" in the address column; otherwise give city/state/country of child's current residence. If deceased, write "deceased" in the address column. If you need more space, continue on separate paper.

Full name of child	Date of birth	Country of birth	Citizenship	A - Number	Address
Adam Stone	6/17/89	U.S.A.	U.S.A.	none	5 Allenby Dr.Madison NJ

Continued on next page

Continued on back

Part 7. Additional eligibility factors.

Please answer each of the following questions. If your answer is **"Yes"**, explain on a separate paper.

1. Are you now, or have you ever been a member of, or in any way connected or associated with the Communist Party, or ever knowingly aided or supported the Communist Party directly, or indirectly through another organization, group or person, or ever advocated, taught, believed in, or knowingly supported or furthered the interests of communism? ☐ Yes ☒ No
2. During the period March 23, 1933 to May 8, 1945, did you serve in, or were you in any way affiliated with, either directly or indirectly, any military unit, paramilitary unit, police unit, self-defense unit, vigilante unit, citizen unit of the Nazi party or SS, government agency or office, extermination camp, concentration camp, prisoner of war camp, prison, labor camp, detention camp or transit camp, under the control or affiliated with:
    a. The Nazi Government of Germany? ☐ Yes ☒ No
    b. Any government in any area occupied by, allied with, or established with the assistance or cooperation of, the Nazi Government of Germany? ☐ Yes ☒ No
3. Have you at any time, anywhere, ever ordered, incited, assisted, or otherwise participated in the persecution of any person because of race, religion, national origin, or political opinion? ☐ Yes ☒ No
4. Have you ever left the United States to avoid being drafted into the U.S. Armed Forces? ☐ Yes ☒ No
5. Have you ever failed to comply with Selective Service laws? ☐ Yes ☒ No
    If you have registered under the Selective Service laws, complete the following information:
    Selective Service Number:_____ Date Registered:_____
    If you registered before 1978, also provide the following:
    Local Board Number:_____ Classification:_____
6. Did you ever apply for exemption from military service because of alienage, conscientious objections or other reasons? ☐ Yes ☒ No
7. Have you ever deserted from the military, air or naval forces of the United States? ☐ Yes ☒ No
8. Since becoming a permanent resident, have you ever failed to file a federal income tax return? ☐ Yes ☒ No
9. Since becoming a permanent resident, have you filed a federal income tax return as a nonresident or failed to file a federal return because you considered yourself to be a nonresident? ☐ Yes ☒ No
10. Are deportation proceedings pending against you, or have you ever been deported, or ordered deported, or have you ever applied for suspension of deportation? ☐ Yes ☒ No
11. Have you ever claimed in writing, or in any way, to be a United States citizen? ☐ Yes ☒ No
12. Have you ever:
    a. been a habitual drunkard? ☐ Yes ☒ No
    b. advocated or practiced polygamy? ☐ Yes ☒ No
    c. been a prostitute or procured anyone for prostitution? ☐ Yes ☒ No
    d. knowingly and for gain helped any alien to enter the U.S. illegally? ☐ Yes ☒ No
    e. been an illicit trafficker in narcotic drugs or marijuana? ☐ Yes ☒ No
    f. received income from illegal gambling? ☐ Yes ☒ No
    g. given false testimony for the purpose of obtaining any immigration benefit? ☐ Yes ☒ No
13. Have you ever been declared legally incompetent or have you ever been confined as a patient in a mental institution? ☐ Yes ☒ No
14. Were you born with, or have you acquired in same way, any title or order of nobility in any foreign State? ☐ Yes ☒ No
15. Have you ever:
    a. knowingly committed any crime for which you have not been arrested? ☐ Yes ☒ No
    b. been arrested, cited, charged, indicted, convicted, fined or imprisoned for breaking or violating any law or ordinance excluding traffic regulations? ☐ Yes ☒ No

(If you answer yes to 15 , in your explanation give the following information for each incident or occurrence the **city**, **state**, and **country**, where the offense took place, the **date** and **nature** of the offense, and the **outcome** or **disposition** of the case).

Part 8. Allegiance to the U.S.

If your answer to any of the following questions is **"NO"**, attach a full explanation:

1. Do you believe in the Constitution and form of government of the U.S.? ☒ Yes ☐ No
2. Are you willing to take the full Oath of Allegiance to the U.S.? (see instructions) ☐ Yes ☒ No
3. If the law requires it, are you willing to bear arms on behalf of the U.S.? ☐ Yes ☒ No
4. If the law requires it, are you willing to perform noncombatant services in the Armed Forces of the U.S.? ☐ Yes ☒ No
5. If the law requires it, are you willing to perform work of national importance under civilian direction? ☒ Yes ☐ No

---

Continued on back

Part 9. Memberships and organizations.

A. List your present and past membership in or affiliation with every organization, association, fund, foundation, party, club, society, or similar group in the United States or in any other place. Include any military service in this part. If none, write "none". Include the name of organization, location, dates of membership and the nature of the organization. If additional space is needed, use separate paper.

Part 10. Complete only if you checked block " C " in Part 2.

How many of your parents are U.S. citizens? ☐ One ☐ Both (Give the following about one U.S. citizen parent:)

Family Name	Given Name	Middle Name

Address

Basis for citizenship:
☐ Birth
☐ Naturalization Cert. No.

Relationship to you (check one): ☐ natural parent ☐ adoptive parent
☐ parent of child legitimated after birth

If adopted or legitimated after birth, give date of adoption or, legitimation: *(month/day/year)*

Does this parent have legal custody of you? ☐ Yes ☐ No

(Attach a copy of relating evidence to establish that you are the child of this U.S. citizen and evidence of this parent's citizenship.)

Part 11. Signature. *(Read the information on penalties in the instructions before completing this section).*

I certify or, if outside the United States, I swear or affirm, under penalty of perjury under the laws of the United States of America that this application, and the evidence submitted with it, is all true and correct. I authorize the release of any information from my records which the Immigration and Naturalization Service needs to determine eligibility for the benefit I am seeking.

Signature *Carla R. Stone*

Date October 25, 1992

Please Note: *If you do not completely fill out this form, or fail to submit required documents listed in the instructions, you may not be found eligible for naturalization and this application may be denied.*

Part 12. Signature of person preparing form if other than above. *(Sign below)*

I declare that I prepared this application at the request of the above person and it is based on all information of which I have knowledge.

Signature	Print Your Name	Date

Firm Name
and Address

DO NOT COMPLETE THE FOLLOWING UNTIL INSTRUCTED TO DO SO AT THE INTERVIEW

I swear that I know the contents of this application, and supplemental pages 1 through_____, that the corrections , numbered 1 through_____, were made at my request, and that this amended application, is true to the best of my knowledge and belief.

Subscribed and sworn to before me by the applicant.

_____
(Examiner's Signature) Date

_____
(Complete and true signature of applicant)

Carla considered herself a nonviolent person and was a member of a religious group that was opposed to war and to participation in any activities related to military service. Even though she knew that as a mother she would never be called upon to serve, Carla felt that she could not in good conscience check "yes" as the answer to questions 2, 3, and 4 of Part 8.

She attached the following statement to her form N-400:

As a member of the Religious Society of Friends, I am constrained by training and belief from participating in any of the activities of the armed forces. As a loyal citizen of the United States, I will be happy to serve my country as needed in any activity totally unconnected to the military.

Having graduated from high school and college in the United States, Carla was confident of her English ability and of the adequacy of her knowledge of U.S. history and government. She could have passed an oral exam very easily, but she chose to take the New Citizens Project English and Citizenship Examination because she knew that this would be a far less stressful way to prove her knowledge than would be the interview/examination.

Of course she passed the written test and received the official notice that she had passed.

Carla had herself photographed and fingerprinted, completed a new form G-325 A, and made more photocopies of her passport, birth certificate and translation, and I-551 alien registration card. She also included a copy of the official notice that she had already passed the English and Citizenship Examination. She enclosed a check and sent off the package by certified mail.

The INS is very busy, so seven months passed before Carla was called for her naturalization interview. As it happened, Carla was scheduled for her naturalization interview on the day of her birthday. She wore a new suit and a very pretty blouse for the important event and arrived at the INS offices 15 minutes before her scheduled appointment. The interviewer was running behind schedule, however, and Carla had to wait two hours before she was finally called. The interviewer asked Carla what she especially liked about the United States, and Carla replied that she appreciated the opportunity to improve her social and economic status and to assume as much responsibility as she might wish. The interviewer also questioned Carla about her religious upbringing and her beliefs. These questions were prompted by her responses in Part 8 of her form N-400. Obviously Carla satisfied the interviewer with her answers. At the end of the interview, the examiner signed the N-400 and shook Carla's hand with a welcoming smile.

Six weeks later, Carla received an invitation to appear before a naturalization judge to take the oath of allegiance. Carla, David, and the baby dressed up for the occasion and appeared before the judge. Carla took her oath. Then, while still in the building, she picked up a Form I-130, Petition for Alien Relative so that she could begin the process of bringing her mother to join her family. That evening, Carla and David hired a baby sitter and went out to dinner to celebrate.

Carla's Naturalization Certificate arrived in the mail three weeks later. She promptly entered her naturalization certificate number on the otherwise completed I-130 and prepared to file the petition for her mother. The printed instructions accompanying this form say that original papers must be filed with the form. If this rule were still in effect, Carla would have filed the form in person. She was not prepared to let her new Naturalization Certificate out of her hands. However, rules have changed since the instructions were printed. The INS will now accept photocopies, so Carla filed by mail following the usual precautions of keeping a full pho-tocopied record of the filing and making use of certified mail and return receipts. Along with the I-130 and photocopy of her naturalization certificate, Carla includ-ed a copy of her own birth certificate to prove her relationship to her mother, one more G-325A for herself and a G-325A completed by her mother, sets of photos of herself and of her mother, and the required fee.

A copy of the I-130 that Carla filed for her mother begins on p. 55.

If you have read carefully through the book to this page, you should understand the pro-cedure for remaining in the United States legally, for changing from nonimmigrant to immigrant, that is, from temporary to permanent resident status, and for applying for and attaining naturalization. The next chapter will help you to prepare for the U.S. govern-ment and history portions of whatever exam you choose and will give you practical instruction for answering multiple-choice questions. The forms appendix at the back of the book includes printed instructions that accompany the forms. By seeing the forms and instructions in advance, you can gather documents that may be hard to find and can get practice in filling in the spaces. If you find some questions or some requirements to be troublesome for you, you can seek advice from an attorney who specializes in immi-gration matters. If you have prepared your questions in advance, you can take less of the attorney's time, and the consultation will cost you less money.

U.S. Department of Justice
Immigration and Naturalization Service (INS)

OMB #1115–0054
Petition for Alien Relative

DO NOT WRITE IN THIS BLOCK – FOR EXAMINING OFFICE ONLY		
Case ID#	Action Stamp	Fee Stamp
A#		
G–28 or Volag #		

Section of Law:
☐ 201 (b) spouse   ☐ 203 (a)(1)
☐ 201 (b) child   ☐ 203 (a)(2)
☐ 201 (b) parent   ☐ 203 (a)(4)
                        ☐ 203 (a)(5)
AM CON: _____

Petition was filed on: _____ (priority date)
☐ Personal Interview   ☐ Previously Forwarded
☐ Pet. ☐ Ben. "A" File Reviewed   ☐ Stateside Criteria
☐ Field Investigations   ☐ I-485 Simultaneously
☐ 204 (a)(2)(A) Resolved   ☐ 204 (h) Resolved

Remarks:

A. Relationship

1. The alien relative is my
☐ Husband/Wife ☒ Parent ☐ Brother/Sister ☐ Child

2. Are you related by adoption?
☐ Yes ☒ No

3. Did you gain permanent residence through adoption?
☐ Yes ☒ No

B. Information about you

1. Name (Family name in CAPS) (First) (Middle)
STONE   Carla   Rojas

2. Address (Number and Street) (Apartment Number)
5 Allenby Drive   none
(Town or City) (State/Country) (ZIP/Postal Code)
Madison, New Jersey   07941

3. Place of Birth (Town or City) (State/Country)
Buenos Aires, Pampas, Argentina

4. Date of Birth (Mo/Day/Yr) 6/6/66
5. Sex ☐ Male ☒ Female
6. Marital Status ☒ Married ☐ Single ☐ Widowed ☐ Divorced

7. Other Names Used (including maiden name)
Carla A. Rojas

8. Date and Place of Present Marriage (if married)
8/2/87 Madison, New Jersey

9. Social Security Number
246-80-1234
10. Alien Registration Number (if any)
N/A

11. Names of Prior Husbands/Wives
none
12. Date(s) Marriage(s) Ended

13. If you are a U.S. citizen, complete the following:
My citizenship was acquired through (check one)
☐ Birth in the U.S.
☒ Naturalization (Give number of certificate, date and place it was issued)
#987654 Newark, NJ   8/22/93
☐ Parents
Have you obtained a certificate of citizenship in your own name?
☐ Yes ☐ No
If "Yes", give number of certificate, date and place it was issued.

14a. If you are a lawful permanent resident alien, complete the following:
Date and place of admission for, or adjustment to, lawful permanent residence, and class of admission:

14b. Did you gain permanent resident status through marriage to a United States citizen or lawful permanent resident? ☐ Yes ☐ No

C. Information about your alien relative

1. Name (Family name in CAPS) (First) (Middle)
DEL CAMPO   Martina   C.

2. Address (Number and Street) (Apartment Number)
1160 Camino Cruz Blanca   1
(Town or City) (State/Country) (ZIP/Postal Code)
Buenos Aires, Pampas, Argentina

3. Place of Birth (Town or City) (State/Country)
Buenos Aires, Pampas, Argentina

4. Date of Birth (Mo/Day/Yr) 9/21/37
5. Sex ☐ Male ☒ Female
6. Marital Status ☐ Married ☐ Single ☐ Widowed ☒ Divorced

7. Other Names Used (including maiden name)
Martina del Campo y Rojas

8. Date and Place of Present Marriage (if married)
N/A

9. Social Security Number
none
10. Alien Registration Number (if any)
none

11. Names of Prior Husbands/Wives
Simon Rojas
12. Date(s) Marriage(s) Ended
December 1978

13. Has your relative ever been in the U.S.?
☒ Yes ☐ No

14. If your relative is currently in the U.S., complete the following: He or she last arrived as a (visitor, student, stowaway, without inspection, etc.)
J-1 exchange student
Arrival/Departure Record (I-94) Number   Date arrived (Month/Day/Year)
1 3 8 — 5 6 2 1 0 9 8 6   8/10/81
Date authorized stay expired, or will expire, as shown on Form I-94 or I-95
September 1, 1983

15. Name and address of present employer (if any)
Colegio Militario de Buenos Aires
Date this employment began (Month/Day/Year)
January 2, 1972

16. Has your relative ever been under immigration proceedings?
☐ Yes ☒ No   Where _____ When _____
☐ Exclusion ☐ Deportation ☐ Recission ☐ Judicial Proceedings

INITIAL RECEIPT	RESUBMITTED	RELOCATED		COMPLETED		
		Rec'd	Sent	Approved	Denied	Returned

C. (continued) Information about your alien relative

16. List husband/wife and all children of your relative (if your relative is your husband/wife, list only his or her children).

(Name)	(Relationship)	(Date of Birth)	(Country of Birth)
none			

17. Address in the United States where your relative intends to live

(Number and Street)	(Town or City)	(State)
5 Allenby Drive	Madison	New Jersey

18. Your relative's address abroad

(Number and Street)	(Town or City)	(Province)	(Country)	(Phone Number)
1160 Camino Cruz Blance, Buenos Aires, Pampas, Argentina				011-54-1-97531

19. If your relative's native alphabet is other than Roman letters, write his or her name and address abroad in the native alphabet:

(Name)	(Number and Street)	(Town or City)	(Province)	(Country)
				N/A

20. If filing for your husband/wife, give last address at which you both lived together: From To

(Name) (Number and Street) (Town or City) (Province) (Country) (Month) (Year) (Month) (Year)

21. Check the appropriate box below and give the information required for the box you checked:

☒ Your relative will apply for a visa abroad at the American Consulate in Buenos Aires, Argentina
(City)   (Country)

☐ Your relative is in the United States and will apply for adjustment of status to that of a lawful permanent resident in the office of the Immigration and Naturalization Service at _____ . If your relative is not eligible for adjustment of status, he or she will
(City)   (State)

apply for a visa abroad at the American Consulate in _____ .
(City)   (Country)

(Designation of a consulate outside the country of your relative's last residence does not guarantee acceptance for processing by that consulate. Acceptance is at the discretion of the designated consulate.)

D. Other Information

1. If separate petitions are also being submitted for other relatives, give names of each and relationship.

   N/A

2. Have you ever filed a petition for this or any other alien before?   ☐ Yes   ☒ No
   If "Yes," give name, place and date of filing, and result.

Warning: The INS investigates claimed relationships and verifies the validity of documents. The INS seeks criminal prosecutions when family relationships are falsified to obtain visas.

Penalties: You may, by law be imprisoned for not more than five years, or fined $250,000, or both, for entering into a marriage contract for the purpose of evading any provision of the immigration laws and you may be fined up to $10,000 or imprisoned up to five years or both, for knowingly and willfully falsifying or concealing a material fact or using any false document in submitting this petition.

Your Certification: I certify, under penalty of perjury under the laws of the United States of America, that the foregoing is true and correct. Furthermore, I authorize the release of any information from my records which the Immigration and Naturalization Service needs to determine eligibility for the benefit that I am seeking.

Signature *Carla R. Stone*   Date 9/13/93   Phone Number (201)123-4567

Signature of Person Preparing Form if Other than Above

I declare that I prepared this document at the request of the person above and that it is based on all information of which I have any knowledge.

Print Name _____ (Address) _____ (Signature) _____ (Date) _____

G–28 ID Number _____

Volag Number _____

NOTICE TO PERSONS FILING FOR SPOUSES IF MARRIED LESS THAN TWO YEARS

Pursuant to section 216 of the Immigration and Nationality Act, your alien spouse may be granted conditional permanent resident status in the United States as of the date he or she is admitted or adjusted to conditional status by an officer of the Immigration and Naturalization Service. Both you and your conditional permanent resident spouse are required to file a petition, Form I–751, Joint Petition to Remove Conditional Basis of Alien's Permanent Resident Status, during the ninety day period immediately before the second anniversary of the date your alien spouse was granted conditional permanent residence.

Otherwise, the rights, privileges, responsibilities and duties which apply to all other permanent residents apply equally to a conditional permanent resident. A conditional permanent resident is not limited to the right to apply for naturalization, to file petitions in behalf of qualifying relatives, or to reside permanently in the United States as an immigrant in accordance with the immigration laws.

> **Failure to file Form I–751, Joint Petition to Remove the Conditional Basis of Alien's Permanent Resident Status, will result in termination of permanent residence status and initiation of deportation proceedings.**

NOTE: You must complete Items 1 through 6 to assure that petition approval is recorded. Do not write in the section below item 6.

---

1. **Name of relative (Family name in CAPS)** (First) (Middle)
   DelCAMPO   Martina   C.

2. **Other names used by relative** (including maiden name)
   Martina delCampo y Rojas

3. **Country of relative's birth**   4. **Date of relative's birth** (Month/Day/Year)
   Argentina   September 21, 1937

5. **Your name (Last name in CAPS)** (First) (Middle)   6. **Your phone number**
   STONE   Carla   R.   (201) 123-4567

Action Stamp

SECTION
- ☐ 201 (b)(spouse)
- ☐ 201 (b)(child)
- ☐ 201 (b)(parent)
- ☐ 203 (a)(1)
- ☐ 203 (a)(2)
- ☐ 203 (a)(4)
- ☐ 203 (a)(5)

DATE PETITION FILED

☐ **STATESIDE**
CRITERIA GRANTED

SENT TO CONSUL AT;

CHECKLIST

Have you answered each question?
Have you signed the petition?
Have you enclosed:

- ☑ The filing fee for each petition?
- ☑ Proof of your citizenship or lawful permanent residence?
- ☑ All required supporting documents for each petition?

If you are filing for your husband or wife have you included:

- ☑ Your picture?
- ☑ His or her picture?
- ☑ Your G–325A?
- ☑ His or her G–325A?

Relative Petition Card
Form I–130A (Rev. 10/01/89) Y

Preparing for the Examination

If you are reading this book so as to learn how to become a U.S. citizen, you must be able to read English very well. Probably if you read so well, you also know how to write English. If you are less certain of your ability to write what you hear, then you should practice by having a friend read you short sentences that you can write. The Guide to the New Citizens Project English and Citizenship Examination which you will receive when you request registration forms, offers the following information and sample sentences:

Writing a Sentence in English

The person giving the New Citizens Project Examination will read one (1) sentence aloud two times. You will be asked to write the sentence so that someone could easily read it. These are samples of the kinds of sentences you will be asked to copy or write.
1. The birthday of the United States is on July 4th.
2. The President lives in the White House.
3. The Constitution gives freedom to people in the United States.
4. The American people live in freedom.
5. I want to live in the United States.

If you choose to take the interview/examination instead of the New Citizens Project exam, the interviewer will dictate a sentence for you to write. The sentence will be similar to the sample sentences above in terms of length and difficulty. You must be able to write what you hear, but the task is not complicated. You need only basic ability to pass this part.

The requirements in terms of knowledge of U.S. government and history are more demanding. You need to answer only a very few questions but the body of knowledge covered is great, and you have no way of knowing in advance what questions will be asked and what you personally will be expected to know. You really do have to study for this portion of the examination. When you have finished studying, you will have much more information than you need to pass the exam. More knowledge and understanding of the history and government you share with other citizens will help you to live a fuller life as a citizen.

We quote again, with permission, from the Guide to the New Citizens Project English and Citizenship Examination:

Facts on United States History and Citizenship Likely to be Covered on the New Citizens Project Examination:

Discovery and Settlement

• Christopher Columbus discovered America in 1492.
• Early settlers came from England in the 1600s.

• The original people were American Indians.
• Settlers were called colonists.
• The original 13 states were called colonies.
• The original colonies were mainly along the Atlantic or Eastern sea coast.
• The first settlers in the Southwest were Spanish.

Revolutionary War and Independence

• In the 1770s, colonists went to war with England over unfair laws.
• George Washington led the colonists in the Revolutionary War.
• On July 4, 1776, people from the 13 colonies made a statement called the Declaration of Independence.
• They met at Independence Hall in Philadelphia.
• Thomas Jefferson wrote the Declaration of Independence, which declared the colonies to be independent of England.
• The Colonial Army won the Revolutionary War.
• July 4 is a national holiday called Independence Day.
• On the American flag, each state is represented by a star. The 13 stripes represent the first 13 states.

National Government and the Constitution

• The first government in the 13 states did not work well.
• A meeting was held at Independence Hall to write a new constitution.
• This Constitution was accepted by all the states in 1789.
• This Constitution set up a strong national government that has three branches.
• The Legislative Branch makes laws.
• The Legislative Branch, called Congress, meets in the United States Capitol building in Washington, DC.
• Congress is made up of two elected bodies, the Senate and the House of Representatives.
• In the Senate each state has two members.
• In the House of Representatives, states that have more people have more members.
• The Judicial Branch includes the Supreme Court and other federal courts.
• These courts interpret and apply the Constitution and federal laws passed by Congress.
• The Executive Branch sees that the laws are carried out.
• The chief executive is the President.
• The President is elected every four years.
• The President's duties include those of Commander-in-Chief of the Armed Forces of the United States.
• George Washington was the first President.
• Each of these branches is meant to keep the other branches in balance. For example, the President may veto (not approve) a law passed by Congress. Congress can still pass the law if two-thirds of its members favor it.
• The Constitution can be changed (amended). These changes are called amendments.
• The first 10 amendments passed in 1791 are called the Bill of Rights.
• These amendments guarantee (assure) rights and liberties such as freedom of speech, freedom of press, and freedom of religion.
• According to these amendments, people are free to meet together and make public their views.
• Another amendment to the Constitution gave women the right to vote.

- All citizens who are 18 years of age have the right to vote.
- After a required period of lawful permanent residence, a person may apply for citizenship.
- All persons earning money must file tax forms.

State and Local Government

- Each state has its own constitution.
- State governments are also divided into three branches.
- The Legislative Branch usually has two elected groups, which in many states are called the Senate and the Assembly.
- The Executive Branch is headed by the Governor who is elected by the people.
- The Judicial Branch is made up of the state courts which interpret and apply state laws.
- All states have equal rights.
- No state can leave the Union.
- The national government cannot do away with any state.
- Each state sets up counties, towns, and cities to provide for local government.
- The elected head of a city is most often called a Mayor.

United States History Since 1800

- The Union was tested in the 1860s when the South attempted to leave the Union.
- This led to a bloody civil war which the North (or Union) Army finally won.
- Slavery was one of the issues that led to this war.
- Abraham Lincoln was the President who led the forces that saved the Union.
- After the Civil War, slavery was prohibited by an amendment to the United States Constitution.
- After the Civil War, the United States grew rapidly and expanded to the West with large numbers of people from other countries.
- The United States has fought several wars to protect its interests.
- In World War II (1941-45), the United States joined other nations in fighting Japan and Germany.
- World War II began for the United States with the Japanese bombing of Pearl Harbor, a naval base in Hawaii.
- Since 1945, the United States has been in wars against Communist forces in Korea and Vietnam.
- Martin Luther King, Jr. was a leader in a national civil rights movement to get rid of laws and practices that are unfair to African-American and other minority group members.

A VERY SHORT HISTORY OF THE UNITED STATES

Europeans came to America soon after its discovery by Christopher Columbus in 1492. The Spanish began exploring Mexico, Central America, and parts of North America as early as 1510. Ponce de Leon landed on the east coast of Florida a few years later.

England sent a number of expeditions to explore the new world, largely on the east coast of North America. Later a full-scale effort to establish English colonies in the New World began.

The first large group of settlers to leave England came here in 1620 in search of religious freedom. About 100 people set out from Plymouth, England, on a ship named the

Mayflower. The ship had been headed for the area of Virginia which has a mild climate. Instead, it landed in America in Cape Cod Bay in Massachusetts. The settlers decided to remain despite the hardships presented by their lack of preparation for the harsh winters of the region. Before going ashore, this group, known as "Pilgrims" drew up a document they called the Mayflower Compact. A modern restatement of the meaning of the Mayflower Compact reads:

—We whose names are underwritten, having undertaken a voyage to plant the first colony in the northern parts of Virginia, do by these present, solemnly and mutually in the presence of God and one of another, covenant and combine ourselves together into a civil body politic, for our better ordering and preservation; and by virtue hereof to enact, constitute, and frame such just and equal laws, ordinances, acts, constitutions, and offices, from time to time, as shall be thought most meet and convenient for the general good of the colony; unto which we promise all due submission and obedience.—

This group of religious dissenters had, in their simple way, created a new government, in effect the first American government, with no laws controlling religious beliefs. This feature of the Mayflower Compact found its way into the Bill of Rights of the United States Constitution in 1791.

English merchants in search of new markets encouraged emigration to the New World, and between 1660 and 1760 England had established 13 colonies in North America. Settlers from other nations arrived as well. Among the new settlers were French, Irish, Germans, and Dutch. With them came new cultures and lifestyles. Thus began the wonderful mix of peoples who became Americans.

During the period of colonization from 1660 to 1760, most colonists continued to look to England for leadership. The northern colonies, those in New England, Pennsylvania, and New York became the commercial region while the South remained agricultural. Farming was hard and expensive. Southern farmers came to rely on the use of slaves as a source of abundant, cheap labor. By 1740, there were about 150,000 slaves in the South.

Meanwhile, the thirteen colonies were growing and were functioning to a large extent independent from the king. However, in 1752, the French, with the assistance of Indians hostile to the English, began to battle the English. By the end of the French and Indian Wars which coincided with the end of the Seven Years' War in Europe (1763), England was heavily in debt. Because of the need for more revenue, England began to tighten its control in the colonies. The colonies were expected to help the English economy by paying more taxes.

As trouble developed between the colonists and the British Army, some Americans began to suggest independence from England. The First Continental Congress met in Philadelphia in September of 1774. The Congress drew up a petition to the King, the "Declaration of Rights," in which it asked for specific changes in England's attitude toward the colonies.

The Revolutionary War

England had been the "mother country" of most of the colonists. They did not all agree that they wished to become independent. The colonists' main objection was to the concept of "taxation without representation." They felt that if they had representatives in the English government they would be able to explain which taxes they found to be offensive and to propose ways in which the colonies could contribute to the well being of the English economy. England, however, would not permit colonial representation in

Parliament. In fact, in January 1775, England ordered armed troops to fire upon colonists who were rebelling against taxes in the Massachusetts colony. That incident has been called "the shot heard round the world." Most colonists who had wanted to remain loyal subjects of England quickly rallied to the cause of freedom. The American Revolution had begun. It was to last for seven years before England finally granted independence to the thirteen colonies.

The Continental Congress named George Washington, a military leader during the French and Indian Wars, to serve as commander-in chief of the Continental forces. Then, among its earliest acts, the Continental Congress asked Thomas Jefferson, who later became our third President, to draft a Declaration of Independence. The Declaration was adopted on July 4, 1776. We now observe July 4 every year as the birthdate of our nation. The Declaration of Independence is a powerful document. It first makes clear the reluctance with which the colonies are declaring their independence. Then it sets forth a clear philosophy of human rights and catalogs all the misdeeds of the King of England. The language of the Declaration is the language of 1776, but once you understand the Declaration, you will understand the causes of the Revolution and the basic roots of American government. Here is the full text of the Declaration of Independence:

"When in the course of human events, it becomes necessary for one people to dissolve the political bands which have connected them with another, and to assume among the powers of the earth, the separate and equal station to which the laws of Nature and of Nature's God entitle them, a decent respect to the opinions of mankind requires that they should declare the causes which impel them to separation.

We hold these truths to be self-evident, that all men are created equal, that they are endowed by their Creator with certain unalienable rights, that among these are life, liberty and the pursuit of happiness. That to secure these rights, governments are instituted among men, deriving their just powers from the consent of the governed,—That whenever any form of government becomes destructive of these ends, it is the right of the people to alter or to abolish it, and to institute new government, laying its foundation on such principles and organizing its powers in such form, as to them shall seem most likely to effect their safety and happiness. Prudence, indeed, will dictate that governments long established should not be changed for light and transient causes; and accordingly all experience hath shown, that man-kind are more disposed to suffer, while evils are sufferable, than to right themselves by abolishing the forms to which they are accustomed. But when a long train of abuses and usurpations, pursuing invariably the same object evinces a design to reduce them under absolute despotism, it is their right, it is their duty , to throw off such government, and to provide new guards for their future security.—Such has been the patient sufferance of these Colonies; and such is now the necessity which constrains them to alter their former systems of government. The history of the present King of Great Britain is a history of repeated injuries and usurpations, all having in direct object the establishment of an absolute tyranny over these States. To prove this, let facts be submitted to a candid world.

He has refused his assent to laws, the most wholesome and necessary for the public good.

He has forbidden his Governors to pass laws of immediate and pressing importance, unless suspended in their operation till his assent should be obtained; and when so suspended, he has utterly neglected to attend to them.

He has refused to pass other laws for the accommodation of large districts of people, unless those people would relinquish the right of representation in the legislature, a right inestimable to them and formidable to tyrants only.

He has called together legislative bodies at places unusual, uncomfortable, and distant from the depository of their public records, for the sole purpose of fatiguing them into compliance with his measures.

He has dissolved Representative Houses repeatedly, for opposing with manly firmness his invasions on the rights of the people.

He has refused for a long time, after such dissolutions, to cause others to be elected; whereby the legislative powers, incapable of annihilation, having returned to the people at large for their exercise; the State remaining in the mean time exposed to all the dangers of invasion from without, and convulsions within.

He has endeavoured to prevent the population of these States; for that purpose obstructing the laws for naturalization of foreigners; refusing to pass others to encourage their migrations hither, and raising the conditions of new appropriations of lands.

He has obstructed the administration of justice, by refusing his assent to laws for establishing judiciary powers.

He has made judges dependent on his will alone, for the tenure of their offices, and the amount and payment of their salaries.

He has erected a multitude of new offices, and sent hither swarms of officers to harass our people, and eat out their substance.

He has kept among us, in times of peace, standing armies without the consent of our legislatures.

He has affected to render the military independent of and superior to the civil power.

He has combined with others to subject us to a jurisdiction foreign to our constitution, and unacknowledged by our laws; giving his assent to their acts of pretended legislation:

For quartering large bodies of armed troops among us:

For protecting them, by a mock trial, from punishment for any murders which they should commit on the inhabitants of these States:

For cutting off our trade with all parts of the world:

For imposing taxes on us without our consent:

For depriving us in many cases, of the benefits of trial by jury:

For transporting us beyond seas to be tried for pretended offenses:

For abolishing the free system of English laws in a neighbouring province, establishing therein an arbitrary government, and enlarging its boundaries so as to render it at once an example and fit instrument for introducing the same absolute rule into these colonies:

For taking away our charters, abolishing our most valuable laws, and altering fundamentally the forms of our governments:

For suspending our own legislatures, and declaring themselves invested with power to legislate for us in all cases whatsoever.

He has abdicated government here, by declaring us out of his protection and waging war against us.

He has plundered our seas, ravaged our coasts, burnt our towns, and destroyed the lives of our people.

He is at this time transporting large armies of foreign mercenaries to complete the works of death, desolation and tyranny, already begun with circumstances of cruelty and perfidy scarcely paralleled in the most barbarous ages, and totally unworthy the head of a civilized nation.

He has constrained our fellow citizens taken captive on the high seas to bear arms against their country, to become the executioners of their friends and brethren, or to fall themselves by their hands.

He has excited domestic insurrections amongst us, and has endeavoured to bring on the inhabitants of our frontiers, the merciless Indian savages, whose known rule of warfare is an undistinguished destruction of all ages, sexes and conditions.

In every stage of these oppressions we have petitioned for redress in the most humble terms: Our repeated petitions have been answered only by repeated injury. A prince, whose character is thus marked by every act which may define a tyrant, is unfit to be the ruler of a free people.

Nor have we been wanting in attentions to our British brethren. We have warned them from time to time of attempts by their legislature to extend an unwarrantable jurisdiction over us. We have reminded them of the circumstances of our emigration and settlement here. We have appealed to their native justice and magnanimity, and we have conjured them by the ties of our common kindred to disavow these usurpations, which would inevitably interrupt our connections and correspondence. They too have been deaf to the voice of justice and of consanguinity. We must, therefore, acquiesce in the necessity which denounces our separation, and hold them, as we hold the rest of mankind, enemies in war, in peace friends.

WE, THEREFORE, the Representatives of the United States of America, in General Congress, Assembled, appealing to the Supreme Judge of the world for the rectitude of our intentions, do, in the name, and by authority of the good people of these Colonies, solemnly publish and declare, That these United Colonies are, and of right ought to be FREE AND INDEPENDENT STATES; that they are absolved from all allegiance to the British Crown, and that all political connection between them and the State of Great Britain, is and ought to be totally dissolved; and that as free and independent States, they have full power to levy war, conclude peace, contract alliances, establish commerce, and to do all other acts and things which independent States may of right do. And for the support of this Declaration, with a firm reliance on the protection of Divine Providence, we mutually pledge to each other our lives, our fortunes and our sacred honor."

Having declared itself a new nation, the United States found that it had to fight a war against England and learn to govern itself at the same time. Members of the Continental Congress drew up a document called the "Articles of Confederation." When the war for independence was over, in 1783, they set about the task of governing the nation under the Articles of Confederation. The Articles had created a very loose federation of states with almost no national government. The country could not pay its debts. Without a strong national government to coordinate the country, a United States of America could not function. The whole country would soon fall apart. A Constitutional Convention met in Philadelphia's Independence Hall throughout the summer of 1787. James Madison, later to become our fourth President, wrote draft after draft, and the delegates argued and debated until they finally agreed upon the Constitution under which the United States is still governed today. Many delegates to the convention were concerned that the Constitution as drafted set up an efficient means for governing the country but neglected the whole area of human rights. They felt that the new Constitution did not offer safeguards against the kinds of activities with which King George III of England had oppressed them. The fears of these delegates were set aside with a firm promise that a Bill of Rights would be presented as a set of Amendments to the Constitution as soon as possible. The Bill of Rights was indeed adopted in 1791. There was also much controversy and discussion on the subject of slavery. Most delegates from the northern states agreed that slavery was wrong, that one person should not be owned by another. Delegates from southern states argued that the whole southern economy and indeed that of the United States would falter without the contribution of slave labor. For some time it appeared that the delegates from the two sections of the country would never agree on a Constitution. They finally arrived at a compromise by which slavery would be permitted to continue and slaves continue to be imported into the United States until at least 1808. The delegates assumed that by 1808 the economy would be in better shape and a fully functioning Congress could legislate according to the needs and conscience of the country at that time. The delegates to the Constitutional Convention agreed that the new Constitution would go into effect when it had been ratified, that is approved, by the legislatures of nine of the states. The Constitution actually did go into effect in March of

1789, followed two years later by the Bill of Rights which had by then been ratified by three-fourths of the states as required by Article V of the Constitution itself.

The Constitution is a short document. It states its business in a few well-chosen words. Perhaps its clarity and simplicity is the secret of its endurance. The body of the Constitution consists of a Preamble stating its purpose and seven articles establishing the framework of the government, defining relationships among the states and between the states and the federal government, and prescribing the amendment process.

The entire Preamble is as follows:

WE THE PEOPLE of the United States, in order to form a more perfect Union, establish justice, insure domestic tranquility, provide for the common defense, promote the general welfare, and secure the blessings of liberty to ourselves and our posterity, do ordain and establish this Constitution for the United States of America.

Your citizenship examination will probably include some questions about the Constitution, but it will not require you to know details nor precisely where to find specific facts. The commentary that accompanies the full text of the Constitution on the following pages will highlight the information that it is important for you to know.

ARTICLE I

SECTION 1. All legislative powers herein granted shall be vested in a Congress of the United States, which shall consist of a Senate and House of Representatives.

SECTION 2. The House of Representatives shall be composed of members chosen every second year by the people of the several States, and the electors in each State shall have the qualifications requisite for electors of the most numerous branch of the State Legislature. [**Members of the House of Representatives serve for two years, then must present themselves for reelection.**]

No person shall be a representative who shall not have attained to the age of twenty-five years, and been seven years a citizen of the United States, and who shall not, when elected, be an inhabitant of that State in which he shall be chosen. [**Members of the House of Representatives must be at least 25 years old and must live in the state that they represent.**]

Representatives and direct taxes shall be apportioned among the several States which may be included within this Union, according to their respective numbers, which shall be determined by adding to the whole number of free persons, including those bound to service for a term of years, and excluding Indians not taxed, three-fifths of all other persons. The actual enumeration shall be made within three years after the first meeting of the Congress of the United States, and within every subsequent term of ten years, in such manner as they shall by law direct. The number of representatives shall not exceed one for every thirty thousand, but each State shall have at least one representative; and until such enumeration shall be made, the State of New Hampshire shall be entitled to choose three, Massachusetts eight, Rhode Island and Providence Plantations one, Connecticut five, New York six, New Jersey four, Pennsylvania eight, Delaware one, Maryland six, Virginia ten, North Carolina five, South Carolina five, and Georgia three. [**This paragraph requires that state delegations to the House of Representatives are to be based on population. It provides for a population census to be made every ten years. The paragraph also states that Indians need pay no taxes but that if they are not taxed they are not counted as persons and that slaves count as three-fifths of a person. This method of counting the population for representation in Congress was one**] of the major compromises reached in drafting a Constitution acceptable to delegates from all regions of the colonies.]

When vacancies happen in the representation from any State, the Executive authority thereof shall issue writs of election to fill such vacancies.

The House of Representatives shall choose their Speaker and other officers; and shall have the sole power of impeachment. **[Impeachment is the means for removing the President, Vice President, and federal judges from office. All impeachment proceedings must begin in the House of Representatives.]**

SECTION 3. The Senate of the United States shall be composed of two senators from each State, chosen by the legislature thereof, for six years and each senator shall have one vote. **[Senators serve a six-year term. The Constitution as originally written and passed provided that Senators be elected by state legislatures rather than by the people. This method of electing Senators was changed in 1913 by the 17th Amendment.]**

Immediately after they shall be assembled in consequence of the first election, they shall be divided as equally as may be into three classes. The seats of the senators of the first class shall be vacated at the expiration of the second year, of the second class at the expiration of the fourth year, and of the third class at the expiration of the sixth year, so that one-third may be chosen every second year; and if vacancies happen by resignation, or otherwise, during the recess of the legislature of any State, the executive thereof may make temporary appointments until the next meeting of the legislature, which shall then fill such vacancies. **[Terms of Senators are staggered so that only one-third of the Senate is elected every two years. This paragraph sets the mechanism in motion.]**

No person shall be a senator who shall not have attained to the age of thirty years, and been nine years a citizen of the United States, and who shall not, when elected, be an inhabitant of that State for which he shall be chosen. **[A Senator must be at least 30 years old and must live in the state from which elected.]**

The Vice President of the United States shall be President of the Senate, but shall have no vote, unless they be equally divided. **[The Vice President presides over the Senate and has the power to vote to break a tie.]**

The Senate shall choose their other officers, and also a President pro tempore, in the absence of the Vice President, or when he shall exercise the office of President of the United States.

The Senate shall have the sole power to try all impeachments. When sitting for that purpose, they shall be on oath or affirmation. When the President of the United States is tried, the Chief Justice shall preside: And no person shall be convicted without the concurrence of two thirds of the members present. **[If the House of Representative votes to impeach the President, Vice President, or another impeachable official, the Senate conducts a trial. The vote of two-thirds of the voting Senators is required for conviction.]**

Judgment in cases of impeachment shall not extend further than to removal from office, and disqualification to hold and enjoy any office or honor, trust or profit under the United States; but the party convicted shall nevertheless be liable and subject to indictment, trial, judgment and punishment, according to law.

SECTION 4. The times, places and manner of holding elections for senators and representatives, shall be prescribed in each State by the legislature thereof; but the Congress may at any time by law make or alter such regulations, except as to the places of choosing senators.

The Congress shall assemble at least once in every year, and such meeting shall be on the first Monday in December, unless they shall by law appoint a different day.

SECTION 5. Each house shall be the judge of the elections, returns and qualifications of its own members, and a majority of each shall constitute a quorum to do business; but a smaller number may adjourn from day to day, and may be authorized to compel the attendance of absent members, in such manner, and under such penalties as each house may provide.

Each house may determine the rules of its proceedings, punish its members for disorderly behaviour, and, with the concurrence of two-thirds, expel a member.

Each house shall keep a journal of its proceedings, and from time to time publish the same, excepting such parts as may in their judgment require secrecy; and the yeas and the nays of the members of either house on any question shall, at the desire of one-fifth of those present, be entered on the journal. [**One-fifth of the members present at a vote taken in either house of Congress may demand that a roll-call vote be taken rather than simply a voice vote of yeas and nays. A roll-call vote allows for certainty as to whether or not the measure has passed and makes each member's vote a matter of public record. From the published record, the voters can follow the activities of their representatives in Congress and can make informed decisions on which to base their votes at the next election.**]

Neither house, during the session of Congress, shall, without the consent of the other, adjourn for more than three days, nor to any other place than that in which the two houses shall be sitting.

SECTION 6. The senators and representatives shall receive a compensation for their services, to be ascertained by law, and paid out of the Treasury of the United States. They shall in all cases, except treason, felony and breach of the peace, be privileged from arrest during their attendance at the session of their respective houses, and in going to and returning from the same; and for any speech or debate in either house, they shall not be questioned in any other place. [**In the interest of free and open debate, members of Congress may express any ideas or opinions without fear of lawsuit or punishment.**]

No senator or representative shall, during the time for which he was elected, be appointed to any civil office under the authority of the United States, which shall have been created, or the emoluments whereof shall have been increased during such time, and no person holding any office under the United States, shall be a member of either house during his continuance in office. [**In effect, a person cannot serve in Congress and hold an appointive office at the same time.**]

SECTION 7. All bills for raising revenue shall originate in the House of Representatives; but the Senate may propose or concur with amendments as on other bills. [**The special power of the House of Representatives is initial control over raising and spending of money. The House of Representatives is said to have the "Power of the purse." All other legislation may begin in either the House of Representatives or the Senate.**]

Every bill which shall have passed the House of Representatives and the Senate, shall, before it become a law, be presented to the President of the United States; if he approves he shall sign it, but if not he shall return it, with his objections to that house in which it shall have originated, who shall enter for the objections at large on their journal, and proceed to reconsider it. If after such reconsideration two thirds of the House shall agree to pass the bill, it shall be sent, together with the objections, to the other House, by which it shall likewise be reconsidered, and if approved by two thirds of that House, it shall become a law. But in all cases the votes of both Houses shall be determined by yeas and nays, and the names of the persons voting for and against the bill shall be entered on the journal of each House respectively. If any bill shall not be returned by the President within ten days (Sundays excepted) after it shall have been presented to him, the same shall be a law, in like manner as if had signed it, unless the Congress by their adjournment prevent its return, in which case it shall not be a law. [**Every bill that has been passed by both Houses of Congress must be sent to the President. The President has ten days (not including Sunday) to approve the bill and sign it into law or to reject the bill and return it to the body which proposed it. If, upon reconsideration, both houses**

pass the bill by majorities of two-thirds or greater, the bill becomes law even over the objections of the President. If the President neither signs nor returns the bill within ten days, it becomes law automatically unless Congress adjourns within that time, in which case the bill does not become law. This last situation is called a "Pocket Veto."]

Every order, resolution, or vote to which the concurrence of the Senate and House of Representatives may be necessary (except on a question of adjournment) shall be presented to the President of the United States; and before the same shall take effect, shall be approved by him, or being disapproved by him, shall be repassed by two thirds of the Senate and House of Representatives, according to the rules and limitations prescribed in the case of a bill.

SECTION 8. The Congress shall have power to lay and collect taxes, duties, imposts and excises, to pay the debts and provide for the common defense and general welfare of the United States; but all duties, imposts and excises shall be uniform throughout the United States; **[Congress can raise money to pay for all the business of government. The only restriction is that all states be treated equally with regard to collection of revenue.]**

To borrow money on the credit of the United States;

To regulate commerce with foreign nations, and among the several States, and with the Indian tribes;

To establish a uniform rule of naturalization, **(this affects you),** and uniform laws on the subject of bankruptcies throughout the United States;

To coin money, regulate the value thereof, and of foreign coin, and fix the standard of weights and measures;

To provide for the punishment of counterfeiting the securities and current coin of the United States;

To establish post offices and post roads;

To promote the progress of science and useful arts, by securing for limited times to authors and inventors the exclusive right to their respective writings and discoveries; **[This clause provides for patenting of inventions and copyrighting of written works.]**

To constitute tribunals inferior to the Supreme Court; **[Aside from the Supreme Court, which is established in Article III, the Congress is in charge of setting up a federal court system.]**

To define and punish piracies and felonies committed on the high seas, and offenses against the law of nations;

To declare war, grant letters of marque and reprisal, and make rules concerning captures on land and water; **[ONLY Congress has the power to declare war.]**

To raise and support armies, but no appropriation of money to that use shall be for a longer term than two years;

To provide and maintain a Navy;

To make rules for the government and regulation of the land and naval forces;

To provide for calling forth the militia to execute the laws of the Union, suppress insurrections and repel invasions;

To provide for organizing, arming, and disciplining the militia, and for governing such part of them as may be employed in the service of the United States, reserving to the States respectively, the appointment of officers, and the authority of training the militia according to the discipline prescribed by Congress;

To exercise exclusive legislation in all cases whatsoever, over such district (not exceeding ten miles square) as may, by cession of particular States, and the acceptance of Congress, become the seat of the Government of the United States, and to exercise like authority over all places purchased by the consent of the legislature of the State in which the same shall be, for the erection of forts, magazines, arsenals, dock-yards, and other needful buildings; **[This is the authority by which the Federal Government governs the District of Columbia (Washington, DC) and military bases throughout the country.]** — And

To make all laws which shall be necessary and proper for carrying into execution the foregoing powers and all other powers vested by this Constitution in the Government of the United States, or in any department or officer thereof.

SECTION 9. The migration or importation of such persons as any of the States now existing shall think proper to admit, shall not be prohibited by the Congress prior to the year one thousand eight hundred and eight, but a tax or duty may be imposed on such importation, not exceeding ten dollars for each person. **[Slaves may be imported into any of the original 13 states at least until 1808, but there may be a tax of up to $10 per slave imported. (For purposes of census, a slave is considered three-fifths of a person, but for purposes of taxation, each slave is a person.)]**

The privilege of the writ of habeas corpus shall not be suspended, unless when in cases of rebellion or invasion the public safety may require it.

No bill of attainder or ex post facto law shall be passed.

No capitation, or other direct, tax shall be laid, unless in proportion to the census or enumeration herein before directed to be taken.

No tax or duty shall be laid on articles exported from any State.

No preference shall be given by any regulation of commerce revenue to the ports of one State over those of another: nor shall vessels bound to, or from, one State, be obliged to enter, clear, or pay duties in another. **[There is to be free trade among the States.]**

No money shall be drawn from the Treasury, but in consequence of appropriations made by law; and a regular statement and account of the receipts and expenditures of all public money shall be published from time to time.

No title of nobility shall be granted by the United States: And no person holding any office of profit or trust under them, shall, without consent of the Congress, accept of any present, emolument, office, or title, of any kind whatever, from any King, Prince, or foreign State.

SECTION 10. No State shall enter into any treaty, alliance, or confederation, grant letters of marque and reprisal; coin money; emit bills of credit; make any thing but gold and silver coin a tender in payment of debts, pass any bill of attainder, ex post facto law, or law impairing the obligation of contracts, or grant any title of nobility.

No State shall, without the consent of the Congress, lay any imposts or duties on imports or exports, except what may be absolutely necessary for executing its inspection laws: and the net produce of all duties and imposts, laid by any State on imports or exports, shall be for the use of the Treasury of the United States; and all such laws shall be subject to the revision and control of the Congress.

No State shall, without the consent of Congress, lay any duty of tonnage, keep troops, or ships of war in time of peace, enter into any agreement or compact with another State, or with a foreign power, or engage in war, unless actually invaded, or in such imminent danger as will not admit of delay.

ARTICLE II

SECTION 1. The executive power shall be vested in a President of the United States of America. He shall hold his office during the term of four years, and, together with the Vice President, chosen for the same term, be elected, as follows:

Each State, shall appoint in such manner as the legislature thereof may direct, a number of electors, equal to the whole number of senators and representatives to which the State may be entitled in the Congress; but no senator or representative, or person holding an office of trust or profit under the United States, shall be appointed an elector.

The electors shall meet in their respective States, and vote by ballot for two persons, of whom one at least shall not be an inhabitant of the same State with themselves. And they shall make a list of all the persons voted for, and of the number of votes for each; which list they shall sign and certify, and transmit sealed to the seat of the Government of the United States, directed to the President of the Senate. The President of the Senate shall, in the presence of the Senate and House of Representatives, open all the certificates, and the votes shall then be counted. The person having the greatest number of votes shall be the President, if such number be a majority of the whole number of electors appointed; and if there be more than one who have such majority, and have an equal number of votes, then the House of Representatives shall immediately choose by ballot one of them for President; and if no person have a majority, then from the five highest on the list the said House shall in like manner choose the President. But in choosing the President, the votes shall be taken by States, the representation from each State having one vote; a quorum for this purpose shall consist of a member or members from two thirds of the States, and a majority of all the States shall be necessary to a choice. In every case, after the choice of the President, the person having the greatest number of votes of the electors shall be the Vice President. But if there should remain two or more who have equal votes, the Senate shall choose from them by ballot the Vice President. [**This method of choosing President and Vice President was changed in 1804 with the passage of the Twelfth Amendment. The President and Vice President must be able to cooperate and to work effectively together. Under the original provisions, the President and Vice President tended to be rivals. Under the current system, each Presidential nominee's choice is well known, and electors vote separately for President and for the President's choice as Vice President.**]

The Congress may determine the time of choosing the electors, and the day on which they shall give their votes; which day shall be the same throughout the United States.

No person except a natural born citizen, or a citizen of the United States, at the time of the adoption of this Constitution, shall be eligible to the office of President; neither shall any person be eligible to that office who shall not have attained to the age of thirty-five years, and been fourteen years a resident within the United States. [**The President must be at least 35 years old and may not be a naturalized citizen.**]

In case of the removal of the President from office, or of his death, resignation, or inability to discharge the powers and duties of the said office, the same shall devolve on the Vice President, and the Congress may by law provide for the case of removal, death, resignation or inability, both of the President and Vice President, declaring what officer shall then act as President, and such officer shall act accordingly, until the disability be removed, or a President shall be elected.

The President shall, at stated times, receive for his services, a compensation, which shall neither be increased nor diminished during the period for which he shall have been elected, and he shall not receive within that period any other emolument from the United States, or any of them.

Before he enter on the execution of his office, he shall take the following oath or affirmation:—"I do solemnly swear (or affirm) that I will faithfully execute the office of President of the United States, and will to the best of my ability, preserve, protect and defend the Constitution of the United States."

SECTION 2. The President shall be Commander in Chief of the Army and Navy of the United States, and of the militia of the several States, when called into the actual service of the United States; he may require the opinion, in writing, of the principal officer in each of the Executive Departments, upon any subject relating to the duties of their respective offices, and he shall have power to grant reprieves and pardons for offenses against the United States, except in cases of impeachment.

He shall have power, by and with the advice and consent of the Senate, to make treaties, provided two-thirds of the Senators present concur; and he shall nominate, and by and with the advice and consent of the Senate, shall appoint ambassadors, other public ministers and consuls, Judges of the Supreme Court, and all other officers of the United States, whose appointments are not herein otherwise provided for, and which shall be established by law: but the Congress may by law vest the appointment of such inferior officers, as they think proper, in the President alone, in the courts of law, or in the heads of departments. **[Just as the President must approve all acts of Congress before they may become law, so the Senate must approve treaties into which the President hopes to enter and must approve all of the President's appointments to positions of power and authority. This system by which those in one branch of the government must ratify actions by persons in another branch is called the system of "Checks and Balances." By instituting these checks and balances, the framers of the Constitution hoped to avoid abuse of power by members of any one branch— Executive, Legislative, or Judiciary.]**

The President shall have power to fill up all vacancies that may happen during the recess of the Senate, by granting commissions which shall expire at the end of their next session.

SECTION 3. He shall from time to time give to the Congress information of the state of the Union, and recommend to their consideration such measures as he shall judge necessary and expedient; he may, on extraordinary occasions, convene both houses, or either of them, and in case of disagreement between them, with respect to the time of adjournment, he may adjourn them to such time as he shall think proper; he shall receive ambassadors and other public ministers; he shall take care that the laws be faithfully executed, and shall commission all the officers of the United States.

SECTION 4. The President, Vice President and all civil officers of the United States, shall be removed from office on impeachment for, and conviction of, treason, bribery, or other high crimes or misdemeanors.

ARTICLE III

SECTION 1. The judicial power of the United States, shall be vested in one Supreme Court, and in such inferior courts as the Congress may from time to time ordain and establish. The judges, both of the supreme and inferior courts, shall hold their offices during good behaviour, and shall, at stated times, receive for their services, a compensation, which shall not be diminished during their continuance of office. **[Federal judges serve in lifetime appointments. The reason for the lifetime appointments is the desire to have a judiciary department totally without political influence or any outside interference. Federal judges do not need to satisfy any appointing authority nor the public at large. They are free to exercise their judgment in deliberations and decisions. This is the concept of an "Independent Judiciary."]**

SECTION 2. The judicial power shall extend to all cases, in law and equity, arising under this Constitution, the laws of the United States, and treaties made, or which shall be made, under their authority; to all cases affecting ambassadors, other public ministers and consuls; to all cases of admiralty and maritime jurisdiction; to controversies to which the United States shall be a party; to controversies between two or more States; between a State and citizens of another State; between citizens of different States; between citizens of the same State claiming lands under grants of different States, and between a State, or the citizens thereof, and foreign States, citizens or subjects.

In all cases affecting ambassadors, other public ministers and consuls, and those in which a State shall be a party, the Supreme Court shall have original jurisdiction. In all the other cases before mentioned, the Supreme Court shall have appellate jurisdiction, both as to law and fact, with such exceptions, and under such regulations as the Congress shall make.

The trial of all crimes, except in cases of impeachment, shall be by jury; and such trial shall be held in the State where the said crimes shall have been committed; but when not committed within any State, the trial shall be at such place or places as the Congress may by law have directed.

SECTION 3. Treason against the United States, shall consist only in levying war against them, or in adhering to their enemies, giving them aid and comfort. No person shall be convicted of treason unless on the testimony of two witnesses to the same overt act, or on confession in open court.

The Congress shall have power to declare the punishment of treason, but no attainder of treason shall work corruption of blood, or forfeiture except during the life of the person attained. **[Only the individual actually convicted of treason (or, for that matter, any other crime) is guilty, and only the guilty may be punished. The family of the guilty party bears no guilt unless also tried and convicted.]**

ARTICLE IV

SECTION 1. Full faith and credit shall be given in each State to the public acts, records, and judicial proceedings of every other State. And the Congress may by general laws prescribe the manner in which such acts, records and proceedings shall be proved, and the effect thereof. **[This section constitutes what is known as the "Full faith and credit clause." Each state is entitled to make and interpret its own laws; all other states must respect those laws and rulings.]**

SECTION 2. The citizens of each State shall be entitled to all privileges and immunities of citizens in the several States. **[A citizen of any state is a citizen of the United States and when within any state other than his or her own is to be treated in the same way as is a citizen of that state.]**

A person charged in any State with treason, felony, or other crime, who shall flee from justice, and be found in another State, shall on demand of the executive authority of the State from which he fled, be delivered up, to be removed to the State having jurisdiction of the crime. **[Article III, Section 2 provides that trial take place in the state in which the crime was committed. This section provides for "extradition" of an accused who may have fled the state of commission in hope of avoiding trial.]**

No person held to service or labour in one State, under the laws thereof, escaping into another, shall, in consequence of any law or regulation therein, be discharged from such service or labour, but shall be delivered up on claim of the party to whom such service or labour may be due. **[Slaves presented a special problem which the Constitution addressed as a specific issue. In some states slavery was entirely legal. Under the laws of those states a slave was property. If a slave managed to escape from his or her home state to a state in which slavery was not legally protected, was the slave to be afforded the privileges and immunities of a citizen of that state or were the laws of the state from which the slave had fled to be afforded full faith and credit? In this special case, full faith and credit of the home state's laws was to be upheld, and the slave was to be returned to the slave state from which he or she had fled.]**

SECTION 3. New States may be admitted by the Congress into this Union; but no new State shall be formed or erected within the jurisdiction of any other State; nor any State be formed by the junction of two or more States, or parts of States, without the consent of the legislatures of the States concerned as well as of the Congress.

The Congress shall have power to dispose of and make all needful rules and regulations respecting the Territory or other property belonging to the United States; and nothing in this Constitution shall be so construed as to prejudice any claims of the United States, or of any particular State.

SECTION 4. The United States shall guarantee to every State in this Union a republican form of Government, and shall protect each of them against invasion; and on application of the legislature, or of the executive (when the legislature cannot be convened) against domestic violence.

ARTICLE V

The Congress, whenever two thirds of both Houses shall deem it necessary, shall propose amendments to this Constitution, or on the application of the legislatures of two thirds of the several States, shall call a convention for proposing amendments, which, in either case, shall be valid to all intents and purposes, as part of the Constitution, when ratified by the legislatures of three fourths of the several States, or by conventions in three fourths thereof, as the one or the other mode of ratification may be proposed by the Congress; provided that no amendment which may be made prior to the year one thousand eight hundred and eight shall in any manner affect the first and fourth clauses in the Ninth Section of the First Article; and that no State, without its consent, shall be deprived of its equal suffrage in the Senate.

ARTICLE VI

All debts contracted and engagements entered into, before the adoption of this Constitution, shall be as valid against the United States under this Constitution, as under the Confederation.

This Constitution, and the laws of the United States which shall be made in pursuance thereof; and all treaties made, or which shall be made, under the authority of the United States, shall be the supreme law of the land; and the judges in every State shall be bound thereby, any thing in the Constitution or laws of any State to the contrary notwithstanding. **[The Constitution (along with U.S. treaties) is the SUPREME LAW OF THE LAND. All Congressional acts and all state laws must comply with the provisions of the Constitution. If a citizen feels that Congress has enacted a law which is contrary to the intent of the Constitution, the citizen may disobey that law, be convicted, and challenge the law through appeals. Appeals must pass through the appeals process upwards from the court in which the citizen was convicted. If all state courts maintain the conviction, the appeal may be brought to the Supreme Court for final determination as to the Constitutionality of the law. This process is known as "Judicial Review." This is another aspect of the system of checks and balances.]**

The senators and representatives before mentioned, and the members of the several State legislatures, and all executive and judicial officers, both of the United States and of the several States, shall be bound by oath or affirmation, to support this Constitution; but no religious test shall ever be required as a qualification to any office or public trust under the United States. **[Adherence to any particular religion, or to any religion at all, is not a qualification nor disqualification for any office.]**

ARTICLE VII

The ratification of the conventions of nine States shall be sufficient for the establishment of this Constitution between the States so ratifying the same.

Done in convention by the unanimous consent of the States present the seventeenth day of September in the year of our Lord one thousand seven hundred and eighty seven and of the Independence of the United States of America the twelfth. In witness whereof we have hereunto subscribed our names,

(here follow the signatures)

AMENDMENTS

ARTICLE I

Congress shall make no law respecting an establishment of religion, or prohibiting the free exercise thereof; or abridging the freedom of speech, or of the press; or the right of the people peaceably to assemble, and to petition the Government for a redress of grievances. [**Many people feel that it is the protections of the First Amendment that make America great.**]

ARTICLE II

A well regulated militia, being necessary to the security of a free State, the right of the people to keep and bear arms, shall not be infringed. [**This amendment authorizes federal and state militias for purposes of security. It is often misinterpreted by people who claim that the amendment gives all citizens the right to arm themselves as individuals.**]

ARTICLE III

No soldier shall, in time of peace be quartered in any house, without the consent of the owner, nor in time of war, but in a manner to be prescribed by law.

ARTICLE IV

The right of the people to be secure in their persons, houses, papers, and effects, against unreasonable searches and seizures, shall not be violated, and no warrants shall issue, but upon probable cause, supported by oath or affirmation, and particularly describing the place to be searched, and the persons or things to be seized. [**This article guarantees personal privacy and protection from search unless the reason for the search can be justified.**]

ARTICLE V

No person shall be held to answer for a capital, or otherwise infamous crime, unless on a presentment or indictment of a Grand Jury, except in cases arising in the land or naval forces, or in the militia, when in actual service in time of war or public danger; nor shall any person be subject for the same offense to be twice put in jeopardy of life or limb; nor shall be compelled in any criminal case to be a witness against himself, nor be deprived of life, liberty, or property, without due process of law; nor shall private property be taken for public use, without just compensation. [**You should be aware of two protections of this article: The protection against double jeopardy means that once acquitted, a person cannot be tried again on the same charge, even if new evidence may point toward guilt. The other protection of importance to the citizenship test-taker is that which permits an accused to refuse to serve as a witness against him- or herself.**]

ARTICLE VI

In all criminal prosecutions, the accused shall enjoy the right to a speedy and public trial, by an impartial jury of the State and district wherein the crime shall have been committed, which district shall have been previously ascertained by law, and to be informed of the nature and cause of the accusation; to be confronted with the witnesses against him; to have compulsory process for obtaining witnesses in his favor, and to have the assistance of counsel for his defense. [**This amendment is important for guaranteeing**

rights and protections to the accused, particularly the right to trial by jury, the right to confront and interrogate witnesses against him or her, and the right to counsel (an attorney)].

ARTICLE VII

In suits at common law, where the value in controversy shall exceed twenty dollars, the right of trial by jury shall be preserved, and no fact tried by a jury, shall be otherwise reexamined in any court of the United States, than according to the rules of the common law.

ARTICLE VIII

Excessive bail shall not be required, nor excessive fines imposed, nor cruel and unusual punishments inflicted. [**The punishment must be appropriate to the crime.**]

ARTICLE IX

The enumeration in the Constitution, of certain rights, shall not be construed to deny or disparage others retained by the people.

ARTICLE X

The powers not delegated to the United States by the Constitution, nor prohibited by it to the States, are reserved to the States respectively, or to the people.

ARTICLE XI

The judicial power of the United States shall not be construed to extend to any suit in law or equity, commenced or prosecuted against one of the United States by citizens of another State, or by citizens or subjects of any foreign State.

ARTICLE XII

The electors shall meet in their respective States, and vote by ballot for President and Vice President, one of whom, at least, shall not be an inhabitant of the same State with themselves; they shall name in their ballots the person voted for as President, and in distinct ballots the person voted for as Vice President, and they shall make distinct lists of all persons voted for as President, and of all persons voted for as Vice President, and of the number of votes for each, which lists they shall sign and certify, and transmit sealed to the seat of the government of the United States, directed to the President of the Senate;—The President of the Senate shall, in the presence of the Senate and House of Representatives, open all the certificates and the votes shall then be counted;—The person having the greatest number of votes for President, shall be the President, if such number be a majority of the whole number of electors appointed; and if no person have such majority, then from the persons having the highest numbers not exceeding three on the list of those voted for as President, the House of Representatives shall choose immediately, by ballot, the President. But in choosing the President, the votes shall be taken by States, the representation from each State having one vote; a quorum for this purpose shall consist of a member or members from two-thirds of the States, and a majority of all the States shall be necessary to a choice. And if the House of Representatives shall not choose a President whenever the right of choice shall devolve upon them, before the fourth day of March next following, then the Vice President shall act as President, as in the case of the death or other constitutional disability of the President.—The person having the greatest number of votes as Vice President, shall be the Vice President, if such number be a majority of the whole number of electors appointed, and if no person have a majority, then from the two highest numbers on the list, the Senate shall choose the Vice

President; a quorum for the purpose shall consist of two-thirds of the whole number of Senators, and a majority of the whole number shall be necessary to a choice. But no person constitutionally ineligible to the office of President shall be eligible to that of Vice President of the United States. **[This amendment changes the methods of voting for President and Vice President originally described in Article II, Section 1. The March 4 date by which a President must be chosen was later changed by the twenty-second amendment to January 20.]**

ARTICLE XIII

SECTION 1. Neither slavery nor involuntary servitude, except as a punishment for crime whereof the party shall have been duly convicted, shall exist within the United States, or any place subject to their jurisdiction. **[This amendment proposed in February and ratified in December of 1865, following the Civil War, abolished slavery in the United States.]**

SECTION 2. Congress shall have power to enforce this article by appropriate legislation.

ARTICLE XIV

SECTION 1. All persons born or naturalized in the United States, and subject to the jurisdiction thereof, are citizens of the United States and of the State wherein they reside. No State shall make or enforce any law which shall abridge the privileges or immunities of citizens of the United States; nor shall any State deprive any person of life, liberty, or property, without due process of law; nor deny to any person within its jurisdiction the equal protection of the laws. **[This section defines citizenship and extends protections of the Constitution to all citizens. States are not permitted to discriminate among citizens in the application of state laws.]**

SECTION 2. Representatives shall be apportioned among the several States according to their respective numbers, counting the whole number of persons in each State, excluding Indians not taxed. But when the right to vote at any election for the choice of electors for President and Vice President of the United States, Representatives in Congress, the executive and judicial officers of a State, or the members of the legislature thereof, is denied to any of the male inhabitants of such State, being twenty-one years of age, and citizens of the United States, or in any way abridged, except for participation in rebellion, or other crime, the basis of representation therein shall be reduced in the proportion which the number of such male citizens shall bear to the whole number of male citizens twenty-one years of age in such State. **[Each state may define qualifications of its voters, but where a state disqualifies any group of male citizens over the age of 21 for other than cause such as criminal conviction, then that state's apportionment of seats in the House of Representatives may be reduced accordingly.]**

SECTION 3. No person shall be a Senator or Representative in Congress, or elector of President and Vice President, or hold any office, civil or military, under the United States, or under any State, who, having previously taken an oath, as a member of Congress, or as an officer of the United States, or as member of any State legislature, or as an executive or judicial officer of any State, to support the Constitution of the United States, shall have engaged in insurrection or rebellion against the same, or given aid or comfort to the enemies thereof. But Congress may by a vote of two-thirds of each house, remove such disability. **[This section was meant to penalize participation in the Civil War by persons who had formerly been in power in federal or state government. In effect the section accused of treason those who had taken an oath to support the Constitution of the United States and who had then engaged in insurrection or rebellion. While condemning these "traitors," the section also gave Congress the power to forgive.]**

SECTION 4. The validity of the public debt of the United States, authorized by law, including debts incurred for payment of pensions and bounties for services in suppressing insurrection or rebellion, shall not be questioned. But neither the United States nor any State shall assume or pay any debt or obligation incurred in aid of insurrection or rebellion against the United States, or any claim for the loss or emancipation of any slave; but all such debts, obligations and claims shall be held illegal and void.

SECTION 5. The Congress shall have power to enforce, by appropriate legislation, the provisions of this article.

ARTICLE XV

SECTION 1. The right of citizens of the United States to vote shall not be denied or abridged by the United States or by any State on account of race, color, or previous condition of servitude. [**Former slaves and all other U.S. male citizens regardless of race or skin color were given the right to vote in this amendment. At this time in U.S. history, women were still not empowered to vote.**]

SECTION 2. The Congress shall have power to enforce this article by appropriate legislation.

ARTICLE XVI

The Congress shall have power to lay and collect taxes on incomes, from whatever source derived, without apportionment among the several States, and without regard to any census or enumeration. [**By this amendment we got the personal income tax by which the federal government gathers revenues directly from the people in order to pay for the business and services of the government.**]

ARTICLE XVII

SECTION 1. The Senate of the United States shall be composed of two senators from each State, elected by the people thereof, for six years; and each senator shall have one vote. The electors in each State shall have the qualifications requisite for electors of the most numerous branch of the State legislatures. [**This amendment provides for the direct election of Senators by the people. Originally, the Constitution provided for election of Senators by the state legislatures. The amendment also provides that a person who is qualified by state law to vote for members of the most numerous house of the state legislature is qualified to vote for that state's Senators.**]

SECTION 2. When vacancies happen in the representation of any State in the senate, the executive authority of such State shall issue writs of election to fill such vacancies: Provided that the legislature of any State may empower the executive thereof to make temporary appointments until the people fill the vacancies by election as the legislature may direct.

SECTION 3. This amendment shall not be so construed as to affect the election or term of any senator chosen before it becomes valid as part of the Constitution.

ARTICLE XVIII

SECTION 1. After one year from the ratification of this article the manufacture, sale, or transportation of intoxicating liquors within, the importation thereof into, or the exportation thereof from the United States and all territory subject to the jurisdiction thereof for beverage purposes is hereby prohibited. [**With ratification of this amendment began the period known as "Prohibition."**]

SECTION 2. The Congress and the several States shall have concurrent power to enforce this article by appropriate legislation.

SECTION 3. This article shall be inoperative unless it shall have been ratified as an amendment to the Constitution by the legislatures of the several States, as provided in the Constitution, within seven years from the date of the submission hereof to the States by the Congress. [**The amendment was sent to the states in December of 1917; was ratified by three-quarters of the states by January 16, 1919; and became an effective part of the Constitution on January 16, 1920.**]

ARTICLE XIX

The right of citizens of the United States to vote shall not be denied or abridged by the United States or by any State on account of sex. [**Women finally got the vote.**]

ARTICLE XX

SECTION 1. The terms of the President and Vice President shall end at noon on the 20th day of January, and the terms of Senators and Representatives at noon on the 3d day of January, of the years in which such terms would have ended if this article had not been ratified; and the terms of their successors shall then begin. [**You may recall that under the Twelfth Amendment the terms of President and Vice President began on March 4. Experience over the years showed that a President who had not been reelected in November had very little power over the new Congress at the beginning of the year. (He was as powerless as a "lame duck.") For this reason the date that the new Presidential term took effect was moved closer to the beginning of the Congressional year.**]

SECTION 2. The Congress shall assemble at least once in every year, and such meeting shall begin at noon on the 3d day of January, unless they shall by law appoint a different day. [**The required annual meeting of Congress was moved from the first Monday in December (Article I, Section 4) to allow just enough time for internal organization within the new Congress before the President takes office.**]

SECTION 3. If, at the time fixed for the beginning of the term of the President, the President elect shall have died, the Vice President elect shall become President. If a President shall not have been chosen before the time fixed for the beginning of his term, or if the President elect shall have failed to qualify, then the Vice President elect shall act as President until a President shall have qualified; and the Congress may by law provide for the case wherein neither a President elect nor a Vice President elect shall have qualified, declaring who shall then act as President, or the manner in which one who is to act shall be selected, and such person shall act accordingly until a President or Vice President shall have qualified.

SECTION 4. The Congress may by law provide for the case of the death of any of the persons from whom the House of Representatives may choose a President whenever the right of choice shall have devolved upon them, and for the case of the death of any of the persons from whom the Senate may choose a Vice President whenever the right of choice shall have devolved upon them.

SECTION 5. Sections 1 and 2 shall take effect on the 15th day of October following the ratification of this article.

SECTION 6. This article shall be inoperative unless it shall have been ratified as an amendment to the Constitution by the legislatures of three-fourths of the several States within seven years from the date of its submission.

ARTICLE XXI

SECTION 1. The eighteenth article of amendment to the Constitution of the United States is hereby repealed. [**Prohibition as a matter of national, Constitutional policy was a failure, and the amendment making it such was repealed.**]

SECTION 2. The transportation or importation into any State, Territory, or possession of the United States for delivery or use therein of intoxicating liquors, in violation of the laws thereof, is hereby prohibited. [**Even though the Tenth Amendment specifically grants to the states or to the people all rights not expressly given to the federal government, this section of the amendment repealing prohibition makes a point of granting to the states the right to institute prohibition within their own borders under Constitutional protection.**]

SECTION 3. This article shall be inoperative unless it shall have been ratified as an amendment to the Constitution by conventions in the several States, as provided in the Constitution, within seven years from the date of the submission hereof to the States by the Congress.

ARTICLE XXII

SECTION 1. No person shall be elected to the office of the President more than twice, and no person who has held the office of President, or acted as President, for more than 2 years of a term to which some other person was elected President shall be elected to the office of the President more than once. But this Article shall not apply to any person holding the office of President when this Article was proposed by the Congress, and shall not prevent any person who may be holding the office of President, or acting as President, during the term within which this Article becomes operative from holding the office of President or acting as President during the remainder of such term. [**This amendment served to limit future Presidents to two terms in office. The only President to be elected to more than two terms was Franklin D. Roosevelt who served three full terms and was elected to a fourth. He died in office during his fourth term.**]

SECTION 2. This Article shall be inoperative unless it shall have been ratified as an amendment to the Constitution by the legislatures of three-fourths of the several States within 7 years from the date of its submission to the States by the Congress.

ARTICLE XXIII

SECTION 1. The District constituting the seat of Government of the United States shall appoint in such manner as the Congress may direct:

A number of electors of President and Vice President equal to the whole number of Senators and Representatives in Congress to which the District would be entitled if it were a State, but in no event more than the least populous State; they shall be in addition to those appointed by the States, but they shall be considered, for the purposes of the election of President and Vice President, to be electors appointed by a State; and they shall meet in the District and perform such duties as provided by the twelfth article of amendment. [**By the terms of this amendment, citizens of the District of Columbia became able to vote for President of the United States. They had never had this right before because they are not citizens of any state, and the Constitution as originally adopted provided only for electors appointed by states.**]

SECTION 2. The Congress shall have power to enforce this article by appropriate legislation.

ARTICLE XXIV

SECTION 1. The right of citizens of the United States to vote in any primary or other election for President or Vice President, for electors for President or Vice President, or for Senator or Representative in Congress, shall not be denied or abridged by the United States or any State by reason of failure to pay any poll tax or other tax. [**Some states had chosen to discriminate against the poor or the poorly informed by requiring the** payment of a poll tax at some time before the election. **The poorly informed did not hear of the requirement or of the time and place for payment; the poor were unable to pay. Thus the poor were effectively denied the right to vote. At the same time, politicians were able to get the information to those expected to vote the "right way" and to pay the tax for poor people who agreed to vote for their candidates or their issues thereby affecting the outcome of the vote. This source of discrimination and corruption was eliminated by the 24th Amendment.]**

SECTION 2. The Congress shall have power to enforce this article by appropriate legislation.

ARTICLE XXV

SECTION 1. In case of the removal of the President from office or of his death or resignation, the Vice President shall become President.

SECTION 2. Whenever there is a vacancy in the office of the Vice President, the President shall nominate a Vice President who shall take office upon confirmation by a majority vote of both Houses of Congress.

SECTION 3. Whenever the President transmits to the President pro tempore of the Senate and the Speaker of the House of Representatives his written declaration that he is unable to discharge the powers and duties of his office, and until he transmits to them a written declaration to the contrary, such powers and duties shall be discharged by the Vice President as Acting President.

SECTION 4. Whenever the Vice President and a majority of either the principal officers of the executive departments or of such other body as Congress may by law provide, transmit to the President pro tempore of the Senate and the Speaker of the House of Representatives their written declaration that the President is unable to discharge the powers and duties of his office, the Vice President shall immediately assume the powers and duties of the office of Acting President.

Thereafter, when the President transmits to the President pro tempore of the Senate and the Speaker of the House of Representatives his written declaration that no inability exists, he shall resume the powers and duties of his office unless the Vice President and a majority of either the principal officers of the executive departments or of such other body as Congress may by law provide, transmit within four days to the President pro tempore of the Senate and Speaker of the House of Representatives their written declaration that the President is unable to discharge the powers and duties of his office. Thereupon Congress shall decide the issue, assembling within forty-eight hours for that purpose if not in session. If the Congress, within twenty-one days after receipt of the latter written declaration, or if Congress is not in session, within twenty-one days after Congress is required to assemble, determines by two-thirds vote of both Houses that the President is unable to discharge the powers and duties of his office, the Vice President shall continue to discharge the same as Acting President; otherwise the President shall resume the powers and duties of his office.

ARTICLE XXVI

SECTION 1. The right of citizens of the United States, who are eighteen years of age or older, to vote shall not be denied or abridged by the United States or by any state on account of age. **[Any citizens who are old enough to fight and die for their country should be able to vote for those leaders who have the power to send them to war.]**

SECTION 2. The Congress shall have power to enforce this article by appropriate legislation.

The ninth state to ratify the new Constitution, New Hampshire, did so in June of 1788. The unanimous election of George Washington to the office of President followed. (This was the only time that a President was elected unanimously.) Because of his role as leader of the victorious Revolutionary army and as first President, George Washington has been called "The Father of Our Country."

While the thirteen original colonies were forming themselves into the United States, adventurous Americans were exploring lands to the south and west, establishing farms and towns. The areas they settled petitioned to join the Union and were admitted as new states. The vast midsection of the country, from the Mississippi River to the Rocky Mountains and from the Gulf of Mexico to the Canadian border had been explored and claimed by France. The United States acquired this large land mass by buying it from France. This acquisition was known as the Louisiana Purchase and the territory was called the Louisiana Territory, even though the current state of Louisiana is only a tiny part of it. Westward exploration and expansion continued through the nineteenth century (the 1800s), including the entire Pacific coast by 1853 and adding the Alaska purchase in 1867 and Hawaii in 1898. Groups of communities formed themselves into states and, one-by-one joined the Union. In 1912, Arizona joined the Union as the 48th state. Much later, Alaska became the 49th state in January 1959 and Hawaii the 50th in August of 1959. **The United States now consists of 50 states represented on the flag by 13 alternating red and white stripes (7 red and 6 white) for the 13 original states and 50 white stars on a blue field for the total number of states.** Each state has its own constitution, a legislature, a governor, and a judiciary system.

The locations, climates, and geographic features of the various states led to great diversity among lifestyles. Its long winters, rocky soil, and deep sea ports for trade with Europe, led the north to industrialize and to depend on manufacturing and trade for its livelihood rather than depending on agriculture. The fast moving rivers created water power for the mills, and small towns clustered around these mills while larger cities grew along the coast. Many immigrants came from Europe to work in these mills and to establish new lives in America.

The climate and soil of the southern states lent itself to large scale planting of a few profitable crops. Tobacco and even more so cotton were grown on large plantations. Cultivating and harvesting these crops was backbreaking work. Slave labor was available and, from the standpoint of the plantation owners, very economical. Thus the development of the southern states was very different from that of the northern states.

With expansion to the west, more economic styles developed. The center of the country proved to be well suited for growing food crops. In fact, the midwest is commonly called "America's breadbasket." The southwestern regions proved to be the perfect areas for raising sheep and cattle. Each area had its own labor needs. As the territories spread out and as new states joined the Union, slavery became an important issue. From 1808 onward, the right to import and own slaves was a constant point of debate in the Congress. Compromises were made with regard to the admission of each new state, but tempers often rose. The slavery question was eventually settled by the Civil War.

Even while the United States was growing, all was not peaceful. Westward expansion involved displacement of the native American Indians who had lived there before settlers arrived. In some cases relations were friendly, but many times they were hostile. There were attacks, small battles and even minor wars.

Wars with the Indians were not the only problem. In 1812, the United States declared war against England. The main reason for this war was the issue of freedom of the high seas. England had been stopping American ships and taking American seamen from them to serve in the British navy. The United States won the war, but not before the British had burned down the entire new city of Washington, DC. **The War of 1812 was the last war to be fought with a European power on American soil.** This was not, unfortunately, the last foreign war on American soil. **The Mexican War, which began in 1846, was the last. When the United States defeated Mexico, it gained parts of California and New Mexico.**

The problems of the United States did not all disappear with defeat of its foreign enemies. The struggle between the North and South was highlighted by differences over slavery, but there were many other differences as well. The argument can be summed up as a dispute over "States' Rights." The southern states felt that the federal government was wielding too much power. They felt that they should have more rights as individual states. The southern states threatened to secede (to separate themselves) from the Union and backed up their threat by attacking Fort Sumter in South Carolina. The federal government refused to accept the idea that some states could resign from the Union and treated the attackers as rebellious states rather than as another nation. Eleven states declared that they had seceded and formed the Confederate States of America. **The member states of the Confederacy were: South Carolina, Mississippi, Florida, Alabama, Georgia, Louisiana, Texas, Virginia, Arkansas, North Carolina, and Tennessee. Their President was Jefferson Davis.** Four other slave states—Delaware, Kentucky, Maryland, and Missouri—chose to remain in the Union. The Civil War, also known as "The War Between the States," lasted from 1861 to 1865. This was a very unhappy period in the history of the United States. Since there had been no border restrictions among the states, members of families were often scattered in different parts of the nation. This meant that in the Civil War fathers might be fighting against sons, and brothers against brothers. Medical science was inadequate for the wounds inflicted, and sanitation was almost nonexistent. Casualties were high, and the land itself was devastated.

By the **Emancipation Proclamation** on January 1, 1863, President Abraham Lincoln declared that all slaves in any parts of the country that were in rebellion against the United States were now free. Slaves in states that had remained loyal to the United States were not affected by the Emancipation Proclamation. These slaves were freed by the thirteenth amendment.

The Civil War ended in 1865, and the reunited country began a process of reconstruction. Agriculture was revived, industrialization proceeded at a very rapid pace, and the population grew quickly. Immigrants contributed significantly to the progress of the nation.

Aside from involvement in the Spanish-American War in 1898, provoked when the Spanish destroyed the U.S. battleship Maine in Havana harbor, times were relatively peaceful. But it was a busy time for industry, for labor, for Congress, and for the American people.

Between the end of the Civil War in 1865 and our entry into World War I in 1917 the country as a whole grew and prospered, and the United States became a powerful nation among the nations of the world. Immigrants flowed into the country and rapidly found their way into American society and the American economy. The United States absorbed so many immigrants that it was called a "melting pot." In this period labor began to organize, and legislation was passed in attempts to control child labor and to encourage safe working conditions for coal miners. Amendments to the Constitution clarified ways in which Constitutional protections governed the actions of the states and how they extended directly to the people. Other amendments defined citizenship and extended its rights, including the right to vote, to former slaves. This was also the era of "Prohibition," the time in which production and sale of liquor was Constitutionally prohibited throughout the United States, but it was nevertheless a time of fun, happiness, and lively music and dance.

Americans were pleased with their own lives. Their attitude toward Europe and its problems was that Europe was far away. Americans wanted to remain isolated even as Europe was at war.

In 1915 a German submarine sank the passenger liner Lusitania with many American civilians aboard. This action led many Americans to change their minds, and in 1917 the United States entered the war. (You will notice that the sinking of ships brought the United States into a number of wars. Sinking of the battleship Maine led to the Spanish American War; sinking of the liner Lusitania drew us into the First World War; and the bombing of Pearl Harbor and the total destruction of the aircraft carrier Arizona along with many other ships caused our entry into the Second World War.)

The First World War was over in 1918. It had been a very expensive war for all the countries involved. Recovery was also expensive and money was mishandled. On October 24, 1929, the American stock market fell in a "great crash" and many banks failed. There was no money with which to pay workers, so millions of Americans lost their jobs. Unemployment was high and poverty spread rapidly. This was the period of the "Great Depression" which continued from 1929 to 1939. The great depression was not limited to the United States. Europe was undergoing a similar depression.

In Europe the depression and misery led the people to turn to dictators who promised a better life. In the United States, people elected as president Franklin D. Roosevelt. President Roosevelt was a strong leader with many ideas for social programs and federally funded work projects to help people to recover and to improve the economy.

The rise of dictatorship in Europe did indeed make for many improvements in the lives of the people for a short period. However, dictatorship and the power that accompanies it tends to lead to a desire for still more power. The German dictator, Adolph Hitler, was the most ruthless of the dictators. He led his armies to occupy one European country after another imposing his own cruel morality on citizens of occupied countries. American "isolationists" did their best to keep the United States from becoming involved. We were just emerging from the depression and wanted a chance to recover in peace. At the same time, the Japanese government was attempting to dominate the Far East just as the German government was attempting to absorb all of Europe. The Japanese forced the United States to join the war by carrying out a surprise attack on the U.S. naval base at Pearl Harbor, Hawaii, on December 7, 1941. The surprise attack early on a Sunday morning caused over 3,300 American deaths. President Roosevelt called December 7 "a date that will live in infamy." Congress promptly declared war against both Japan and Germany. The United States entered World War II as a major participant.

The war in Europe was won by the allied forces of the United States, England, Canada, and soldiers of European nations. The war in the Far East was ended abruptly with the dropping of an atomic bomb on the Japanese island of Hiroshima followed three days later by an atomic bomb's destruction of Nagasaki. President Harry Truman, who had succeeded President Franklin Roosevelt, made the difficult decision to use atomic weapons on civilian populations in order to save thousands of American servicemen's lives.

When the war ended, the victorious nations met and discussed forming some sort of world government which could help prevent such a devastating war from occurring again. They hoped to develop a "United Nations" that could solve problems through discussion, debate, and compromise. They hoped that a multinational peacekeeping force could stop tiny conflicts and prevent them from growing into full-scale wars. The United Nations was established with its headquarters in New York City. It has had successes as well as failures, and still exists today.

With the end of World War II in 1945 came new governments and new alliances. Russian Communism emerged as a new form of dictatorship and threatened to expand throughout Europe. The hostility and strained relations that developed between the United States and Russia was called the **Cold War.** At the same time another style of Communism, Chinese Communism, was taking hold in Asia and was spreading into North Korea and the northern part of the Indochinese peninsula.

In 1950 North Korea attacked its neighbor, South Korea. The United States went to war to help defend South Korea, but this time as a member of the international United Nations forces rather than as an individual nation. The Korean War ended in 1953.

The American government was very opposed to Communism. It felt that once Communist governments gained control they tended to spread their influence rapidly and threatened the peace of the entire world. Because of this fear, the United States attempted to stop the spread of Communism in Southeast Asia by assisting the South Vietnamese in their war against the North Vietnamese. The Vietnamese war extended from 1964 to 1973. It was an unpopular war. Many Americans felt that we were fighting an undefined enemy for an undefined reason. They felt that we were interfering in a Vietnamese civil war and had no business there. They did not want the United States to become a nation that was always at war. When the war was finally over, the American people wanted to show the world how kindhearted and peaceful we really are. The United States opened its doors to war refugees and to victims of tyranny and oppression. We became much more hospitable and friendly to immigrants. Now you can benefit from this friendly attitude.

This brief history has dwelt heavily on the wars in which the United States has been involved. Wars and their dates and circumstances tend to offer good anchor dates for discussion of what was happening in the United States and abroad at a given time. War has not, however, been the chief motivating force of the American government or the American people. Americans are devoted to the goals of justice and equality and to an ever improving quality of life. Between and even during wars, amendments and legislation granted greater equality, civil rights, and human rights to members of minority groups, to women, to the elderly, to the handicapped, and even to those accused of crimes.

UNITED STATES CITIZENSHIP QUIZZER

The question and answer method is a good way to learn facts which are important for you to know. Some of the following questions are based on the short history that you just studied. Other questions are asked just so that you may now learn their answers. Read through the questions and answers for yourself a few times. You probably already know many of the answers. Study any that are new to you. Then hand this book to a friend and ask your friend to read the questions one by one. After each question, tell your friend the answer. You will probably answer many correctly. Let your friend mark questions you were unable to answer by making a checkmark in the book next to the question number. Then you will be able to study some more.

If you plan to be examined in an interview, this is the way that questions will be asked. The examiner may even ask some of these questions. If you plan to take the New Citizens Project examination, you will be able to choose right answers instead of thinking of them, but you will need the same information. This quizzer should help you to prepare for either style of questioning.

1. Q. Who were the Pilgrims?
   A. The earliest permanent English settlers in America.

2. Q. When did the Pilgrims come to America?
   A. In 1620.

3. Q. Why did the Pilgrims come?
   A. In search of religious freedom.

4. Q. On what boat did the Pilgrims travel?
   A. The Mayflower.

5. Q. Where did the Pilgrims settle?
   A. Massachusetts Bay Colony in Cape Cod Bay.

6. Q. What was the Mayflower Compact?
   A. The set of rules by which the Pilgrims governed themselves.
      This was the first constitution in America.

7. Q. How many colonies originally joined to become the United States?
   A. Thirteen.

8. Q. What were some of the colonists' complaints against England?
   A. Taxation without representation; restriction of trade; quartering armies among the
      colonists; firing upon the citizens.

9. Q. By what document did the colonists declare independence?
   A. The Declaration of Independence, which was debated by the Continental Congress
      and written by Thomas Jefferson.

10. Q. When was the Declaration of Independence effective?
    A. July 4, 1776, our country's birthday. We celebrate this date every year as
       Independence Day.

11. Q. By what document did the new states originally govern themselves?
    A. The Articles of Confederation written by the Continental Congress.

12. Q. What Group wrote the Constitution?
    A. The Congress of the Confederation. The person credited with doing the actual
       writing was James Madison.

13. Q. How long do members of the House of Representatives serve?
    A. Each term is two years.

14. Q. How long do members of the Senate serve?
    A. Each term is six years.

15. Q. How long does the President serve?
    A. A Presidential term is four years. The President is limited to serving two terms.

16. Q. How long do Federal Judges serve?
    A. A Federal Judge serves a lifetime appointment.

17. Q. How many Senators does each state have?
    A. Each state has two Senators.

18. Q. How many Representatives does each state have?
    A. The number of Representatives is based on the state's population as determined
       by a census every ten years. Each state has at least one Representative.

19. Q. What is impeachment?

A. Impeachment is the process by which President, Vice President, and Federal Judges may be removed from office. The impeachment charges are made in the House of Representatives and the official is tried in the Senate.

20. Q. What is the job of the Vice President?
A. The Vice President presides over the Senate and, in case of a tied vote, casts the tie-breaking vote. The Vice President serves as President if the President becomes unable to serve and becomes President if the President dies, resigns, or is impeached.

21. Q. How does a bill become a law?
A. A bill must be approved by majorities in both houses of Congress and be signed by the President.

22. Q. What happens if a President refuses to sign a bill into law?
A. If both houses of Congress pass the bill by votes of two-thirds of voting members, the bill becomes law over the President's veto.

23. Q. Who can declare war?
A. Only Congress.

24. Q. What is Washington, DC?
A. DC stands for District of Columbia. This is the federal district, the seat of the federal government.

25. Q. What are the three branches of government?
A. The Executive, headed by the President; the Legislative, consisting of Congress; and the Judiciary, the courts.

26. Q. Can you describe the Constitution in a few words?
A. The Supreme Law of the land.

27. Q. What is judicial review?
A. The courts have the power to review laws to be certain that they comply with Constitutional requirements and to strike down laws that are unconstitutional.

28. Q. What are checks and balances?
A. The President has the power to approve or veto bills passed by Congress; Congress can override the President's veto; the Senate has the duty to advise and consent when the President appoints judges and cabinet members and other high government officials; the courts exercise judicial review, with the Supreme Court over them all.

29. Q. What is the Bill of Rights?
A. The first ten amendments to the Constitution.

30. Q. What are a few of the rights guaranteed by the Bill of Rights?
A. Freedom of speech; freedom of religion; freedom of the press; freedom from unwarranted search and seizure; freedom against cruel and unusual punishment.

31. Q. What were some causes of the Civil War?
A. Slavery, states' rights, and some economic issues.

32. Q. Who was President during the Civil War?
    A. Abraham Lincoln.

33. Q. How many states seceded from the Union?
    A. Eleven.

34. Q. What did the secessionist states call themselves?
    A. The Confederate States of America. Their President was Jefferson Davis.

35. Q. Who was freed by the Emancipation Proclamation?
    A. All slaves held in the states that had seceded.

36. Q. When was the Great Depression?
    A. 1929 to 1939.

37. Q. What were the effects of the Depression in America?
    A. Unemployment and poverty.

38. Q. What was the result of the Depression in Europe?
    A. The people turned to dictators in search of relief.

39. Q. Which President helped the United States to overcome the Depression?
    A. Franklin D. Roosevelt.

40. Q. Why did the United States enter World War II?
    A. The Japanese bombed our fleet at Pearl Harbor, Hawaii.

41. Q. Who made the decision to drop atomic bombs and why?
    A. President Harry S Truman to stop World War II quickly so as to save American servicemen's lives.

42. Q. What was the Cold War?
    A. The state of tension and suspicion between the United States and the Soviet Union lasting from 1946 to 1989.

43. Q. What happened in Korea?
    A. The communist North with the help of the Chinese attacked South Korea; United Nations peacekeeping forces, with U.S. participation, went to the aid of South Korea.

44. Q. Why did many Americans oppose our involvement in Vietnam?
    A. Congress had not properly declared war, and the conflict was considered to be a civil war in which we were interfering.

45. Q. Where does the President live?
    A. In the White House in Washington, DC.

46. Q. Can you describe the U.S. flag?
    A. Yes. There are 13 alternating red and white stripes representing the 13 original states and 50 white stars on a blue background representing the current 50 states.

47. Q. What are the words of the Pledge of Allegiance?

A. "I pledge allegiance to the Flag of the United States of America and to the Republic for which it stands, one nation under God, indivisible, with liberty and justice for all."

48. Q. How are treaties made with other nations?
    A. The President enters into treaties with the consent (approval) of the Senate.

49. Q. How does an amendment become part of the Constitution?
    A. The amendment must be passed by a two-thirds vote in each house of Congress and by three-fourths of the states.

50. Q. What is a democratic government?
    A. Government by the people through their elected representatives.

51. Q. Who is the head of the Supreme Court?
    A. The Chief Justice.

52. Q. Who is the head of the Armed Forces?
    A. The President is Commander-in-Chief.

53. Q. Can any state make a treaty or alliance with a foreign nation?
    A. No. Only the federal government can do so.

54. Q. How many Senators are there in Congress?
    A. 100; two from each of the 50 states.

55. Q. What is an Amendment?
    A. It is a change or addition to the Constitution.

56. Q. How many justices are there on the U.S. Supreme Court?
    A. Nine.

57. Q. What is the cabinet?
    A. The cabinet is a group of advisors selected by the President with the approval of the Senate to assist in special areas such as education, agriculture, foreign affairs, and to head up executive departments.

58. Q. What bird is the symbol of the United States?
    A. The bald eagle.

59. Q. Can the residents of Washington, DC vote?
    A. Yes, but only for citywide officers and for President and Vice President.

60. Q. Who makes the laws for each state?
    A. The legislature of that state with the approval of its governor.

If you take an interview/examination you might also have to answer questions like the following, so be prepared with the answers before you go the interview.

Q. Who is the President of the United States?
Q. Who is the current Vice President of the United States?
Q. Who is the Governor of your state?

Q. Can you name one of your state's Senators?
Q. Who represents your home district in Congress?

ANSWERING MULTIPLE-CHOICE QUESTIONS

If you choose to take the New Citizens Project examination, you will see questions on subjects similar to those you just answered. Some questions will be asked as questions ending with a question mark. Other questions will appear as incomplete sentences to which you will choose the correct completion. Every question will offer you four answers; only one answer will be correct. No question will have more than one correct answer. There will be a correct answer choice for each question. If you think that two answers might be correct, you must choose the answer that you think is best.

Questions on the New Citizens Project examination are answered by blackening ovals. The directions given along with official practice test questions distributed by the New Citizens Project are as follows:

Instructions: Read each question. Pick the one best answer. Fill in the oval next to the letter (A, B, C, or D) of the correct answer.

Example:

The colors of the United States flag are red, white, and
A. green
B. orange
C. blue
D. brown

A◯ B◯ C● D◯

On the actual examination, the ovals that you darken to mark your answer are on a separate page from the questions. The answer sheet will be scored by a person who has only a key with the correct letter answers or even by a machine. You cannot give any explanations to the person in another location who has only your answer sheet and a key of correct letter answers nor can you explain your answers to a machine, so you must mark the answer sheet clearly and correctly.

Answer the questions one at a time. Read the question slowly. Read each of the four answer choices. Do not choose the first answer that *seems* right; read all the choices to be sure that you choose the best answer. If you are certain of the correct answer,find the question number on the answer sheet. Blacken the oval of the letter that appears before the answer you have chosen for that question. If you are not certain of the answer, try to narrow your choices. Eliminate the choice or choices that you know to be wrong. Then guess from among the remaining choices. If you are guessing from a group of fewer than four, your chances for guessing correctly are improved. If you have no idea of the right answer, guess anyway. In order to pass the test, you must get 12 right. It does not matter how many questions you answer wrong. If you mark no answer at all, you cannot get the answer right. So, answer every question in turn, and answer every question in the correctly numbered space.

Here are the rules for using the answer sheet:

1. Blacken your answer space completely. ● is the only correct way to mark the answer sheet. ◐, ⊗, ⊘, and ∅ are all unacceptable. The machine might not read them at all and might think that you did not answer the question. If the

machine does not read an answer, even if the answer is correct, you will not get a point.

2. Mark only one answer for each question. If you mark more than one answer you will be considered wrong, even if one of the answers is correct. You will not get a point for the correct answer if you marked two answers for the question.

3. If you change your mind, you must erase your mark. Attempting to cross out an incorrect answer like this ✖ will not work. You must erase any incorrect answer completely. An incomplete erasure might be read as a second answer.

4. All of your answers should be in the form of blackened spaces only. Do not write any notes in the margins. Do not make any extra marks on the paper.

5. Answer every question in the right place. Compare the question number with the number of the answer space as you mark each answer.

The following questions supplied by the New Citizens Project are typical of those on the Citizenship Test. Try these practice questions as if you were taking an actual test, using the answer strip which follows the last question. Cover the correct answers with a plain piece of paper while you are taking the practice test. When you have answered all 15 questions, compare your answers with the correct answers.

1. Where were the original 13 American colonies?
   A. On the East Coast
   B. On the West Coast
   C. In the Midwest
   D. In the Southwest

2. When is Independence Day?
   A. May 30
   B. July 4
   C. September 7
   D. November 24

3. The first 10 amendments to the United States Constitution are called
   A. The Bill of Rights
   B. The Rights of States
   C. The Articles of Confederation
   D. The Declaration of Independence

4. Freedom of speech and religion are protected by
   A. The Declaration of Independence
   B. The Bill of Rights
   C. Early laws of Congress
   D. State laws

5. The first President of the United States was
   A. Abraham Lincoln
   B. James Madison
   C. Thomas Jefferson
   D. George Washington

6. During the Civil War, the President was
   A. Ulysses S. Grant
   B. Andrew Jackson
   C. Abraham Lincoln
   D. Theodore Roosevelt

7. An amendment to the Constitution gave to women the right to
   A. vote
   B. free speech
   C. own property
   D. serve in the Army

8. When the Japanese attacked Pearl Harbor, the United States entered
   A. World War I
   B. World War II
   C. The Korean War
   D. The Vietnam War

9. Dr. Martin Luther King, Jr. was a
   A. Senator   C. Medical Scientist
   B. Governor   D. Civil Rights Leader

10. Where is the United States Capitol?
   A. Washington, DC   C. Philadelphia, PA
   B. New York City   D. Boston, MA

11. The head of the executive branch of the United States government is the
   A. Governor   C. Chief Justice
   B. President   D. Speaker of the House

12. A President is elected every
   A. year   C. four years
   B. two years   D. six years

13. The United States Congress is made up of the Senate and the
   A. Assembly   C. House of Commons
   B. Lower House   D. House of Representatives

14. A state government is headed by a
   A. Governor   C. President
   B. Secretary of State   D. Senator

15. A mayor governs a
   A, city   C. province
   B. county   D. region

ANSWER STRIP FOR NEW CITIZENS PROJECT
PRACTICE QUESTIONS

1 Ⓐ Ⓑ Ⓒ Ⓓ   4 Ⓐ Ⓑ Ⓒ Ⓓ   7 Ⓐ Ⓑ Ⓒ Ⓓ   10 Ⓐ Ⓑ Ⓒ Ⓓ   13 Ⓐ Ⓑ Ⓒ Ⓓ
2 Ⓐ Ⓑ Ⓒ Ⓓ   5 Ⓐ Ⓑ Ⓒ Ⓓ   8 Ⓐ Ⓑ Ⓒ Ⓓ   11 Ⓐ Ⓑ Ⓒ Ⓓ   14 Ⓐ Ⓑ Ⓒ Ⓓ
3 Ⓐ Ⓑ Ⓒ Ⓓ   6 Ⓐ Ⓑ Ⓒ Ⓓ   9 Ⓐ Ⓑ Ⓒ Ⓓ   12 Ⓐ Ⓑ Ⓒ Ⓓ   15 Ⓐ Ⓑ Ⓒ Ⓓ

CORRECT ANSWERS

1. A	4. B	7. A	10. A	13. D
2. B	5. D	8. B	11. B	14. A
3. A	6. C	9. D	12. C	15. A

A passing score on these New Citizens Project practice questions is 9 correct out of 15. The passing score on an actual test is 12 correct out of 20.

ARCO PRACTICE TEST

The following multiple-choice questions will give you still more practice with this question style and with the subject matter of the citizenship test. These are not actual questions from the exam, but they are very similar. Some may even appear on the exam that you take. There are 20 questions on each of the New Citizens Project exams that you may take on the same day. These are represented here by Part A and Part B. You are permitted 30 minutes in which to answer the 20 questions on each exam. Limit yourself to the regulation 30 minutes to answer questions on Part A and another 30 minutes to answer those on Part B. Answer every question. If you are not certain of an answer, eliminate answers that you are sure are wrong and choose from those remaining. When you finish, compare your answers with those provided. You must correctly answer 12 questions on one exam (or here on one part) to pass. If you cannot answer 12 questions correctly, or if you feel that you just made many lucky guesses, then you should return to the Federal Textbooks on Citizenship listed in the section called "Prepare Yourself by Individual Study" in the chapter, APPLYING FOR NATURALIZATION, (page 37). You may also find it very helpful to reread this entire chapter, especially the "Very Short History of the United States" and the "U.S. Citizenship Quizzer." Use the answer strip following question 20 to mark your answers for Part A.

PART A

1. In order to vote, a person must be 18 years of age or older and be a
    A. property owner C. citizen
    B. woman   D. taxpayer

2. A person cannot become Vice President unless he or she was born
    A. in one of the original 13 states C. later than the President
    B. in the United States   D. in the same state as the President

3. The system of checks and balances gives the
    A. President power to overrule state governors
    B. Supreme Court the power to amend the Constitution
    C. House of Representatives power to pass bills that the Senate refuses to approve
    D. Senate power to approve treaties

4. In which war was the city of Washington, DC burned down?
    A. War of 1812   C. Revolutionary War
    B. Civil War   D. Spanish-American War

5. A member of the Senate may not at the same time
    A. serve as an Ambassador
    B. own a home outside of the state from which he or she was elected
    C. travel abroad
    D. campaign for office

6. The state most recently admitted to the Union is
    A. Alaska   C. Delaware
    B. Hawaii   D. Washington

7. The number of congressmen in the House of Representatives is
    A. 100   C. 435
    B. 109   D. 535

8. The amendment to the Constitution that protects citizens from unwarranted search of their homes or seizure of their property is the
    A. First   C. Fourth
    B. Second   D. Sixth

9. The President of the United States must be a native-born citizen and must be at least how many years old?
   A. 25
   B. 30
   C. 35
   D. 39

10. The National Anthem of the United States is called
    A. "America the Beautiful"
    B. "Star Spangled Banner"
    C. "Battle Hymn of the Republic"
    D. "God Bless America"

11. If a federal official is impeached and is found guilty, he or she will
    A. go to prison
    B. be deported
    C. pay a fine
    D. lose his or her job

12. Which of these states did NOT secede from the Union?
    A. Florida
    B. Tennessee
    C. Maryland
    D. Texas

13. Which document begins with the words: "We the People of the United States..."?
    A. Declaration of Independence
    B. Constitution
    C. Mayflower Compact
    D. Bill of Rights

14 The term "President's cabinet" refers to
    A. the piece of furniture in which unsigned bills are filed
    B. congressional committee heads
    C. the President's secretarial staff
    D. a group of advisors

15. Of the following structures, the one that is NOT in Washington, DC is
    A. Independence Hall
    B. White House
    C. Thomas Jefferson Memorial
    D. Washington Monument

16. If the President vetoes a bill, that bill can still become law by a vote of
    A. a majority of both houses meeting in joint session
    B. 2/3 of the members of each house of Congress
    C. 3/4 of the members of each house of Congress
    D. 3/4 of all the states

17. The Civil War was fought in
    A. New England
    B. Central America
    C. the southern United States
    D. Cuba

18. A ruling of the Supreme Court
    A. may be resubmitted to the Supreme Court on appeal
    B. may be appealed directly to the President
    C. may be overturned by a 3/4 vote of both Houses of Congress
    D. must be accepted

19. A divorce granted in one state is recognized as valid in all states by virtue of
    A. the "full faith and credit clause" of the Constitution
    B. a law passed by Congress
    C. the Bill of Rights
    D. the principle of "states' rights"

20. What was the effect of the dropping of the first Atomic Bombs?
    A. The Korean War was begun.
    B. World War II was ended in the Far East.
    C. World War II was ended in Europe.
    D. Members of disadvantaged minority groups rioted in Los Angeles.

ANSWER STRIP — PART A

1 Ⓐ Ⓑ Ⓒ Ⓓ   5 Ⓐ Ⓑ Ⓒ Ⓓ   9 Ⓐ Ⓑ Ⓒ Ⓓ   13 Ⓐ Ⓑ Ⓒ Ⓓ   17 Ⓐ Ⓑ Ⓒ Ⓓ
2 Ⓐ Ⓑ Ⓒ Ⓓ   6 Ⓐ Ⓑ Ⓒ Ⓓ   10 Ⓐ Ⓑ Ⓒ Ⓓ   14 Ⓐ Ⓑ Ⓒ Ⓓ   18 Ⓐ Ⓑ Ⓒ Ⓓ
3 Ⓐ Ⓑ Ⓒ Ⓓ   7 Ⓐ Ⓑ Ⓒ Ⓓ   11 Ⓐ Ⓑ Ⓒ Ⓓ   15 Ⓐ Ⓑ Ⓒ Ⓓ   19 Ⓐ Ⓑ Ⓒ Ⓓ
4 Ⓐ Ⓑ Ⓒ Ⓓ   8 Ⓐ Ⓑ Ⓒ Ⓓ   12 Ⓐ Ⓑ Ⓒ Ⓓ   16 Ⓐ Ⓑ Ⓒ Ⓓ   20 Ⓐ Ⓑ Ⓒ Ⓓ

CORRECT ANSWERS — PART A

1. C	5. A	9. C	13. B	17. C
2. B	6. B	10. B	14. D	18. D
3. D	7. C	11. D	15. A	19. A
4. A	8. C	12. C	16. B	20. B

The $16.00 fee you pay to register for the New Citizens Project English and Citizenship Examination for United States Citizenship entitles you to take two equivalent examinations, Part A and Part B, on the same date. You are not required to take both exams, but it costs you absolutely nothing except an additional 30 minutes. You need to pass only one examination. No harm is done to your application if you fail an exam. Since you cannot be certain that you have passed the first examination, you should give yourself the insurance of taking the second exam as well. Scoring is not done instantly, so you cannot choose to take the second exam on the basis of your score on the first. Give yourself every opportunity to pass. Take the second exam. At the exam site, you will not be able to study between exams. You must be well prepared before you go to take the exam. Right now, however, you have the luxury of study between exams if needed. If you have not already checked your answers on Part A, do so now. If you passed comfortably, just go on to Part B as you will on exam day. If you failed or just barely passed, or if you simply feel uncomfortable, do some more study and review before you try Part B.

PART B

1. The first English settlers in the Massachusetts colony came to this country
    A. instead of serving time in debtor's prison
    B. to escape famine
    C. in search of religious freedom
    D. to avoid paying taxes to the King

2. Why did George Washington serve only two terms as President?
    A. The Constitution limits a President to two terms.
    B. He retired.
    C. He was not reelected.
    D. He died.

3. The call "Remember the Maine" rallied American forces to battle in which war?
    A. French and Indian War   C. Civil War
    B. Spanish-American War   D. World War II

4. The Statue of Liberty may be seen and visited in
   A. Plymouth, Massachusetts
   B. Washington, DC
   C. Philadelphia's Independence Hall
   D. New York harbor

5. What is the term of office served by a federal judge?
   A. six years
   B. thirteen years
   C. his or her lifetime
   D. until the next President is elected

6. In World War II, the group of countries including Germany, Italy, and Japan was called the
   A. Axis   C. Central Powers
   B. Allies   D. United Front

7. The heads of executive departments serve as members of the President's cabinet. One of these, the head of the Department of Justice, is the Attorney General. Every other cabinet member bears the title
   A. Department Head   C. Executive
   B. Secretary   D. General Attorney

8. From the standpoint of the states that seceded from the Union at the start of the Civil War, the chief issue was "states' rights" and their desire to live under laws that favored the southern economy. From the standpoint of the federal government, and most especially that of President Lincoln, the issue over which the war was fought was
   A. slavery   C. the insolubility of the Union
   B. the price of cotton   D. freedom of the seas

9. In the history of the United States, only one President has been impeached, and that President was not convicted by the Senate so he served out the remainder of his term. Who was that President?
   A. Richard Nixon   C. Lyndon Johnson
   B. Andrew Jackson   D. Andrew Johnson

10. The group of men who debated independence was called the
    A. Continental Congress   C. Senate
    B. Mayflower Compact   D. Conference of Governors

11. Who has the power to declare war?
    A. the House of Representatives
    B. the Commander-in-Chief of the Armed Forces
    C. the Senate
    D. Congress

12. The Supreme Law of the Land is
    A. the final ruling of the Supreme Court
    B. the most recent amendment to the Constitution
    C. the Constitution
    D. a joint resolution of Congress

13. Which group received the right to vote most recently?
    A. women   C. poor people
    B. former slaves   D. 18-year-olds

14. Who is called "The Father of Our Country"?
    A. King George III of England   C. Abraham Lincoln
    B. George Washington   D. Martin Luther King

15. Political parties are not mentioned in the Constitution, but the right for the people to peaceably assemble, as granted by the First Amendment, clearly allows for political parties. The two political parties most active in the United States today are the
    A. Liberal Party and the Conservative Party
    B. Labor Party and Conservative Party
    C. Democratic Party and Republican Party
    D. Republican Party and People's Party

16. The right to trial by jury means that
    A. the trial will be fair
    B. a panel of three judges must agree on a verdict
    C. trial judges are elected by a vote of the people
    D. guilt or innocence is determined by ordinary citizens who listen to the evidence

17. What happens if the President dies in office?
    A. The Vice President automatically becomes President.
    B. The Electoral College meets and elects a new President.
    C. The House of Representatives chooses a new President.
    D. The Chief Justice appoints a new President.

18. Since the passage of the Thirteenth Amendment,
    A. a general census has been taken every ten years
    B. slavery has been illegal
    C. naturalized citizens have been permitted to vote
    D. all wage earners have been required to pay an income tax

19. All but one of the following statements are true. Which statement is NOT true?
    A. Every state has its own constitution by which that state is governed.
    B. A state cannot pass and enforce a law that is in conflict with the United States Constitution.
    C. Each state can set its own rules with regard to trade with other states.
    D. Every state has its own judicial system, that is, its own set of courts.

20. If a person who has committed a crime in one state leaves that state and is caught in another state, the state in which the person was caught will
    A. try him or her for the crime
    B. return him or her to the state in which the crime was committed
    C. send him or her to the state of which he or she is a citizen
    D. send him or her to a state in which he or she is unknown so as to assure an impartial jury

ANSWER STRIP — PART B

1 Ⓐ Ⓑ Ⓒ Ⓓ	5 Ⓐ Ⓑ Ⓒ Ⓓ	9 Ⓐ Ⓑ Ⓒ Ⓓ	13 Ⓐ Ⓑ Ⓒ Ⓓ	17 Ⓐ Ⓑ Ⓒ Ⓓ
2 Ⓐ Ⓑ Ⓒ Ⓓ	6 Ⓐ Ⓑ Ⓒ Ⓓ	10 Ⓐ Ⓑ Ⓒ Ⓓ	14 Ⓐ Ⓑ Ⓒ Ⓓ	18 Ⓐ Ⓑ Ⓒ Ⓓ
3 Ⓐ Ⓑ Ⓒ Ⓓ	7 Ⓐ Ⓑ Ⓒ Ⓓ	11 Ⓐ Ⓑ Ⓒ Ⓓ	15 Ⓐ Ⓑ Ⓒ Ⓓ	19 Ⓐ Ⓑ Ⓒ Ⓓ
4 Ⓐ Ⓑ Ⓒ Ⓓ	8 Ⓐ Ⓑ Ⓒ Ⓓ	12 Ⓐ Ⓑ Ⓒ Ⓓ	16 Ⓐ Ⓑ Ⓒ Ⓓ	20 Ⓐ Ⓑ Ⓒ Ⓓ

CORRECT ANSWERS — PART B

1. C	5. C	9. D	13. D	17. A
2. B	6. A	10. A	14. B	18. B
3. B	7. B	11. D	15. C	19. C
4. D	8. C	12. C	16. D	20. B

FORMS APPENDIX

These forms along with their accompanying instructions appear in the order in which they are first mentioned in the text. You should find these copies and instructions very useful as you gather information and documents. You might also practice filling out these copies, adjusting your words and handwriting to fit the spaces. You may NOT use these copies for actual filing. You must request original current forms and fill them out according to their attached instructions. Forms change; instructions change; filing fees change. Complete and file current official forms as you proceed through the process of becoming a United States citizen.

I-538	Certification by Designated School Official
I-765	Application for Employment Authorization
I-539	Application to Extend/Change Nonimmigrant Status
I-134	Affidavit of Support
I-690	Application for Waiver of Grounds of Excludability
I-130	Petition for Alien Relative
I-485	Application to Register Permanent Residence or Adjust Status
G-325A	Biographic Information
9003	Department of the Treasury—Internal Revenue Service Additional Questions
I-693	Medical Examination of Aliens Seeking Adjustment of Status
FD-258	Fingerprint Card
I-751	Petition to Remove the Conditions on Residence
N-300	Application to File Declaration of Intention
N-400	Application for Naturalization

SECTION A. This section must be completed by student as appropriate (Please print or type) :

1. Name:	*(Family in CAPS)*	*(First)*	*(Middle)*	2. Date of birth:

3. Student admission number:	4. Date first granted F-1 or M-1 status:

5. Level of education being sought:	6. Student's major field of study:

7. Describe the proposed employment for practical training:

Beginning date :   Ending date: Number of hours per week:

8. List all periods of previously authorized employment for practical training:

A. Curricular or work/study:	B. Post completion of studies

Signature of student:_____ Date:_____

SECTION B. This Section must be completed by the designated school official of the school the student is attending or was last authorized to attend:

9. I hereby certify that:

The student named above:
- ☐ Is taking a full course of study at this school, and the expected date of completion is:_____
- ☐ Is taking less than a full course of study at this school because:_____
- ☐ Completed the course of study at this school on (date):_____
- ☐ Did not complete the course of study. Terminated attendance on (date):_____

Check one:

☐ A. The employment is for practical training in the student's field of study. The student has been in the educational program for at least 9 months and is eligible for the requested practical training in accordance with INS regulations at 8CFR 214.2(f) (10).

☐ B. The endorsement for off-campus employment is based on the wage-and-labor attestation filed by the employer in accordance with the requirements set forth by the Secretary of Labor. The student has been in F-1 status for at least one year and is in good academic standing. Copy of the employer's attestation is attached.

☐ C. The employment is for an internship with a recognized international organization and is within the scope of the organization's sponsorship. The student has been in F-1 status for at least 9 months and is in good academic standing.

10. Name and title of DSO:	Signature:	Date:

11. Name of school:	School file number:	Telephone no.:

For Official Use only
Microfilm Index Number:

Instructions

A Student seeking authorization for off-campus employment (F-1 only) or practical training (F-1 and M-1) must submit as supporting documentation to Form I-765, Application for Employment Authorization, a certification by the designated school official (DSO) of the school they were last authorized to attend. Certification by the DSO is required of all students (F-1 and M-1) seeking authorization for employment off campus or practical training, including required or optional curricular practical training. The DSO must certify on Form I-538 that the proposed employment is directly related to the student's field of study. A copy of the DSO's certification must be mailed to the STSC date processing center, P.O. Box 140, Highway 25 South, London, Ky. 40741.

All students requesting school certification must complete questions 1 through 6. Students requesting recommendation for practical training must complete questions 7 and 8. Answers to questions 7 through 9 may be continued on this page if needed.

M-1 students seeking extensions of stay must submit a completed Form I-539, Application to Extend time of Temporary Stay, supported by a current Form I-20M-N as appropriate.

Reporting Burden

Public reporting burden for this collection of information is estimated to average 4 minutes per response, including the time for reviewing instructions, searching existing data sources, gathering and maintaining the data needed, and completing and reviewing the collection of information. Send comments regarding this burden estimate or any other aspect of this collection of information, including suggestions for reducing this burden, to: U.S. Department of Justice, Immigration and Naturalization Service (Room 5304), Washington, D.C. 20536; and to the Office Management and Budget, Paperwork Reduction Project, OMB No. 1115-0060 Washington, D.C. 20503.

Comments: _____
_____
_____
_____
_____
_____
_____
_____
_____
_____
_____
_____
_____
_____
_____

U. S. Department of Justice
Immigration and Naturalization Service

OMB # 1115-0163
Application for Employment Authorization

Do Not Write In This Block

Please Complete Both Sides of Form

Case ID#	Action Stamp	Fee Stamp
A#		
Applicant is filing under 274a.12 _____		Remarks

☐ Application Approved. Employment Authorized / Extended (Circle One) _____ (Date).

Subject to the following conditions: _____ until _____ (Date).

☐ Application Denied.
    ☐ Failed to establish eligibility under 8 CFR 274a.12 (a) or (c).
    ☐ Failed to establish economic necessity as required in 8 CFR 274a.12(c), (10), (13), (14).

I am applying for: ☐ Permission to accept employment
    ☐ Replacement (of lost employment authorization document).
    ☐ Extension of my permission to accept employment (attach previous employment authorization document).

1. Name (Family Name in CAPS) (First) (Middle)

2. Other Names Used (Include Maiden Name)

3. Address in the United States (Number and Street) (Apt. Number)

  (Town or City) (State/Country) (ZIP Code)

4. Country of Citizenship

5. Place of Birth (Town or City) (State/Province) (Country)

6. Date of Birth (Month/Day/Year) 7. Sex
    ☐ Male ☐ Female

8. Marital Status ☐ Married ☐ Single
    ☐ Widowed ☐ Divorced

9. Social Security Number (Include all Numbers you have ever used)

10. Alien Registration Number (A-Number) or I-94 Number (if any)

11. Have you ever before applied for employment authorization from INS?
  ☐ Yes (If yes, complete below) ☐ No
  Which INS Office? Date(s)

Results (Granted or Denied - attach all documentation)

12. Date of Last Entry into the U.S. (Month/Day/Year)

13. Place of Last Entry into the U.S.

14. Manner of Last Entry (Visitor, Student, etc.)

15. Current Immigration Status (Visitor, Student, etc.)

16. Go to the Eligibility Section on the reverse of this form and check the box which applies to you. In the space below, place the number of the box you selected on the reverse side:

Eligibility under 8 CFR 274a.12

(   ) (   ) (   )

Complete the reverse of this form before signature.

Your Certification: I certify, under penalty of perjury under the laws of the United States of America, that the foregoing is true and correct. Furthermore, I authorize the release of any information which the Immigration and Naturalization Service needs to determine eligibility for the benefit I am seeking. I have read the reverse of this form and have checked the appropriate block, which is identified in item #16, above.

Signature   Telephone Number   Date

Signature of Person Preparing Form If Other Than Above: I declare that this document was prepared by me at the request of the applicant and is based on all information of which I have any knowledge.

Print Name   Address   Signature   Date

Initial Receipt	Resubmitted	Relocated		Completed		
		Rec'd	Sent	Approved	Denied	Returned

Form I-765 (08/24/89) Page 2

Eligibility

GROUP A

The current immigration laws and regulations permit certain classes of aliens to work in the United States. If you are an alien described within one of the classes below, you do not need to request that employment authorization be granted to you, but you do need to request a document to show that you are able to work in the United States. **NO FEE will be required for your original card. If you need a replacement employment authorization document the fee will be required to process your request.**

Place an **X** in the box next to the number which applies to you.

☐ (a) (3) - I have been admitted to the United States as a refugee.

☐ (a) (4) - I have been paroled into the United States as a refugee.

☐ (a) (5) - My application for asylum has been granted.

☐ (a) (6) - I am the fiancé(e) of a United States citizen and I have K-1 nonimmigrant status; **OR** I am the dependent of a fiancé(e) of a United States citizen and I have K-2 nonimmigrant status.

☐ (a) (7) - I have N-8 or N-9 nonimmigrant status in the United States.

☐ (a) (8) - I am a citizen of the Federated States of Micronesia or of the Marshall Islands.

☐ (a) (9) - I have been granted suspension of deportation and I have not yet been granted lawful permanent resident status in the United States.

☐ (a) (10) - I have been granted withholding of deportation.

☐ (a) (11) - I have been granted extended voluntary departure by the Attorney General.

GROUP C

The immigration law and regulations allow certain aliens to apply for employment authorization. If you are an alien described in one of the classes below you may request employment authorization from the INS and, if granted, you will receive an employment authorization document.

Place an **X** in the box next to the number which applies to you.

☐ (c) (1) - I am the dependent of a foreign government official (A-1 or A-2). I have attached certification from the Department of State recommending employment. **NO FEE.**

☐ (c) (2) - I am the dependent of an employee of the Coordination Council of North American Affairs and I have E-1 nonimmigrant status. I have attached certification of my status from the American Institute of Taiwan. **FEE REQUIRED.**

☐ (c) (3) (i) - I am a foreign student (F-1). I have attached certification from the designated school official recommending employment for economic necessity. I have also attached my INS Form I-20 ID copy. **FEE REQUIRED.**

☐ (c) (3) (ii) - I am a foreign student (F-1). I have attached certification from the designated school official recommending employment for practical training. I have also attached my INS Form I-20 ID copy. **FEE REQUIRED.**

☐ (c) (3) (iii) - I am a foreign student (F-1). I have attached certification from my designated school official and I have been offered employment under the sponsorship of an international organization within the meaning of the International Organization Immunities Act. I have certification from this sponsor and I have also attached my INS Form I-20 ID copy. **FEE REQUIRED.**

☐ (c) (4) - I am the dependent of an officer or employee of an international organization (G-1 or G-4). I have attached certification from the Department of State recommending employment. **NO FEE.**

☐ (c) (5) - I am the dependent of an exchange visitor and I have J-2 nonimmigrant status. **FEE REQUIRED.**

☐ (c) (6) - I am a vocational foreign student (M-1). I have attached certification from the designated school official recommending employment for practical training. I have also attached my INS Form I-20ID Copy. **FEE REQUIRED.**

☐ (c) (7) - I am the dependent of an individual classified as NATO-1 through NATO-7. **FEE REQUIRED.**

☐ (c) (8) - I have filed an application for asylum in the United States and the application is pending. **FEE REQUIRED FOR REPLACEMENT ONLY.**

☐ (c) (9) - I have filed an application for adjustment of status to lawful permanent resident status and the application is pending. **FEE REQUIRED.**

☐ (c) (10) - I have filed an application for suspension of deportation and the application is still pending. **I understand that I must show economic necessity and I will refer to the instructions concerning "Basic Criteria to Establish Economic Necessity." FEE REQUIRED.**

☐ (c) (11) - I have been paroled into the United States for emergent reasons or for reasons in the public interest. **FEE REQUIRED.**

☐ (c) (12) - I am a deportable alien and I have been granted voluntary departure either prior to or after my hearing before the immigration judge. **FEE REQUIRED.**

☐ (c) (13) - I have been placed in exclusion or deportation proceedings. I have not received a final order of deportation or exclusion and I have not been detained. **I understand that I must show economic necessity and I will refer to the instructions concerning "Basic Criteria to Establish Economic Necessity." FEE REQUIRED.**

☐ (c) (14) - I have been granted deferred action by INS as an act of administrative convenience to the government. **I understand that I must show economic necessity and I will refer to the instructions concerning "Basic Criteria to Establish Economic Necessity." FEE REQUIRED.**

☐ (c) (15) (i) - I am a nonimmigrant temporary worker (H-1, H-2, H-3) and I have filed a timely application for extension of my stay. My application for extension has not been adjudicated within 120 days. **FEE REQUIRED.**

☐ (c) (15) (ii) - I am a nonimmigrant exchange visitor (J-1) and I have filed a timely application for extension of my stay. My application for extension has not been adjudicated within 120 days. **FEE REQUIRED.**

☐ (c) (15) (iii) - I am a nonimmigrant intracompany transferee (L-1) and I have filed a timely application for extension of my stay. My application has not been adjudicated within 120 days. **FEE REQUIRED.**

☐ (c) (15) (iv) - I am a nonimmigrant E-1, E-2, I, A-3, or G-5 and I have filed a timely application for extension of my stay. My application has not been adjudicated within 120 days. **FEE REQUIRED.**

FPI-PET

How to File:

A separate application must be filed by each applicant. Applications must be typewritten or clearly printed in ink and completed in full. If extra space is needed to answer any item, attach a continuation sheet and indicate your name, A-number (if any) and the item number.

Note: It is recommended that you retain a complete copy of your application for your records.

Who should file this application?

Certain aliens temporarily in the United States are eligible for employment authorization. Please refer to the ELIGIBILITY SECTION of this application which is found on page three. Carefully review the classes of aliens described in Group A and Group C to determine if you are eligible to apply.

This application should not be filed by lawful permanent resident aliens or by lawful temporary resident aliens.

What is the fee?

Applicants must pay a fee of $35.00 to file this form <u>unless</u> otherwise noted on the reverse of the form. Please refer to page 3. If required, the fee will not be refunded. Pay by cash, check, or money order in the exact amount. All checks and money orders must be payable in U.S. currency in the United States. Make check or money order payable to "Immigration and Naturalization Service." However, if you live in Guam make it payable to "Treasurer, Guam," or if you live in the U.S. Virgin Islands make it payable to "Commissioner of Finance of the Virgin Islands." If the check is not honored the INS will charge you $5.00.

Where should you file this application?

Applications must be presented in person to the nearest Immigration and Naturalization Service (INS) Office that processes employment authorization applications within the jurisdiction over your place of residence. Please bring your INS Form I-94 and any document issued to you by the INS granting you previous employment authorization.

What is our authority for collecting this information?

The authority to require you to file Form I-765, Application for Employment Authorization, is contained in the "Immigration Reform and Control Act of 1986." This information is necessary to determine whether you are eligible for employment authorization and for the preparation of your Employment Authorization Document if you are found eligible. Failure to provide all information as requested may result in the denial or rejection of this application.

The information you provide may also be disclosed to other federal, state, local and foreign law enforcement and regulatory agencies during the course of the investigation required by this Service.

Basic Criteria to Establish Economic Necessity:

Title 45 - Public Welfare, Poverty Guidelines, 45 CFR 1060.2 may be used as the basic criteria to establish eligibility for employment authorization when the applicant's economic necessity is identified as a factor. If you are an applicant who must show economic necessity, you should include a statement listing all of your assets, income, and expenses as evidence of your economic need to work.

Note: Not all applicants are required to establish economic necessity. Carefully review the ELIGIBILITY SECTION of the application. Only aliens who are filing for employment authorization under Group C, items (c)(10), (c)(13), and (c)(14) are required to furnish information on economic need. This information must be furnished on attached sheet(s) and submitted with this application.

What are the penalties for submitting false information?

Title 18, United States Code, Section 1001 states that whoever willfully and knowingly falsifies a material fact, makes a false statement, or makes use of a false document will be fined up to $10,000 or imprisoned up to five years, or both.

Title 18, United States Code, Section 1546(a) states that whoever makes any false statement with respect to a material fact in any document required by the immigration laws or regulations, or presents an application containing any false statement shall be fined or imprisoned or both.

Please Complete Both Sides of Form.

Reporting Burden: Public reporting burden for this collection of information is estimated to average sixty (60) minutes per response, including the time for reviewing instructions, searching existing data sources, gathering and maintaining the data needed, and completing and reviewing the collection of information. Send comments regarding this burden estimate or any other aspect of this collection of information, including suggestions for reducing this burden, to: U.S. Department of Justice, Immigration and Naturalization Service, Room 2011, Washington, D.C. 20536; and to the Office of Management and Budget, Paperwork Reduction Project: OMB No. 1115-0163, Washington, D.C. 20503.

Additional Instructions for
Applicants for an Employment Authorization Document
Form I-765 Instructions Supplement (03/11/93)

These instructions clarify what you must file with your application, and explain *where* you should file your application.

1. Filing at a local INS office.
If you are in proceedings before an Immigration Judge, including any outstanding Order to Show Cause, you must <u>always</u> file your application in person at your local INS office regardless of the basis for your EAD application.

In other situations, file your application at your local INS office *unless* you are applying for a new or extension EAD under one of the categories listed in the next section, titled *Filing at a Service Center.*

When you are filing at a local office, file *in person* and bring the following with you:
* any fee required by the instructions on the application form, the current fee is $60;
* evidence of your identity;
* any Form I-94 issued to you;
* any prior EAD issued to you;
* all evidence of eligibility required in the form instructions;
* if you are in proceedings, also submit a copy of the *Order to Show Cause* or other INS document that placed you in exclusion or deportation proceedings;
* if you are in proceedings, and are filing for an EAD based on an asylum application, include a copy of your asylum application, and attachments, with your EAD application;
* if your Form I-94 and/or prior EAD has been lost or stolen, bring a full written statement of how it was lost or stolen and a copy of the front and back of the document, if you have a copy *(the copy will speed processing).*

Please note: If you are applying at a local INS office, contact that office before going there. Due to demand, many offices must schedule appointments for EAD applications.

2. Filing at a Service Center.
Mail the following types of EAD applications to the appropriate INS Service Center. You must mail your application *with* the initial evidence listed below for the category. With each application you must also submit 2 photographs *(the specifications are listed in Part 4 of these instructions)* and an I-765 signature card. *(If a signature card is not attached to your application, ask your local INS office for one.)* Before you mail your application, sign the card in the blue box marked *signature.* Your signature <u>must</u> fit within the blue box. *DO NOT* fold this card when you mail it with your application.

Please note: In any case where your Form I-94 and/or prior EAD has been lost or stolen, bring a full written statement of how it was lost or stolen and a copy of the front and back of the document, if you have a copy. *The copy will speed processing.*

* **Applicant for asylum- (c)(8).** *(Remember, if you are in exclusion or deportation proceedings, file your asylum application with the Immigration Judge, and your EAD application at your local INS office* <u>with</u> *a copy of your asylum application.)*
  File your application with:
  ○ evidence of your asylum application;

○ if you are filing your initial EAD application *with* your *new* asylum application, simply submit the applications together;
○ if you are filing an initial or extension EAD application *based on a previously filed asylum application* which is still pending, file your EAD application with a copy of the INS receipt notice for that earlier asylum application, or other evidence your asylum application is pending;
○ a copy of any Form I-94 issued to you;
○ an I-765 signature card;
○ if you were previously issued an EAD, submit a copy of the front *and* back of the most recent card;
○ 2 *ADIT* style photos (see Part 4 for specifications); and
○ Fee- There is no fee for an EAD application based on an asylum application, but you will only receive an EAD if your asylum application is found to be non-frivolous. *However,* if you are a national of El Salvador and entered the U.S. before September 19, 1990, or are a national of Guatemala and entered the U.S. on or before October 1, 1990, you can instead file your EAD application based on your asylum application <u>and</u> the A.B.C. settlement by filing it with the $60 application filing fee.
  Please note: If our records do not establish that you have a pending asylum application, we may deny your EAD application or we may return it to you and instruct you to submit it with a complete asylum application.

* **Asylee - (a)(5).** If you have been *granted* asylum in the U.S., and your status has not expired or been revoked, file your application with:
  ○ a copy of the INS notice granting asylum;
  ○ an I-765 signature card;
  ○ if you were previously issued an EAD, submit a copy of the front *and* back of the most recent card;
  ○ 2 *ADIT* style photos (see Part 4 for specifications); and
  ○ Fee. An application fee is not required for your first EAD based on this status. If you are applying for an extension, submit the $60 application fee.

* **Approved Family Unity Status - (a)(13).** If you have been *granted* status under the Family Unity Program, or if you are also enclosing an application (Form I-817) for status under the Family Unity Program, as the spouse or child of a legalized alien, file your application with:
  ○ a copy of the INS notice granting status under the Family Unity Program;
  ○ an I-765 signature card;
  ○ if you were previously issued an EAD, submit a copy of the front *and* back of the most recent card;
  ○ 2 *ADIT* style photos (see Part 4 for specifications); and
  ○ the $60 application filing fee.

* **Family Unity status denied solely because the legalized alien applied after May 5, 1988 - (c)(12).** If you were *denied* status under the Family Unity Program but were granted voluntary departure as the spouse or child of a legalized alien who applied after May 5, 1988, file your application with:
  ○ a copy of the INS notice denying Family Unity status solely on this ground;
  ○ your *original* statement and copies of evidence you wish to submit to establish economic necessity for

employment authorization;

- ○ an I-765 signature card;
- ○ if you were previously issued an EAD, submit a copy of the front *and* back of the most recent card;
- ○ 2 *ADIT* style photos (see Part 4 for specifications); and
- ○ the $60 application filing fee.

- **Applicant for Adjustment of Status- (c)(9).** If you are filing a Form I-485, *Application to Register Permanent Residence or Adjust Status*, and, pursuant to filing instructions for that application, you are mailing that application to a Service Center, or if you already mailed that application and it is still pending at a Service Center, file your EAD application with that same Service Center with:
  - ○ evidence of your I-485 application:
    - ○ if you are filing your initial EAD application *with* your *new* I-485 application, simply submit the applications together;
    - ○ if you are filing an initial or extension EAD application *based on an I-485 previously filed at a Service Center*, file your EAD application with a copy of the INS receipt notice for that earlier I-485, or other evidence your I-485 application is pending;
  - ○ a copy of any Form I-94 issued to you by INS;
  - ○ an I-765 signature card;
  - ○ if you were previously issued an EAD, submit a copy of the front *and* back of the most recent card;
  - ○ 2 *ADIT* style photos (see Part 4 for specifications); and
  - ○ the $60 application filing fee.

Please note: If we issue a decision on your I-485 application within 90 days of filing, your EAD application will be approved, but instead of an EAD you will receive evidence of permanent residence.

- **K-1 fiance(e) nonimmigrant and K-2 dependents - (a)(6).** File your application with:
  - ○ a copy of your Form I-94, *Nonimmigrant Arrival-Departure Record*;
  - ○ an I-765 signature card;
  - ○ if you were previously issued an EAD, submit a copy of the front *and* back of the most recent card;
  - ○ 2 *ADIT* style photos (see Part 4 for specifications); and
  - ○ *Fee-* There is no fee for your *first* EAD based on this status.

- **Dependent of Foreign Government Official or International Organization - (c)(1), (c)(4).** File your application with:
  - ○ a copy of your Form I-94, *Nonimmigrant Arrival-Departure Record*;
  - ○ a copy of the Form I-94 or most recent approval notice for the principal's nonimmigrant status;
  - ○ the required certification from the Department of State recommending employment authorization;
  - ○ an I-765 signature card;
  - ○ if you were previously issued an EAD, submit a copy of the front *and* back of the most recent card;
  - ○ 2 *ADIT* style photos (see Part 4 for specifications); and
  - ○ *Fee-* There is no fee for an EAD based on this status.

- **Dependent of NATO Personnel - (c)(7).** File your application with:
  - ○ a copy of your Form I-94, *Nonimmigrant Arrival-Departure Record*;

- ○ a copy of the Form I-94 or most recent approval notice for the principal's nonimmigrant status;
- ○ the required certification from the Department of State recommending employment authorization;
- ○ an I-765 signature card;
- ○ if you were previously issued an EAD, submit a copy of the front *and* back of the most recent card;
- ○ 2 *ADIT* style photos (see Part 4 for specifications); and
- ○ the $60 application filing fee.

- **Dependent of an employee of the Coordination Council of North American Affairs and having E-1 status - (c)(2).** File your application with:
  - ○ a copy of your Form I-94, *Nonimmigrant Arrival-Departure Record*;
  - ○ a copy of the Form I-94 or most recent approval notice for the principal's nonimmigrant status;
  - ○ the required certification of status from the American Institute of Taiwan;
  - ○ an I-765 signature card;
  - ○ if you were previously issued an EAD, submit a copy of the front *and* back of the most recent card;
  - ○ 2 *ADIT* style photos (see Part 4 for specifications); and
  - ○ the $60 application filing fee.

- **N-8 or N-9 Nonimmigrant - (a)(7).** File your application with:
  - ○ a copy of your Form I-94, *Nonimmigrant Arrival-Departure Record*;
  - ○ an I-765 signature card;
  - ○ if you were previously issued an EAD, submit a copy of the front *and* back of the most recent card;
  - ○ 2 *ADIT* style photos (see Part 4 for specifications); and
  - ○ *Fee-* There is no fee for your *first* EAD based on this status. If you are filing for an extension, include the $60 application filing fee.

- **B-1 Nonimmigrant Domestic Servant of a Nonimmigrant Employer - (c)(17)(1).** File your application with:
  - ○ a copy of your Form I-94, *Nonimmigrant Arrival-Departure Record*;
  - ○ a copy of the Form I-94 or most recent approval notice for the principal's nonimmigrant status;
  - ○ the required certification from the Department of State recommending employment authorization;
  - ○ an I-765 signature card;
  - ○ if you were previously issued an EAD, submit a copy of the front *and* back of the most recent card;
  - ○ 2 *ADIT* style photos (see Part 4 for specifications); and
  - ○ the $60 application filing fee.

- **B-1 Domestic Servant of a U.S. Citizen - (c)(17)(2).** File your application with:
  - ○ a copy of your Form I-94, *Nonimmigrant Arrival-Departure Record*;
  - ○ a copy of the Form I-94 or most recent approval notice for the principal's nonimmigrant status;
  - ○ the required certification from the Department of State recommending employment authorization;
  - ○ an I-765 signature card;
  - ○ if you were previously issued an EAD, submit a copy of the front *and* back of the most recent card;
  - ○ 2 *ADIT* style photos (see Part 4 for specifications); and
  - ○ the $60 application filing fee.

- *B-1 Airline Employee - (c)(17)(3).* File your application. with:
  - o a copy of your Form I-94, *Nonimmigrant Arrival-Departure Record;*
  - o a letter from the airline explaining your duties;
  - o an I-765 signature card;
  - o if you were previously issued an EAD, submit a copy of the front *and* back of the most recent card;
  - o 2 *ADIT* style photos (see Part 4 for specifications); and
  - o the $60 application filing fee.

- *E-1, E-2, H-1, H-2, H-3, I, J-1 or L-1 nonimmigrant with application for extension pending at least 120 days (c)(15)(1), (c)(15)(2), (c)(15)(3) or (c)(15)(4).* File your application with:
  - o a copy of your Form I-94, *Nonimmigrant Arrival-Departure Record;*
  - o evidence your primary application has been pending for at least 120 days;
  - o an I-765 signature card;
  - o if you were previously issued an EAD, submit a copy of the front *and* back of the most recent card;
  - o 2 *ADIT* style photos (see Part 4 for specifications); and
  - o the $60 application filing fee.

File all other EAD applications at your local INS office. If you are in proceedings, file any EAD application at your local office.

3. Photo Specifications.

If you are mailing your application to a Service Center, you must mail it with 2 *ADIT* style natural color photos taken within the past 30 days that:
- have a white background, are unmounted, are printed on thin paper, are glossy and are unretouched;
- show a three-quarter frontal profile of the right side of your face, with your right ear visible and with your head bare *(unless you are wearing a headdress as required by a religious order you belong to);*
- are no larger than 2 X 2 inches, with the distance from the top of the head to just below the chin about 1¼ inches.

Lightly print your name and any A# on the back of each photo with a pencil.

4. Jurisdictions of the Service Centers.

If you are filing for an EAD based on an Asylum Application:
- *If you are in:* Connecticut, Delaware, Maine, Massachusetts, New Hampshire, New Jersey, New York, eastern Pennsylvania, Rhode Island or Vermont, mail your application to:
  USINS Eastern Service Center
  75 Lower Welden Street
  St. Albans, VT 05479-0008

- *If you are in:* Arizona, southern California or southern Nevada, mail your application to:
  USINS Western Service Center
  P.O. Box 10589
  Laguna Niguel, CA 92607-0589

- *If you are in:* Alabama, Arkansas, Colorado, the District of Columbia, Florida, Georgia, Louisiana, Maryland, Mississippi, New Mexico, N. Carolina, western Pennsylvania, Oklahoma, S. Carolina, Tennessee, Utah, Virginia, W. Virginia, Wyoming, the U.S. Virgin Islands or Puerto Rico, mail your

application to:
USINS Southern Service Center
P.O. Box 152122, Department A
Irving, TX 75015-2122

- *If you are* anywhere else in the U.S., mail your application to:
  USINS Northern Service Center
  P.O. Box 82521
  Lincoln, NE 685001-252

If you are mailing your application to a Service Center and your EAD application is not based on an Asylum Application:
- *If you are in:* Connecticut, Delaware, the District of Columbia, Maine, Maryland, Massachusetts, New Hampshire, New Jersey, New York, Pennsylvania, Puerto Rico, Rhode Island, Vermont, Virginia, West Virginia or the U.S. Virgin Islands, mail your application to:
  USINS Eastern Service Center
  75 Lower Welden Street
  St. Albans, VT 05479-0008

- *If you are in:* Arizona, California, Guam, Hawaii or Nevada, mail your application to:
  USINS Western Service Center
  P.O. Box 10589
  Laguna Niguel, CA 92607-0589

- *If you are in:* Alabama, Arkansas, Florida, Georgia, Kentucky, Louisiana, Mississippi, New Mexico, N. Carolina, Oklahoma, S. Carolina, Tennessee or Texas, mail your application to:
  USINS Southern Service Center
  P.O. Box 152122, Department A
  Irving, TX 75015-2122

- *If you are* anywhere else in the U.S., mail your application to:
  USINS Northern Service Center
  P.O. Box 82521
  Lincoln, NE 685001-2521

5. When to apply for an extension.

It may take up to 60 days to process an EAD extension application. If you are filing your extension application at a Service Center, we recommend you file 60 days in advance. If you are filing at a local office we recommend you contact them about how far in advance you should file or schedule to file.

6. Processing at a Service Center.

You will be mailed a receipt after we receive your application. However, if your application is not signed, we will send it back to you. If it is incomplete we may send it back to you or deny the application. If we send back your application, this will delay review of your application and issuance of any Employment Authorization Document.

If you are filing based on a pending asylum application, after initial processing the Service Center will forward your application to the appropriate Asylum Office for a decision.

U.S. Department of Justice
Immigration and Naturalization Service

OMB #1115-0093
Application to Extend/ChangeNonimmigrant Status

START HERE - Please Type or Print

Part 1. Information about you.

Family Name	Given Name	Middle Initial

Address - In Care of: _____

Street # and Name		Apt. #

City	State

Zip Code _____

Date of Birth (month/day/year)	Country of Birth

Social Security # (if any)	A# (if any)

Date of Last Arrival Into the U.S.	I-94#

Current Nonimmigrant Status	Expires on (month/day/year)

Part 2. Application Type.   (See instructions for fee.)

1. **I am applying for:** (check one)
   a. ☐ an extension of stay in my current status
   b. ☐ a change of status. The new status I am requesting is: _____
2. **Number of people included in this application:** (check one)
   a. ☐ I am the only applicant
   b. ☐ Members of my family are filing this application with me.
   The Total number of people included in this application is (complete the supplement for each co-applicant) _____

Part 3. Processing Information.

1. I/We request that my/our current or requested status be extended until (month/day/year) _____
2. Is this application based on an extension or change of status already granted to your spouse, child or parent?
   ☐ No   ☐ Yes (receipt # _____)
3. Is this application being filed based on a separate petition or application to give your spouse, child or parent an extension or change of status?
   ☐ No   ☐ Yes, filed with this application   ☐ Yes, filed previously and pending with INS
4. If you answered yes to question 3, give the petitioner or applicant name:

   _____

   If the application is pending with INS, also give the following information.

   Office filed at _____ Filed on _____ (date)

Part 4. Additional information.

1. For applicant #1, provide passport information:

Country of issuance	Valid to: (month/day/year)

2. Foreign address:

Street # and Name		Apt#

City or Town	State or Province

Country	Zip or Postal Code

Form I-539 (Rev. 12-2-91)   **Continued on back.**

Part 4. Additional Information. *(continued)*

3. Answer the following questions. If you answer yes to any question, explain on separate paper.	Yes	No
a. Are you, or any other person included in this application, an applicant for an immigrant visa or adjustment of status to permanent residence?		
b. Has an immigrant petition ever been filed for you, or for any other person included in this application?		
c. Have you, or any other person included in this application ever been arrested or convicted of any criminal offense since last entering the U.S.?		
d. Have you, or any other person included in this application done anything which violated the terms of the nonimmigrant status you now hold?		
e. Are you, or any other person included in this application, now in exclusion or deportation proceedings?		
f. Have you, or any other person included in this application, been employed in the U.S. since last admitted or granted an extension or change of status?		

If you answered YES to question 3f, give the following information on a separate paper: Name of person, name of employer, address of employer, weekly income, and whether specifically authorized by INS.

If you answered NO to question 3f, fully describe how you are supporting yourself on a separate paper. Include the source and the amount and basis for any income.

Part 5. Signature. *Read the information on penalties in the instructions before completing this section. You must file this application while in the United States.*

I certify under penalty of perjury under the laws of the United States of America that this application, and the evidence submitted with it, is all true and correct. I authorize the release of any information from my records which the Immigration and Naturalization Service needs to determine eligibility for the benefit I am seeking.

Signature	Print your name	Date

Please Note: *If you do not completely fill out this form, or fail to submit required documents listed in the instructions, you cannot be found eligible for the requested document and this application will have to be denied.*

Part 6. Signature of person preparing form if other than above. *(Sign below)*

I declare that I prepared this application at the request of the above person and it is based on all information of which I have knowledge.

Signature	Print Your Name	Date

Firm Name and Address

(Please remember to enclose the mailing label with your application)

Form I-539 (Rev. 12-2-91)

Supplement-1

Attach to Form I-539 when more than one person is included in the petition or application. *(List each person separately. Do not include the person you named on the form).*

Family Name		Given Name	Middle Initial	Date of Birth (month/day/year)
Country of Birth		Social Security No.	A#	
IF IN THE U.S.	Date of Arrival *(month/day/year)*		I-94#	
	Current Nonimmigrant Status:		Expires on *(month/day/year)*	
Country where passport issued		Expiration Date (month/day/year)		

Family Name		Given Name	Middle Initial	Date of Birth (month/day/year)
Country of Birth		Social Security No.	A#	
IF IN THE U.S.	Date of Arrival *(month/day/year)*		I-94#	
	Current Nonimmigrant Status:		Expires on *(month/day/year)*	
Country where passport issued		Expiration Date (month/day/year)		

Family Name		Given Name	Middle Initial	Date of Birth (month/day/year)
Country of Birth		Social Security No.	A#	
IF IN THE U.S.	Date of Arrival *(month/day/year)*		I-94#	
	Current Nonimmigrant Status:		Expires on *(month/day/year)*	
Country where passport issued		Expiration Date (month/day/year)		

Family Name		Given Name	Middle Initial	Date of Birth (month/day/year)
Country of Birth		Social Security No.	A#	
IF IN THE U.S.	Date of Arrival *(month/day/year)*		I-94#	
	Current Nonimmigrant Status:		Expires on *(month/day/year)*	
Country where passport issued		Expiration Date (month/day/year)		

Family Name		Given Name	Middle Initial	Date of Birth (month/day/year)
Country of Birth		Social Security No.	A#	
IF IN THE U.S.	Date of Arrival *(month/day/year)*		I-94#	
	Current Nonimmigrant Status:		Expires on *(month/day/year)*	
Country where passport issued		Expiration Date (month/day/year)		

Purpose Of This Form.

This form is for a nonimmigrant to apply for an extension of stay or change to another nonimmigrant status. However, an employer should file Form I-129 to request an extension/change to E, H, L, O, P, Q or R status for an employee or prospective employee. Dependents of such employees should file for an extension/change of status on this form, not on Form I-129. This form is also for a nonimmigrant F-1 or M-1 student to apply for reinstatement.

This form consists of a basic application and a supplement to list co-applicants.

Who May File.

For extension of stay or change of status.
If you are a nonimmigrant in the U.S., you may apply for an extension of stay or a change of status on this form except as noted above. However, you may not be granted an extension or change of status if you were admitted under the Visa Waiver Program or if your current or proposed status is as:

- an alien in transit (C) or in transit without a visa (TWOV);
- a crewman (D); or
- a fiance(e) or dependent of a fiance(e) (K).

There are additional limits on change of status.

- A J-1 exchange visitor whose status was for the purpose of receiving graduate medical training is ineligible for change of status.
- A J-1 exchange visitor subject to the foreign residence requirement who has not received a waiver of that requirement, is only eligible for a change of status to A or G.
- An M-1 student is not eligible for a change to F-1 status, and is not eligible for a change to any H status if training received as an M-1 student helped him/her qualify for the H status.
- You may not be granted a change to M-1 status for training to qualify for H status.

For F-1 or M-1 student reinstatement. You will only be considered for reinstatement if you establish when filing this application:

- that the violation of status was solely due to circumstances beyond your control or that failure to reinstate you would result in extreme hardship;
- you are pursuing, or will pursue, a full course of study;
- you have not been employed off campus without authorization or, if an F-1 student, that your only unauthorized off-campus employment was pursuant to a scholarship, fellowship, or assistantship, or did not displace a U.S. resident; and
- you are not in deportation proceedings.

Multiple Applicants.

You may include your spouse and your unmarried children under age 21 as co-applicants in your application for the same extension or change of status if you are all in the same status now or they are all in derivative status.

General Filing Instructions.

Please answer all questions by typing or clearly printing in black ink. Indicate that an item is not applicable with "N/A". If the answer is "none," please so state. If you need extra space to answer any item, attach a sheet of paper with your name and your alien registration number (A#), if any, and indicate the number of the item to which the answer refers. Your application must be filed with the required Initial Evidence. Your application must be properly signed and filed with the correct fee. If you are under 14 years of age, your parent or guardian may sign your application.

Copies. If these instructions state that a copy of a document may be filed with this application and you choose to send us the original, we may keep that original for our records.

Translations. Any foreign language document must be accompanied by a full English translation which the translator has certified as complete and correct, and by the translator's certification that he or she is competent to translate from the foreign language into English.

Initial Evidence.

Form I-94, Nonimmigrant Arrival-Departure Record. You must file your application with the original Form I-94, Nonimmigrant Arrival/Departure Record, of each person included in the application, if you are filing for:

- an extension as a B-1 or B-2, or change to such status;
- reinstatement as an F-1 or M-1 or filing for change to F or M status; or
- an extension as a J, or change to such status.

In all other instances, file this application with a copy of the Form I-94 of each person included in the application.

If the required Form I-94 or required copy cannot be submitted, you must file Form I-102, Application for Replacement/Initial Nonimmigrant Arrival/Departure Document, with this application.

Valid Passport. A nonimmigrant who is required to have a passport to be admitted must keep that passport valid during his/her entire nonimmigrant stay. If a required passport is not valid when you file this application, submit an explanation with your application.

Additional Initial Evidence. An application must also be filed with the following evidence.

- If you are filing for an extension/change of status as the dependent of an employee who is an E, H, L, O, P, Q or R nonimmigrant, this application must be filed with:
  - the petition filed for that employee or evidence it is pending with the Service; or
  - a copy of the employee's Form I-94 or approval notice showing that he/she has already been granted status to the period requested in your application.
- If you are requesting an extension/change to A-3 or G-5 status, this application must be filed with:
  - a copy of your employer's Form I-94 or approval notice demonstrating A or G status;
  - an original letter from your employer describing your duties and stating that he/she intends to personally employ you; and
  - an original Form I-566, certified by the Department of State, indicating your employer's continuing accredited diplomatic status.
- If you are filing for an extension/change to other A or G status, you must submit Form I-566, certified by the Department of State to indicate your accredited diplomatic status.
- If you are filing for an extension/change to B-1 or B-2 status, this application must be filed with a statement explaining, in detail,:
  - the reasons for your request;
  - why your extended stay would be temporary including what arrangement you have made to depart the U.S.; and
  - any effect of the extended stay on your foreign employment and residency.
- If you are requesting an extension/change to F-1 or M-1 student status, this application must be filed with an original Form I-20 issued by the school which has accepted you. If you are requesting reinstatement to F-1 or M-1 status, you must also submit evidence establishing that you are eligible for reinstatement.
- If you are filing for an extension/change to I status, this application must be filed with a letter describing the employment and establishing that it is as the representative of qualifying foreign media.
- If you are filing for an extension/change to J-1 exchange visitor status, this application must be filed with an original Form IAP-66 issued by your program sponsor.
- If you are filing for an extension/change to N-1 or N-2 status as the parent or child of an alien admitted as a special immigrant under section 101(a)(27)(I), this application must be filed with a copy of that person's alien registration card.

When To File.

You must submit an application for extension of stay or change of status before your current authorized stay expires. We suggest you file at least 45 days before your stay expires, or as soon as you determine you need to change status. Failure to file before the expiration date may be excused if you demonstrate when you file the application:

- the delay was due to extraordinary circumstances beyond your control;
- the length of the delay was reasonable;
- that you have not otherwise violated your status;
- that you are still a bona fide nonimmigrant; and
- that you are not in deportation proceedings

Additional Instructions for Persons Applying for <u>B-1</u>, <u>F</u>, <u>M</u> or <u>J</u> Nonimmigrant Status, or for an Extension or Reinstatement of such Status

Form I-539 Instructions Supplement (03/01/93)

The instructions on Form I-539 indicate that the following applicants should file their I-539 applications at their local INS office:

- persons filing for <u>B-1</u> or <u>B-2</u> nonimmigrant visitor and their dependents;
- persons filing for <u>F</u> or <u>M</u> nonimmigrant student status, and their dependents; and
- persons filing for <u>J</u> nonimmigrant exchange visitor status, and their dependents.

Effective April 1, 1993, <u>all</u> persons filing a Form I-539 application should mail their application direct to the appropriate INS Service Center. The jurisdictions of the Service Centers are indicated on the attached instructions.

Revised <u>Evidence Instructions</u> for those filing for <u>B</u>, <u>F</u>, <u>M</u> or <u>J</u> status, or for an extension or reinstatement of such status.

- *Form I-94, Nonimmigrant Arrival Document.*
  - *If you are filing your application <u>before</u> September 1, 1993:*
    Mail your original Form I-94 with your application.
  - *If you are filing your application <u>on or after</u> September 1, 1993:*
    Do not mail your original Form I-94 with your application. Instead mail a copy of both sides of this document for each person included in your application plus a copy of any I-797 approval notices changing or extending your status. If we approve your application we will mail you an approval notice that will include a replacement Form I-94.

  If you do not have an original Form I-94, you must file your I-539 application along with a separate Form I-102 application for an I-94. If you did not receive an I-94 when you entered the U.S., along with Form I-102 you must submit a complete explanation of the circumstances of your entry plus copies of any documentation you have showing your admission.

- *Form IAP-66.* If you are applying for J status, or an extension of such status, mail your original Form IAP-66 with your application, but retain the copy of the IAP-66 designated for the J-1.

- *Form I-20.* If you are applying for F or M status, or for reinstatement, mail your original I-20, but retain the copy of the I-20 designated for the student.

- If you are applying for an extension of B-1 or B-2 nonimmigrant visitor status, file your application with a complete written explanation of why you are applying for an extension. Your explanation of why an extension should be given is critical to deciding whether to grant your application.

Processing at a Service Center.

You will be mailed a receipt after we receive your application. If we approve your application you will be mailed an approval notice. You should keep this notice with your Form I-94, and with your copy of the IAP-66 or I-20. While you are in the U.S., this approval notice, combined with your I-94, will demonstrate your status.

You will not need to turn this approval notice in when you leave the U.S. (In most instances you will have to turn in your Form I-94 at time of departure.) Retain the approval notice for your records, and to assist in obtaining any new visa in the same status in order to return to the U.S.

OMB No. 1115-0062

U. S. Department of Justice
Immigration and Naturalization Service

Affidavit of Support

(ANSWER ALL ITEMS: FILL IN WITH TYPEWRITER OR PRINT IN BLOCK LETTERS IN INK.)

I, _____ , residing at _____
(Name)   (Street and Number)

_____
(City)   (State)   (ZIP Code if in U.S.)   (Country)

BEING DULY SWORN DEPOSE AND SAY:

1. I was born on_____at_____
(Date)   (City)   (Country)

    If you are *not* a native born United States citizen, answer the following as appropriate:

    a. If a United States citizen through naturalization, give certificate of naturalization number _____

    b. If a United States citizen through parent(s) or marriage, give citizenship certificate number _____

    c. If United States citizenship was derived by some other method, attach a statement of explanation.

    d. If a lawfully admitted permanent resident of the United States, give "A" number _____

2. That I am_____years of age and have resided in the United States since (date) _____

3. That this affidavit is executed in behalf of the following person:

Name	Sex	Age

Citizen of--(Country)	Marital Status	Relationship to Deponent

Presently resides at--(Street and Number)	(City)	(State)	(Country)

Name of spouse and children accompanying or following to join person:

Spouse	Sex	Age	Child	Sex	Age
Child	Sex	Age	Child	Sex	Age
Child	Sex	Age	Child	Sex	Age

4. That this affidavit is made by me for the purpose of assuring the United States Government that the person(s) named in item 3 will not become a public charge in the United States.

5. That I am willing and able to receive, maintain and support the person(s) named in item 3. That I am ready and willing to deposit a bond, if necessary, to guarantee that such person(s) will not become a public charge during his or her stay in the United States, or to guarantee that the above named will maintain his or her nonimmigrant status if admitted temporarily and will depart prior to the expiration of his or her authorized stay in the United States.

6. That I understand this affidavit will be binding upon me for a period of three (3) years after entry of the person(s) named in item 3 and that the information and documentation provided by me may be made available to the Secretary of Health and Human Services and the Secretary of Agriculture, who may make it available to a public assistance agency.

7. That I am employed as, or engaged in the business of _____with _____
(Type of Business)   (Name of concern)

at _____
(Street and Number)   (City)   (State)   (Zip Code)

I derive an annual income of *(if self-employed, I have attached a copy of my last income tax return or report of commercial rating concern which I certify to be true and correct to the best of my knowledge and belief. See instruction for nature of evidence of net worth to be submitted.)* $_____

I have on deposit in savings banks in the United States $_____

I have other personal property, the reasonable value of which is $_____

Form I-134 (Rev. 12-1-84) Y   OVER

I have stocks and bonds with the following market value, as indicated on the attached list
which I certify to be true and correct to the best of my knowledge and belief. $ _____
I have life insurance in the sum of $ _____
With a cash surrender value of $ _____
I own real estate valued at $ _____
    With mortgages or other encumbrances thereon amounting to $ _____

    Which is located at_____
    (Street and Number)   (City)   (State)   (Zip Code)

8. That the following persons are dependent upon me for support: *(Place an "X" in the appropriate column to indicate whether the person named is **wholly** or **partially** dependent upon you for support.)*

Name of Person	Wholly Dependent	Partially Dependent	Age	Relationship to Me

9. That I have previously submitted affidavit(s) of support for the following person(s). If none, state *"None"*

Name   Date submitted
_____
_____
_____

10. That I have submitted visa petition(s) to the Immigration and Naturalization Service on behalf of the following person(s). If none, state none.

Name   Relationship   Date submitted
_____
_____
_____

11. *(Complete this block only if the person named in item 3 will be in the United States temporarily.)*
That I ☐ do intend   ☐ do not   intend, to make specific contributions to the support of the person named in item 3. *(If you check "do intend", indicate the exact nature and duration of the contributions. For example, if you intend to furnish room and board, state for how long and, if money, state the amount in United States dollars and state whether it is to be given in a lump sum, weekly, or monthly, or for how long.)*
_____
_____
_____

OATH OR AFFIRMATION OF DEPONENT

I acknowledge at that I have read Part III of the Instructions, Sponsor and Alien Liability, and am aware of my responsibilities as an immigrant sponsor under the Social Security Act, as amended, and the Food Stamp Act, as amended.

I swear (affirm) that I know the contents of this affidavit signed by me and the statements are true and correct.

Signature of deponent _____

Subscribed and sworn to (affirmed) before me this _____*day of* _____ , 19_____

at _____ .*My commission expires on* _____

Signature of Officer Administering Oath _____ *Title* _____

If affidavit prepared by other than deponent, please complete the following: I declare that this document was prepared by me at the request of the deponent and is based on all information of which I have knowledge.

_____
(Signature)   *(Address)*   *(Date)*

U. S. Department of Justice
Immigration and Naturalization Service

Affidavit of Support

INSTRUCTIONS

I. EXECUTION OF AFFIDAVIT. A separate affidavit must be submitted for each person. You must sign the affidavit in your full, true and correct name and affirm or make it under oath. If you are **in the United States** the affidavit may be sworn or affirmed before an immigration officer without the payment of fee, or before a notary public or other officer authorized to administer oaths for general purposes, in which case the official seal or certificate of authority to administer oaths must be affixed. If you are **outside the United States** the affidavit must be sworn to or affirmed before a United States consular or immigration officer.

II. SUPPORTING EVIDENCE. The deponent must submit in duplicate evidence of income and resources, as appropriate:

A. Statement from an officer of the bank or other financial institution in which you have deposits giving the following details regarding your account:
1. Date account opened.
2. Total amount deposited for the past year.
3. Present balance.

B. Statement of your employer on business stationery, showing:
1. Date and nature of employment.
2. Salary paid.
3. Whether position is temporary or permanent.

C. If self-employed:
1. Copy of last income tax return filed or,
2. Report of commercial rating concern.

D. List containing serial numbers and denominations of bonds and name of record owner(s).

III. SPONSOR AND ALIEN LIABILITY. Effective October 1, 1980, amendments to section 1614(f) of the Social Security Act and Part A of Title XVI of the Social Security Act establish certain requirements for determining the eligibility of aliens who apply for the first time for Supplemental Security Income (SSI) benefits. Effective October 1, 1981, amendments to section 415 of the Social Security Act establish similar requirements for determining the eligibility of aliens who apply for the first time for Aid to Families with Dependent Children (AFDC) benefits. Effective December 22, 1981, amendments to the Food Stamp Act of 1977 affect the eligibility of alien participation in the Food Stamp Program. These amendments require that the income and resources of any person who, as the sponsor of an alien's entry into the United States, executes an affidavit of support or similar agreement on behalf of the alien, and the income and resources of the sponsor's spouse (*if living with the sponsor*) shall be deemed to be the income and resources of the alien under formulas for determining eligibility for SSI, AFDC, and Food Stamp benefits during the three years following the alien's entry into the United States.

Form I-134 (Rev. 12-1-84) Y

An alien applying for SSI must make available to the Social Security Administration documentation concerning his or her income and resources and those of the sponsor including information which was provided in support of the application for an immigrant visa or adjustment of status. An alien applying for AFDC or Food Stamps must make similar information available to the State public assistance agency. The Secretary of Health and Human Services and the Secretary of Agriculture are authorized to obtain copies of any such documentation submitted to INS or the Department of State and to release such documentation to a State public assistance agency.

Sections 1621(e) and 415(d) of the Social Security Act and subsection 5(i) of the Food Stamp Act also provide that an alien and his or her sponsor shall be jointly and severably liable to repay any SSI, AFDC, or Food Stamp benefits which are incorrectly paid because of misinformation provided by a sponsor or because of a sponsor's failure to provide information. Incorrect payments which are not repaid will be withheld from any subsequent payments for which the alien or sponsor are otherwise eligible under the Social Security Act or Food Stamp Act, except that the sponsor was without fault or where good cause existed.

These provisions do not apply to the SSI, AFDC or Food Stamp eligibility of aliens admitted as refugees, granted political asylum by the Attorney General, or Cuban/Haitian entrants as defined in section 501(e) of P.L. 96-422 and of dependent children of the sponsor or sponsor's spouse. They also do not apply to the SSI or Food Stamp eligibility of an alien who becomes blind or disabled after admission into the United States for permanent residency.

IV. AUTHORITY/USE/PENALTIES. Authority for the collection of the information requested on this form is contained in 8 U.S.C. 1182(a)(15), 1184(a), and 1258. The information will be used principally by the Service, or by any consular officer to whom it may be furnished, to support an alien's application for benefits under the Immigration and Nationality Act and specifically the assertion that he or she has adequate means of financial support and will not become a public charge. Submission of the information is voluntary. It may also, as a matter of routine use, be disclosed to other federal, state, local and foreign law enforcement and regulatory agencies, including the Department of Health and Human Services, the Department of Agriculture, the Department of State, the Department of Defense and any component thereof (if the deponent has served or is serving in the armed forces of the United States), the Central Intelligence Agency, and individuals and organizations during the course of any investigation to elicit further information required to carry out Service functions. Failure to provide the information may result in the denial of the alien's application for a visa, or his or her exclusion from the United States.

U.S. Department of Justice
Immigration and Naturalization Service

Application for Waiver of Grounds of Excludability
(Sec. 245A or Sec. 210 of the Immigration and Nationality Act)

Please begin with item #1, after carefully reading the instructions.　　　The block below is for *Government Use Only.*

Name and Location (City or Town) of Qualified Designated Entity	Fee Stamp
	Fee Receipt No. (This application)
Qualified Designated Entity I.D. No.	**File No. (This applicant)** A -

Applicant: Do not write above this line. See instructions before filling in application. If you need more space to answer fully any question on this form, use a separate sheet and identify each answer with the number of the corresponding question. *Fill in with typewriter or print in block letters in ink.*

1. **Family Name** *(Last Name in CAPITAL Letters)* (First Name) (Middle Name)	2. **Date of Birth** *(Month/Day/Year)*

3. **Address** *(No. and Street)*　　(Apt. No.)　　(City/Town)　　(State/Country)　　(ZIP/Postal Code)

4. **Place of Birth** *(City or Town and County, Province or State)*　　(Country)	5. **Social Security Number**

6. **Date of visa application** *(Month/Day/Year)*—for: ☐ Permanent ☐ Temporary Residence	7. **Visa applied for at:**

8. **I am inadmissable under Section(s):**　　☐ 212 (a) (1)　　☐ 212 (a) (6)　　☐ 212 (a) (19)
　　　☐ 212 (a) (3)　　☐ 212 (a) (12)　　☐ Other 212 (a) *Specify Section* (_____)

9. **List reasons of excludability;** if active or suspected tuberculosis, the reverse of the page must be completed.

10. **List all immediate relatives in the United States (parents, spouse and children):**

Name	Address	Relationship	Immigration Status

11. **I should be granted a waiver because:** *(Describe family unity considerations or humanitarian or public interest reasons for granting a waiver).* If more space is needed attach an additional sheet.

12. **Applicant's Signature**	13. **Date** *(Month/Day/Year)*

I&NS USE ONLY
Recommended by:
(Print or Type Name and Title) _____ Date _____

Signature _____　I.D.# _____　Director, Regional Processing Facility _____

Form I-690 (02/14/87)

A. APPLICANT

Instructions: Leave this side *blank* if your Application for Waiver of Grounds of Excludability is for any reason *other than* active or suspected *tuberculosis*. If your application is due to active or suspected tuberculosis, take this form to any physician or medical facility under contract with the Immigration and Naturalization Service. Have the physician complete Section B. You must sign Section A (below) *in the presence of the physician*.

If medical care will be provided by a physician who checked Box 3 or 4 in Section B, have Section C completed by the local or State Health Officer who has jurisdiction in the area where you reside. Present the form to the Health Officer after Sections A and B on this side, and *all sections on the other side* have been completed.

Statement: I have reported to the physician or health facility named in Section B; have presented all X-Rays used in the Legalization medical examination to substantiate diagnosis; will submit to such examinations, treatment, isolation, and medical regimen as may be required; and will remain under the prescribed treatment or observation whether on inpatient or outpatient basis, until discharged at the discretion of the physician named, or a physician representing the facility named in Section B. Satisfactory financial arrangements have been made. **(NOTE: This statement does not relieve you from submitting evidence to establish that you are not likely to become a public charge.)**

A. Signature of Applicant	Date

B. PHYSICIAN OR HEALTH FACILITY

Instructions: This section of Form I-690 may be executed by a physician in private practice (under contract with the Immigration and Naturalization Service), or a physician employed by a health department, other public health facility, or military hospital.

Complete Section B (below) of this form, and have alien sign and date Section A (above) *in your presence. Please be sure the alien's signature above, and the alien's signature on the other side of this form are identical.*

Statement: I agree to supply any treatment or observation necessary for the proper management of the alien's tuberculous condition. I agree to submit Form CDC 75.18 to the health officer named below (*Section C) within thirty (30) days of the alien's reporting for care, indicating presumptive diagnosis, test results, and plans for future care of the alien. Satisfactory financial arrangements have been made.

I represent *(enter X in the appropriate box and type or legibly print name and address of facility):*

   1. ☐ Local Health Department
   2. ☐ Military Hospital
   3. ☐ Other Public Health Facility
   4. ☐ Private Practice or Private Health Facility under contract with the Immigration and Naturalization Service.

B. Signature of Physician	Date
Print or Type Name and Address of Physician and Facility. (If military, enter name and address of receiving hospital and mail directly to Centers for Disease Control, Atlanta, GA 30333.)	

C. LOCAL OR STATE HEALTH OFFICER

Instructions: If the facility or physician who signed in Section B is not in your health jurisdiction and is not familiar to you, you may wish to contact the health officer responsible for the jurisdiction of the facility or physician prior to endorsing this document.

Statement: This endorsement signifies recognition of the physician or facility for the purpose of providing care for tuberculosis.

C. Signature of Health Officer	Date
Print or Type Name of Health Officer*, and Offical Name and Complete Address of Local Health Department.	

Form I-690 (02/14/87)

Application for Waiver of Grounds of Excludability
Under Sections 245A or 210 of the Immigration and Nationality Act

I-690 Instructions

Please carefully read all of the instructions.
The fee will not be refunded.

1. Filing the Application

The application and supporting documentation should be taken or mailed to an American Consulate if the applicant is outside of the United States and is applying for temporary resident status as a Special Agricultural Worker.

If the applicant is in the United States, a participating Qualified Designated Entity near your place of residence, or

The Service legalization office having jurisdiction over the applicant's place of residence or employment.

If an applicant for permanent residence under Section 245A of the Immigration and Nationality Act, the application should be mailed along with the I-698 application form to the Regional Processing Facility having jurisdiction over the applicant's residence.

2. Fee

A fee of thirty-five dollars ($35.00), is required at the time of filing. The fee is not refundable regardless of the action taken on the application.

A separate cashier's check or money order must be submitted for each application. *All fees must be submitted in the exact amount.* The fee must be in the form of a cashier's check or money order. No cash or personal checks will be accepted. The cashier's check or money order must be made payable to "Immigration and Naturalization Service" unless applicant resides in the Virgin Islands or Guam. (Applicants residing in the Virgin Islands make cashier's check or money order payable to "Commissioner of Finance of the Virgin Islands." Applicants residing in Guam make cashier's check or money order payable to "Treasurer, Guam."

A fee is not required if this application is filed for an alien who:

Is afflicted with tuberculosis;
Is mentally retarded; or
Has a history of mental illness.

3. Applicants with Tuberculosis.

An applicant with active tuberculosis or suspected tuberculosis must complete Statement A on page two of this form. The applicant and his or her sponsor is also responsible for having:

Statement B completed by the physician or health facility which has agreed to provide treatment or observation, and

Statement C, if required, completed by the appropriate local or state health officer.

This form should then be returned to the applicant for presentation to the consular office, or to the appropriate office of the Immigration and Naturalization Service.

Submission of the application without the required fully executed statements will result in the return of the application to the applicant without further action.

4. Applicants with Mental Conditions.

An alien who is mentally retarded or who has a history of mental illness shall attach a statement that arrangements have been made for the submission of a medical report, as follows, to the office where this form is filed:

The medical report shall contain:

A complete medical history of the alien, including details of any hospitalization or institutional care or treatment for any physical or mental condition;

Findings as to the current physical condition of the alien, including reports of chest X-rays and a serologic test if the alien is 15 years of age or older, and other pertinent diagnostic tests; and

Findings as to the current mental condition of the alien, with information as to prognosis and life expectancy and with a report of a psychiatric examination conducted by a psychiatrist who shall, in case of mental retardation, also provide an evaluation of intelligence.

For an alien with a past history of mental illness, the medical report shall also contain available information on which the United States Public Health Service can base a finding as to whether the alien has been free of such mental illness for a period of time sufficient in the light of such history to demonstrate recovery.

The medical report will be referred to the United States Public Health Service for review and, if found acceptable, the alien will be required to submit such additional assurances as the United States Public Health Service may deem necessary in his or her particular case.

U.S. Department of Justice
Immigration and Naturalization Service (INS)

OMB #1115–0054

Petition for Alien Relative

DO NOT WRITE IN THIS BLOCK – FOR EXAMINING OFFICE ONLY

Case ID#	Action Stamp	Fee Stamp
A#		
G–28 or Volag #		

Section of Law:
- ☐ 201 (b) spouse
- ☐ 201 (b) child
- ☐ 201 (b) parent
- ☐ 203 (a)(1)
- ☐ 203 (a)(2)
- ☐ 203 (a)(4)
- ☐ 203 (a)(5)

AM CON: _____

Petition was filed on: _____ (priority date)
- ☐ Personal Interview
- ☐ Pet. ☐ Ben. "A" File Reviewed
- ☐ Field Investigations
- ☐ 204 (a)(2)(A) Resolved
- ☐ Previously Forwarded
- ☐ Stateside Criteria
- ☐ I–485 Simultaneously
- ☐ 204 (h) Resolved

Remarks:

A. Relationship

1. The alien relative is my
   ☐ Husband/Wife   ☐ Parent   ☐ Brother/Sister   ☐ Child

2. Are you related by adoption?   ☐ Yes   ☐ No

3. Did you gain permanent residence through adoption?   ☐ Yes   ☐ No

B. Information about you

1. **Name** (Family name in CAPS)   (First)   (Middle)

2. **Address** (Number and Street)   (Apartment Number)

   (Town or City)   (State/Country)   (ZIP/Postal Code)

3. **Place of Birth** (Town or City)   (State/Country)

4. **Date of Birth** (Mo/Day/Yr)
5. **Sex**   ☐ Male   ☐ Female
6. **Marital Status**   ☐ Married   ☐ Single   ☐ Widowed   ☐ Divorced

7. **Other Names Used** (including maiden name)

8. **Date and Place of Present Marriage** (if married)

9. **Social Security Number**
10. **Alien Registration Number** (if any)

11. **Names of Prior Husbands/Wives**
12. **Date(s) Marriage(s) Ended**

13. If you are a U.S. citizen, complete the following:
    My citizenship was acquired through (check one)
    ☐ Birth in the U.S.
    ☐ Naturalization (Give number of certificate, date and place it was issued)

    ☐ Parents
    Have you obtained a certificate of citizenship in your own name?
    ☐ Yes   ☐ No
    If "Yes", give number of certificate, date and place it was issued.

14a. If you are a lawful permanent resident alien, complete the following:
    Date and place of admission for, or adjustment to, lawful permanent residence, and class of admission:

14b. Did you gain permanent resident status through marriage to a United States citizen or lawful permanent resident? ☐ Yes   ☐ No

C. Information about your alien relative

1. **Name** (Family name in CAPS)   (First)   (Middle)

2. **Address** (Number and Street)   (Apartment Number)

   (Town or City)   (State/Country)   (ZIP/Postal Code)

3. **Place of Birth** (Town or City)   (State/Country)

4. **Date of Birth** (Mo/Day/Yr)
5. **Sex**   ☐ Male   ☐ Female
6. **Marital Status**   ☐ Married   ☐ Single   ☐ Widowed   ☐ Divorced

7. **Other Names Used** (including maiden name)

8. **Date and Place of Present Marriage** (if married)

9. **Social Security Number**
10. **Alien Registration Number** (if any)

11. **Names of Prior Husbands/Wives**
12. **Date(s) Marriage(s) Ended**

13. Has your relative ever been in the U.S.?   ☐ Yes   ☐ No

14. If your relative is currently in the U.S., complete the following: He or she last arrived as a (visitor, student, stowaway, without inspection, etc.)

    Arrival/Departure Record (I-94) Number   Date arrived (Month/Day/Year)

    Date authorized stay expired, or will expire, as shown on Form I-94 or I-95

15. Name and address of present employer (if any)

    Date this employment began (Month/Day/Year)

16. Has your relative ever been under immigration proceedings?
    ☐ Yes   ☐ No   Where _____   When _____
    ☐ Exclusion   ☐ Deportation   ☐ Recission   ☐ Judicial Proceedings

INITIAL RECEIPT	RESUBMITTED	RELOCATED		COMPLETED		
		Rec'd	Sent	Approved	Denied	Returned

Form I-130 (Rev. 10/01/89) Y

C. (continued) Information about your alien relative

16. List husband/wife and all children of your relative (if your relative is your husband/wife, list only his or her children).

(Name)	(Relationship)	(Date of Birth)	(Country of Birth)

17. Address in the United States where your relative intends to live

(Number and Street)	(Town or City)	(State)

18. Your relative's address abroad

(Number and Street)	(Town or City)	(Province)	(Country)	(Phone Number)

19. If your relative's native alphabet is other than Roman letters, write his or her name and address abroad in the native alphabet:

(Name)	(Number and Street)	(Town or City)	(Province)	(Country)

20. If filing for your husband/wife, give last address at which you both lived together: From   To

(Name)	(Number and Street)	(Town or City)	(Province)	(Country)	(Month)	(Year)	(Month)	(Year)

21. Check the appropriate box below and give the information required for the box you checked:

☐ Your relative will apply for a visa abroad at the American Consulate in _____

                                                            (City)   (Country)

☐ Your relative is in the United States and will apply for adjustment of status to that of a lawful permanent resident in the office of the Immigration and Naturalization Service at _____ . If your relative is not eligible for adjustment of status, he or she will

                       (City)   (State)

apply for a visa abroad at the American Consulate in _____ .

                                      (City)   (Country)

(Designation of a consulate outside the country of your relative's last residence does not guarantee acceptance for processing by that consulate. Acceptance is at the discretion of the designated consulate.)

D. Other Information

1. If separate petitions are also being submitted for other relatives, give names of each and relationship.

2. Have you ever filed a petition for this or any other alien before?   ☐ Yes   ☐ No
If "Yes," give name, place and date of filing, and result.

Warning: The INS investigates claimed relationships and verifies the validity of documents. The INS seeks criminal prosecutions when family relationships are falsified to obtain visas.

Penalties: You may, by law be imprisoned for not more than five years, or fined $250,000, or both, for entering into a marriage contract for the purpose of evading any provision of the immigration laws and you may be fined up to $10,000 or imprisoned up to five years or both, for knowingly and willfully falsifying or concealing a material fact or using any false document in submitting this petition.

Your Certification: I certify, under penalty of perjury under the laws of the United States of America, that the foregoing is true and correct. Furthermore, I authorize the release of any information from my records which the Immigration and Naturalization Service needs to determine eligibility for the benefit that I am seeking.

Signature _____ Date _____ Phone Number _____

Signature of Person Preparing Form if Other than Above

I declare that I prepared this document at the request of the person above and that it is based on all information of which I have any knowledge.

Print Name _____ (Address) _____ (Signature) _____ (Date) _____

G–28 ID Number _____

Volag Number _____

NOTICE TO PERSONS FILING FOR SPOUSES IF MARRIED LESS THAN TWO YEARS

Pursuant to section 216 of the Immigration and Nationality Act, your alien spouse may be granted conditional permanent resident status in the United States as of the date he or she is admitted or adjusted to conditional status by an officer of the Immigration and Naturalization Service. Both you and your conditional permanent resident spouse are required to file a petition, Form I–751, Joint Petition to Remove Conditional Basis of Alien's Permanent Resident Status, during the ninety day period immediately before the second anniversary of the date your alien spouse was granted conditional permanent residence.

Otherwise, the rights, privileges, responsibilities and duties which apply to all other permanent residents apply equally to a conditional permanent resident. A conditional permanent resident is not limited to the right to apply for naturalization, to file petitions in behalf of qualifying relatives, or to reside permanently in the United States as an immigrant in accordance with the immigration laws.

> **Failure to file Form I–751, Joint Petition to Remove the Conditional Basis of Alien's Permanent Resident Status, will result in termination of permanent residence status and initiation of deportation proceedings.**

NOTE: You must complete Items 1 through 6 to assure that petition approval is recorded. Do not write in the section below item 6.

---

1. **Name of relative** (Family name in CAPS)   (First)   (Middle)

2. **Other names used by relative** (including maiden name)

3. **Country of relative's birth**   4. **Date of relative's birth** (Month/Day/Year)

5. **Your name** (Last name in CAPS) (First) (Middle)   6. **Your phone number**

Action Stamp

SECTION
- ☐ 201 (b)(spouse)
- ☐ 201 (b)(child)
- ☐ 201 (b)(parent)
- ☐ 203 (a)(1)
- ☐ 203 (a)(2)
- ☐ 203 (a)(4)
- ☐ 203 (a)(5)

DATE PETITION FILED

☐ **STATESIDE CRITERIA GRANTED**

SENT TO CONSUL AT;

CHECKLIST

Have you answered each question?
Have you signed the petition?
Have you enclosed:

- ☐ The filing fee for each petition?
- ☐ Proof of your citizenship or lawful permanent residence?
- ☐ All required supporting documents for each petition?

If you are filing for your husband or wife have you included:

- ☐ Your picture?
- ☐ His or her picture?
- ☐ Your G–325A?
- ☐ His or her G–325A?

Relative Petition Card
Form I–130A (Rev. 10/01/89) Y

Instructions

Read the instructions carefully. If you do not follow the instructions, we may have to return your petition, which may delay final action. If more space is needed to complete an answer continue on separate sheet of paper.

1. Who can file?
A citizen or lawful permanent resident of the United States can file this form to establish the relationship of certain alien relatives who may wish to immigrate to the United States. You must file a separate form for each eligible relative.

2. For whom can you file?
A. If you are a citizen, you may file this form for:
1) your husband, wife, or unmarried child under 21 years old
2) your unmarried child over 21, or married child of any age
3) your brother or sister if you are at least 21 years old
4) your parent if you are at least 21 years old.
B. If you are a lawful permanent resident you may file this form for:
1) your husband or wife
2) your unmarried child
Note: If your relative qualifies under instruction A(2) or A(3) above, separate petitions are not required for his or her husband or wife or unmarried children under 21 years old. If your relative qualifies under instruction B(2) above, separate petitions are not required for his or her unmarried children under 21 years old. These persons will be able to apply for the same type of immigrant visa as your relative.

3. For whom can you not file?
You cannot file for people in the following categories:
A. An adoptive parent or adopted child, if the adoption took place after the child became 16 years old, or if the child has not been in the legal custody and living with the parent(s) for at least two years.
B. A natural parent if the United States citizen son or daughter gained permanent residence through adoption.
C. A stepparent or stepchild, if the marriage that created this relationship took place after the child became 18 years old.
D. A husband or wife, if you were not both physically present at the marriage ceremony, and the marriage was not consummated.
E. A husband or wife if you gained lawful permanent resident status by virtue of a prior marriage to a United States citizen or lawful permanent resident unless:
1) a period of five years has elapsed since you became a lawful permanent resident; OR
2) you can establish by clear and convincing evidence that the prior marriage (through which you gained your immigrant status) was not entered into for the purpose of evading any provision of the immigration laws; OR
3) your prior marriage (through which you gained your immigrant status) was terminated by the death of your former spouse.
F. A husband or wife if he or she was in exclusion, deportation, rescission, or judicial proceedings regarding his or her right to remain in the United States when the marriage took place, unless such spouse has resided outside the United States for a two-year period after the date of the marriage.
G. A husband or wife if the Attorney General has determined that such alien has attempted or conspired to enter into a marriage for the purpose of evading the immigration laws.
H. A grandparent, grandchild, nephew, niece, uncle, aunt, cousin, or in-law.

4. What documents do you need?
You must give INS certain documents with this form to prove you are eligible to file. You must also give the INS certain documents to prove the family relationship between you and your relative.
A. For each document needed, give INS the original and one copy. However, because it is against the law to copy a Certificate of Naturalization, a Certificate of Citizenship or an Alien Registration Receipt Card (Form I–151 or I–551) give INS the original only. **Originals will be returned to you.**
B. If you do not wish to give INS the original document, you may give INS a copy. The copy must be certified by:
1) an INS or U.S. consular officer, or
2) an attorney admitted to practice law in the United States, or
3) an INS accredited representative (INS may still require originals).
C. Documents in a foreign language must be accompanied by a complete English translation. The translator must certify that the translation is accurate and that he or she is competent to translate.

5. What documents do you need to show you are a United States citizen?
A. If you were born in the United States, give INS your birth certificate.
B. If you were naturalized, give INS your original Certificate of Naturalization.
C. If you were born outside the United States, and you are a U.S. citizen through your parents, give INS:
1) your original Certificate of Citizenship, or
2) your Form FS–240 (Report of Birth Abroad of a United States Citizen).
D. In place of any of the above, you may give INS your valid unexpired U.S. passport that was initially issued for at least 5 years.
E. If you do not have any of the above and were born in the United States, see instruction under 8 below. *"What if a document is not available?"*

6. What documents do you need to show you are a permanent resident?
You must give INS your alien registration receipt card (Form I–151 or Form I–551). Do not give INS a photocopy of the card.

7. What documents do you need to prove family relationship?
You have to prove that there is a family relationship between your relative and yourself.

In any case where a marriage certificate is required, if either the husband or wife was married before, you must give INS documents to show that all previous marriages were legally ended. In cases where the names shown on the supporting documents have changed, give INS legal documents to show how the name change occurred (for example a marriage certificate, adoption decree, court order, etc.)

Find the paragraph in the following list that applies to the relative for whom you are filing.

If you are filing for your:

A. **husband or wife,** give INS
   1) your marriage certificate
   2) a color photo of you and one of your husband or wife, taken within 30 days of the date of this petition. These photos must have a white background. They must be glossy, unretouched, and not mounted. The dimension of the facial image should be about 1 inch from chin to top of hair in 3/4 frontal view, showing the right side of the face with the right ear visible. Using pencil or felt pen, lightly print name (and Alien Registration Number, if known) on the back of each photograph.
   3) a completed and signed G–325A (Biographic Information) for you and one for your husband or wife. Except for name and signature, you do not have to repeat on the G–325A the information given on your I–130 petition.

B. **child** and you are the **mother,** give the child's birth certificate showing your name and the name of your child.

C. **child** and you are the **father or stepparent,** give the child's birth certificate showing both parents' names and your marriage certificate. **Child** born out of wedlock and you are the **father,** give proof that a parent/child relationship exists or existed. For example, the child's birth certificate showing your name and evidence that you have financially supported the child. (A blood test may be necessary).

D. **brother or sister,** your birth certificate and the birth certificate of your brother or sister showing both parents' names. If you do not have the same mother, you must also give the marriage certificates of your father to both mothers.

E. **mother,** give your birth certificate showing your name and the name of your mother.

F. **father,** give your birth certificate showing the names of both parents, and your parents' marriage certificate.

G. **stepparent,** give your birth certificate showing the names of both natural parents and the marriage certificate of your parent to your stepparent.

H. **adoptive parent or adopted child,** give a certified copy of the adoption decree, the legal custody decree if you obtained custody of the child before adoption, and a statement showing the dates and places you have lived together with the child.

8. **What if a document is not available?**
   If the documents needed above are not available, you can give INS the following instead. (INS may require a statement from the appropriate civil authority certifying that the needed document is not available.)

   A. Church record: A certificate under the seal of the church where the baptism, dedication, or comparable rite occurred within two months after birth, showing the date and place of child's birth, date of the religious ceremony, and the names of the child's parents.

   B. School record: A letter from the authorities of the school attended (preferably the first school), showing the date of admission to the school, child's date and place of birth, and the names and places of birth parents, if shown in the school records.

   C. Census record: State or federal census record showing the names, place of birth, and date of birth or the age of the person listed.

   D. Affidavits: Written statements sworn to or affirmed by two persons who were living at the time and who have personal knowledge of the event you are trying to prove; for example, the date and place of birth, marriage, or death. The persons making the affidavits need not be citizens of the United States. Each affidavit should contain the following information regarding the person making the affidavit: his or her full name, address, date and place of birth, and his or her relationship to you, if any; full information concerning the event; and complete details concerning how the person acquired knowledge of the event.

9. **How should you prepare this form?**
   A. Type or print legibly in ink.
   B. If you need extra space to complete any item, attach a continuation sheet, indicate the item number, and date and sign each sheet.
   C. Answer all questions fully and accurately. If any item does not apply, please write "N/A".

10. **Where should you file this form?**
    A. If you live in the United States, send or take the form to the INS office that has jurisdiction over where you live.
    B. If you live outside the United States, contact the nearest American Consulate to find out where to send or take the completed form.

11. **What is the fee?**
    You must pay forty dollars ($40.00) to file this form. **The fee will not be refunded, whether the petition is approved or not.** DO NOT MAIL CASH. All checks or money orders, whether U.S. or foreign, must be payable in U.S. currency at a financial institution in the United States. When a check is drawn on the account of a person other than yourself, write your name on the face of the check. If the check is not honored, INS will charge you $5.00.

    Pay by check or money order in the exact amount. Make the check or money order payable to "Immigration and Naturalization Service". However,

    A. if you live in Guam: Make the check or money order payable to "Treasurer, Guam", or

    B. if you live in the U.S. Virgin Islands: Make the check or money order payable to "Commissioner of Finance of the Virgin Islands".

12. **When will a visa become available?**
    When a petition is approved for the husband, wife, parent, or unmarried minor child of a United States citizen, these relatives do not have to wait for a visa number, as they are not subject to the immigrant visa limit. However, for a child to qualify for this category, all processing must be completed and the child must enter the United States before his or her 21st birthday.

    For all other alien relatives there are only a limited number of immigrant visas each year. The visas are given out in the order in which INS receives properly filed petitions. To be considered properly filed, a petition must be completed accurately and signed, the required documents must be attached, and the fee must be paid.

    For a monthly update on the dates for which immigrant visas are available, you may call (202) 647–0508.

13. **What are the penalties for committing marriage fraud or submitting false information or both?**
    Title 8, United States Code, Section 1325 states that any individual who knowingly enters into a marriage contract for the purpose of evading any provision of the immigration laws shall be imprisoned for not more than five years, or fined not more than $250,000.00 or both.

    Title 18, United States Code, Section 1001 states that whoever willfully and knowingly falsifies a material fact, makes a false statement, or makes use of a false document will be fined up to $10,000 or imprisoned up to five years, or both.

14. **What is our authority for collecting this information?**
    We request the information on the form to carry out the immigration laws contained in Title 8, United States Code, Section 1154(a). We need this information to determine whether a person is eligible for immigration benefits. The information you provide may also be disclosed to other federal, state, local, and foreign law enforcement and regulatory agencies during the course of the investigation required by this Service. You do not have to give this information. However, if you refuse to give some or all of it, your petition may be denied.

15. **Reporting Burden.**
    Public reporting burden for this collection of information is estimated to average 30 minutes per response, including the time for reviewing instructions, searching existing data sources, gathering and maintaining the data needed, and completing and reviewing the collection of information. Send comments regarding this burden estimate or any other aspect of this collection of information, including suggestions for reducing this burden, to: U.S. Department of Justice, Immigration and Naturalization Service (Room 2011), Washington, D.C. 20536; and to the Office of Management and Budget, Paperwork Reduction Project, OMB No. 1115–0054, Washington, D.C. 20503.

It is not possible to cover all the conditions for eligibility or to give instructions for every situation. If you have carefully read all the instructions and still have questions, please contact your nearest INS office.

U.S. Department of Justice
Immigration and Naturalization Service

OMB No. 1115-0053

Application to Register Permanent Residence or Adjust Status

START HERE - Please Type or Print

Part 1. Information about you.

Family Name	Given Name	Middle Initial

Address - C/O

Street Number and Name	Apt. #

City

State	Zip Code

Date of Birth (month/day/year)	Country of Birth

Social Security #	A # (if any)

Date of Last Arrival (month/day/year)	I-94 #

Current INS Status	Expires on (month/day/year)

Part 2. Application Type. *(check one)*

I am applying for adjustment to permanent resident status because:

a. ☐ an immigrant petition giving me an immediately available immigrant visa number has been approved (attach a copy of the approval notice), or a relative, special immigrant juvenile, or special immigrant military visa petition filed with this application will give me an immediately available visa number if approved.

b. ☐ My spouse or parent applied for adjustment of status or was granted lawful permanent residence in an immigrant visa category which allows derivative status for spouses and children.

c. ☐ I entered as a K-1 fiance(e) of a U.S. citizen whom I married within 90 days of entry, or I am the K-2 child of such a fiance(e) (attach a copy of the fiance(e) petition approval notice and the marriage certificate).

d. ☐ I was granted asylum or derivative asylum status as the spouse or child of a person granted asylum and am eligible for adjustment.

e. ☐ I am a native or citizen of Cuba admitted or paroled into the U.S. after January 1, 1959, and thereafter have been physically present in the U.S. for at least 1 year.

f. ☐ I am the husband, wife, or minor unmarried child of a Cuban described in (e) and am residing with that person, and was admitted or paroled into the U.S. after January 1, 1959, and thereafter have been physically present in the U.S. for at least 1 year.

g. ☐ I have continuously resided in the U.S. since before January 1, 1972.

h. ☐ Other-explain _____

I am already a permanent resident and am applying to have the date I was granted permanent residence adjusted to the date I originally arrived in the U.S. as a nonimmigrant or parolee, or as of May 2, 1964, whichever is later, and: *(Check one)*

i. ☐ I am a native or citizen of Cuba and meet the description in (e), above.

j. ☐ I am the husband, wife or minor unmarried child of a Cuban, and meet the description in (f), above.

Form I-485 (09-09-92)N   *Continued on back.*

Part 3. Processing Information.

A. City/Town/Village of birth _____ | Current occupation _____

Your mother's first name _____ | Your father's first name _____

Give your name exactly how it appears on your Arrival /Departure Record (Form I-94)

_____

Place of last entry into the U.S. (City/State)	In what status did you last enter? *(Visitor, Student, exchange alien, crewman, temporary worker, without inspection, etc.)*
Were you inspected by a U.S. Immigration Officer? ☐ Yes ☐ No	
Nonimmigrant Visa Number	Consulate where Visa was issued

Date Visa was Issued (month/day/year)	Sex: ☐ Male ☐ Female	Marital Status: ☐ Married ☐ Single ☐ Divorced ☐ Widowed

Have you ever before applied for permanent resident status in the U.S? ☐ No ☐ Yes (give date and place of filing and final disposition):

B. List your present husband/wife, all of your sons and daughters (if you have none, write "none". If additional space is needed, use separate paper).

Family Name	Given Name	Middle Initial	Date of Birth (month/day/year)
Country of birth	Relationship	A #	Applying with you? ☐ Yes ☐ No
Family Name	Given Name	Middle Initial	Date of Birth (month/day/year)
Country of birth	Relationship	A #	Applying with you? ☐ Yes ☐ No
Family Name	Given Name	Middle Initial	Date of Birth (month/day/year)
Country of birth	Relationship	A #	Applying with you? ☐ Yes ☐ No
Family Name	Given Name	Middle Initial	Date of Birth (month/day/year)
Country of birth	Relationship	A #	Applying with you? ☐ Yes ☐ No
Family Name	Given Name	Middle Initial	Date of Birth (month/day/year)
Country of birth	Relationship	A #	Applying with you? ☐ Yes ☐ No

C. List your present and past membership in or affiliation with every political organization, association, fund, foundation, party, club, society, or similar group in the United States or in any other place since your 16th birthday. Include any foreign military service in this part. If none, write "none". Include the name of organization, location, dates of membership from and to, and the nature of the organization. If additional space is needed, use separate paper.

_____

_____

_____

_____

_____

_____

_____

_____

Form I-485 (Rev. 09-09-92) N   Continued On Next Page

Part 3. Processing Information. (Continued)

Please answer the following questions. (If your answer is **"Yes"** on any one of these questions, explain on a separate piece of paper. Answering **"Yes"** does not necessarily mean that you are not entitled to register for permanent residence or adjust status).

1. Have you ever, in or outside the U. S.:
    a. knowingly committed any crime of moral turpitude or a drug-related offense for which you have not been arrested?
    b. been arrested, cited, charged, indicted, fined, or imprisoned for breaking or violating any law or ordinance, excluding traffic violations?
    c. been the beneficiary of a pardon, amnesty, rehabilitation decree, other act of clemency or similar action?
    d. exercised diplomatic immunity to avoid prosecution for a criminal offense in the U. S.?   ☐ Yes ☐ No

2. Have you received public assistance in the U.S. from any source, including the U.S. government or any state, county, city, or municipality (other than emergency medical treatment) , or are you likely to receive public assistance in the future?   ☐ Yes ☐ No

3. Have you ever:
    a. within the past 10 years been a prostitute or procured anyone for prostitution, or intend to engage in such activities in the future?
    b. engaged in any unlawful commercialized vice, including, but not limited to, illegal gambling?
    c. knowingly encouraged, induced, assisted, abetted or aided any alien to try to enter the U.S. illegally?
    d. illicitly trafficked in any controlled substance, or knowingly assisted, abetted or colluded in the illicit trafficking of any controlled substance?   ☐ Yes ☐ No

4. Have you ever engaged in, conspired to engage in, or do you intend to engage in, or have you ever solicited membership or funds for, or have you through any means ever assisted or provided any type of material support to, any person or organization that has ever engaged or conspired to engage, in sabotage, kidnapping, political assassination, hijacking, or any other form of terrorist activity?   ☐ Yes ☐ No

5. Do you intend to engage in the U.S. in:
    a. espionage?
    b. any activity a purpose of which is opposition to, or the control or overthrow of, the Government of the United States, by force, violence or other unlawful means?
    c. any activity to violate or evade any law prohibiting the export from the United States of goods, technology or sensitive information?   ☐ Yes ☐ No

6. Have you ever been a member of, or in any way affiliated with, the Communist Party or any other totalitarian party?   ☐ Yes ☐ No

7. Did you, during the period March 23, 1933 to May 8, 1945, in association with either the Nazi Government of Germany or any organization or government associated or allied with the Nazi Government of Germany, ever order, incite, assist or otherwise participate in the persecution of any person because of race, religion, national origin or political opinion?   ☐ Yes ☐ No

8. Have you ever engaged in genocide, or otherwise ordered, incited, assisted or otherwise participated in the killing of any person because of race, religion, nationality, ethnic origin, or political opinion?   ☐ Yes ☐ No

9. Have you ever been deported from the U.S., or removed from the U.S. at government expense, excluded within the past year, or are you now in exclusion or deportation proceedings?   ☐ Yes ☐ No

10. Are you under a final order of civil penalty for violating section 274C of the Immigration Act for use of fraudulent documents, or have you, by fraud or willful misrepresentation of a material fact, ever sought to procure, or procured, a visa, other documentation, entry into the U.S., or any other immigration benefit?   ☐ Yes ☐ No

11. Have you ever left the U.S. to avoid being drafted into the U.S. Armed Forces?   ☐ Yes ☐ No

12. Have you ever been a J nonimmigrant exchange visitor who was subject to the 2 year foreign residence requirement and not yet complied with that requirement or obtained a waiver?   ☐ Yes ☐ No

13. Are you now withholding custody of a U.S. Citizen child outside the U.S. from a person granted custody of the child? .   ☐ Yes ☐ No

14. Do you plan to practice polygamy in the U.S.?   ☐ Yes ☐ No

Part 4. Signature. *(Read the information on penalties in the instructions before completing this section. You must file this application while in the United States.)*

I certify under penalty of perjury under the laws of the United States of America that this application, and the evidence submitted with it, is all true and correct. I authorize the release of any information from my records which the Immigration and Naturalization Service needs to determine eligibility for the benefit I am seeking.

Signature	*Print Your Name*	*Date*	*Daytime Phone Number*

Please Note: *If you do not completely fill out this form, or fail to submit required documents listed in the instructions, you may not be found eligible for the requested document and this application may be denied.*

Part 5. Signature of person preparing form if other than above. *(Sign Below)*

I declare that I prepared this application at the request of the above person and it is based on all information of which I have knowledge.

Signature	**Print Your Name**	*Date*	*Day time Phone Number*

**Firm Name
and Address**

FPI-LOM

Purpose of this Form.
This form is for a person who is in the United States to apply to adjust to permanent resident status or register for permanent residence while in the U.S. It may also be used by certain Cuban nationals to request a change in the date their permanent residence began.

Who May File.
Based on an immigrant petition. You may apply to adjust your status if:
- an immigrant visa number is immediately available to you based on an approved immigrant petition; or
- you are filing this application with a complete relative, special immigrant juvenile, or special immigrant military petition which if approved, would make an immigrant visa number immediately available to you.

Based on being the spouse or child of another adjustment applicant or of a person granted permanent residence . You may apply to adjust status if you are the spouse or child of another adjustment applicant, or of a lawful permanent resident, if the relationship existed when that person was admitted as a permanent resident in an immigrant category which allows derivative status for spouses and children.

Based on admission as the fiance(e) of a U.S. citizen and subsequent marriage to that citizen. You may apply to adjust status if you were admitted to the U.S. as the K-1 fiance(e) of a U.S. citizen and married that citizen within 90 days of your entry. If you were admitted as the K-2 child of such a fiance(e), you may apply based on your parent's adjustment application.

Based on asylum status. You may apply to adjust status if you have been granted asylum in the U.S. and are eligible for asylum adjustment. [Note: In most cases you become eligible after being physically present in the U.S. for one year after the grant of asylum if you still qualify as a refugee or as the spouse or child of refugee.]

Based on Cuban citizenship or nationality. You may apply to adjust status if:
- you are a native or citizen of Cuba, were admitted or paroled into the U.S. after January 1, 1959, and thereafter have been physically present in the U.S. for at least one year; or
- you are the spouse or unmarried child of a Cuban described above, and you were admitted or paroled after January 1, 1959, and thereafter have been physically present in the U.S. for at least one year.

Based on continuous residence since before January 1, 1972. You may apply for permanent residence if you have continuously resided in the U.S. since before January 1, 1972.

Other basis of eligibility. If you are not included in the above categories, but believe you may be eligible for adjustment or creation of record of permanent residence, contact your local INS office.

Applying to change the date your permanent residence began. If you were granted permanent residence in the U.S. prior to November 6, 1966, and are a native or citizen of Cuba, his or her spouse or unmarried minor child, you may ask to change the date your lawful permanent residence began to your date of arrival in the U.S. or May 2, 1964, whichever is later.

Persons Who Are Ineligible.
Unless you are applying for creation of record based on continuous residence since before 1/1/72, or adjustment of status under a category in which special rules apply (such as asylum adjustment, Cuban adjustment, special immigrant juvenile adjustment, or special immigrant military personnel adjustment), **you are not eligible for adjustment of status if any of the following apply to you:**
- you entered the U.S. in transit without a visa;
- you entered the U.S. as a nonimmigrant crewman;
- you were not admitted or paroled following inspection by an immigration officer;
- your authorized stay expired before you filed this application, you were employed in the U.S. , prior to filing this application, without INS authorization, or you otherwise failed to maintain your nonimmigrant status, other than through no fault of your own or for technical reasons; unless you are applying because you are an immediate relative of a U.S. citizen (parent, spouse, widow, widower, or unmarried child under 21 years old), a K-1 fiance(e) or K-2 fiance(e) dependent who married the U.S. petitioner within 90.

days of admission, or an "H" or "I" special immigrant (foreign medical graduates, international organization employees or their derivative family members);
- you are or were a J-1 or J-2 exchange visitor, are subject to the two-year foreign residence requirement, and have not complied with or been granted a waiver of the requirement;
- you have A, E or G nonimmigrant status, or have an occupation which would allow you to have this status, unless you complete Form I-508 (I-508F for French nationals) to waive diplomatic rights, privileges and immunities, and if you are an A or G nonimmigrant, unless you submit a completed Form I-566;
- you were admitted to Guam as a visitor under the Guam visa waiver program;
- you were admitted to the U.S. as a visitor under the Visa Waiver Pilot Program, unless you are applying because you are an immediate relative of a U.S. citizen (parent, spouse, widow, widower, or unmarried child under 21 years old);
- you are already a conditional permanent resident;
- you were admitted as a K-1 fiance(e) but did not marry the U.S. citizen who filed the petition for you, or were admitted as the K-2 child of a fiance(e) and your parent did not marry the U.S. citizen who filed the petition.

General Filing Instructions.
Please answer all questions by typing or clearly printing in black ink. Indicate that an item is not applicable with **"N/A"**. If the answer is **"none"**, write **"none"**. If you need extra space to answer any item, attach a sheet of paper with your name and your alien registration number (A#), if any, and indicate the number of the item to which the answer refers. You must file your application with the required **Initial Evidence**. Your application must be properly signed and filed with the correct fee. If you are under 14 years of age, your parent or guardian may sign your application.

Translations. Any foreign language document must be accompanied by a full English translation which the translator has certified as complete and correct, and by the translator's certification that he or she is competent to translate from the foreign language into English.

Copies. If these instructions state that a copy of a document may be filed with this application, and you choose to send us the original, we may keep the original for our records.

Initial Evidence.
You must file your application with following evidence:

- **Birth certificate.** Submit a copy of your birth certificate or other record of your birth.
- **Photos.** Submit two (2) identical natural color photographs of yourself, taken within 30 days of this application [Photos must have a white background, be unmounted, printed on thin paper, and be glossy and unretouched. They must show a three-quarter frontal profile showing the right side of your face, with your right ear visible and with your head bare. You may wear a headdress if required by a religious order of which you are a member. The photos must be no larger than 2 X 2 inches, with the distance from the top of the head to just below the chin about 1 and 1/4 inches. Lightly print your A# (or your name if you have no A#) on the back of each photo, using a pencil.].
- **Fingerprints.** Submit a complete set of fingerprints on Form FD-258 if you are between the ages of 14 and 75 [Do not bend, fold, or crease the fingerprint chart. You should complete the information on the top of the chart and write your A# (if any) in the space marked "Your no. OCA" or "Miscellaneous no. MNU". You should not sign the chart until you have been fingerprinted, or are told to sign by the person who takes your fingerprints. The person who takes your fingerprints must also sign the chart and write his/her title and the date you are fingerprinted in the space provided on the chart. You may be fingerprinted by police, sheriff, or INS officials or other reputable person or organization. You should call the police, sheriff, organization or INS office before you go there, since some offices do not take fingerprints or may take fingerprints only at certain times.].

- **Medical Examination.** Submit a medical examination report on the form you have obtained from INS [Not required if you are applying for creation of record based on continuous residence since before 1/1/72, or if you are a K-1 fiance(e) or K-2 dependent of a fiance(e) who had a medical examination within the past year as required for the nonimmigrant fiance(e) visa.].
- **Form G-325A,** Biographic Information Sheet. You must submit a completed G-325A if you are between 14 and 79 years of age.
- **Evidence of status.** Submit a copy of your Form I-94, Nonimmigrant Arrival/Departure Record, showing your admission to the U.S. and current status, or other evidence of your status.
- **Employment letter/Affidavit of Support.** Submit a letter showing you are employed in a job that is not temporary, an affidavit of support from a responsible person in the U.S., or other evidence that shows that you are not likely to become a public charge [Not required if you are applying for creation of record based on continuous residence since before 1/1/72, asylum adjustment, or a Cuban or a spouse or unmarried child of a Cuban who was admitted after 1/1/59].
- **Evidence of eligibility.**
  - **Based on an immigrant petition.** Attach a copy of the approval notice for an immigrant petition which makes a visa number immediately available to you, or submit a complete relative, special immigrant juvenile, or special immigrant military petition which, if approved, will make a visa number immediately available to you.
  - **Based on admission as the K-1 fiance(e) of a U.S. citizen and subsequent marriage to that citizen.** Attach a copy of the fiance(e) petition approval notice and a copy of your marriage certificate.
  - **Based on asylum status.** Attach a copy of the letter or Form I-94 which shows the date you were granted asylum.
  - **Based on continuous residence in the U.S. since before 1/1/72.** Attach copies of evidence that shows continuous residence since before 1/1/72.
  - **Based on Cuban citizenship or nationality.** Attach evidence of your citizenship or nationality, such as a copy of your passport, birth certificate or travel document.
  - **Based on you being the spouse or child of another adjustment applicant or person granted permanent residence based on issuance of an immigrant visa.** File your application with the application of that other applicant, or with evidence it is pending with the Service or has been approved, or evidence your spouse or parent has been granted permanent residence based on an immigrant visa and:
    - If you are applying as the spouse of that person, also attach a copy of your marriage certificate and copies of documents showing the legal termination of all other marriages by you and your spouse; or
    - If you are applying as the child of that person, also attach a copy of your birth certificate, and, if the other person is not your natural mother, copies of evidence, (such as a marriage certificate and documents showing the legal termination of all other marriages, and an adoption decree), to demonstrate that you qualify as his or her child.
  - **Other basis for eligibility.** Attach copies of documents proving that you are eligible for the classification.

Where To File.
File this application at the local INS office having jurisdiction over your place of residence.

Fee. The fee for this application is $120, except that it is $95 if you are less than 14 years old. The fee must be submitted in the exact amount. It cannot be refunded. **DO NOT MAIL CASH.** All checks and money orders must be drawn on a bank or other institution located in the United States and must be payable in United States currency. The check or money order should be made payable to the Immigration and Naturalization Service, except that:
- If you live in Guam, and are filing this application in Guam, make your check or money order payable to the "Treasurer, Guam."

- If you live in the Virgin Islands, and are filing this application in the Virgin Islands, make your check or money order payable to the "Commissioner of Finance of the Virgin Islands."

Checks are accepted subject to collection. An uncollected check will render the application and any document issued invalid. A charge of $5.00 will be imposed if a check in payment of a fee is not honored by the bank on which it is drawn.

Processing Information.
Acceptance. Any application that is not signed, or is not accompanied by the correct fee, will be rejected with a notice that the application is deficient. You may correct the deficiency and resubmit the application. An application is not considered properly filed until accepted by the Service.

Initial processing. Once an application has been accepted, it will be checked for completeness, including submission of the required initial evidence. If you do not completely fill out the form, or file it without required initial evidence, you will not establish a basis for eligibility, and we may deny your application.

Requests for more information. We may request more information or evidence. We may also request that you submit the originals of any copy. We will return these originals when they are no longer required.

Interview. After you file your application you will be notified to appear at an INS office to answer questions about the application. You will be required to answer these questions under oath or affirmation. You must bring your Arrival-Departure Record (Form I-94) and any passport to the interview.

Decision. You will be notified in writing of the decision on your application.

Travel Outside the U.S. If you plan to leave the U.S. to go to any other country, including Canada or Mexico, before a decision is made on your application, contact the INS office processing your application before you leave. In many cases, leaving the U.S. without advance written permission will result in automatic termination of your application. Also, you may experience difficulty upon returning to the U.S. if you do not have written permission to reenter.

Penalties.
If you knowingly and willfully falsify or conceal a material fact or submit a false document with this request, we will deny the benefit you are filing for, and may deny any other immigration benefit. In addition, you will face severe penalties provided by law, and may be subject to criminal prosecution.

Privacy Act Notice.
We ask for the information on this form, and associated evidence, to determine if you have established eligibility for the immigration benefit you are filing for. Our legal right to ask for this information is in 8 USC 1255 and 1259. We may provide this information to other government agencies. Failure to provide this information, and any requested evidence, may delay a final decision or result in denial of your request.

Paperwork Reduction Act Notice.
We try to create forms and instructions that are accurate, can be easily understood, and which impose the least possible burden on you to provide us with information. Often this is difficult because some immigration laws are very complex. The estimated average time to complete and file this application is computed as follows: (1) **20** minutes to learn about the law and form; (2) **25** minutes to complete the form; and (3) **270** minutes to assemble and file the application, including the required interview and travel time; for a total estimated average of **5** hours and **15** minutes per application. If you have comments regarding the accuracy of this estimate, or suggestions for making this form simpler, you can write to both the Immigration and Naturalization Service, 425 I Street, N.W., Room 5304, Washington, D.C. 20536; and the Office of Management and Budget, Paperwork Reduction Project, OMB No. 1115-0053, Washington, D.C. 20503.

SUPPLEMENTAL INFORMATION FOR FILING I-485

UNMARRIED MINOR CHILDREN OF USC'S

PARENTS OF USC'S

CERTAIN EMPLOYMENT BASED PREFERENCES AND
DERIVATIVE SPOUSE & CHILDREN

1. Medical exam (I-693) completed by a medical doctor on the INS
list, signed by you and by the doctor. If you are unable to have
an X-ray due to pregnancy, the doctor on the INS list may be
willing to give:

   - A tine Test or
   - A PPD Test (Purified Protein Derivative).

2. Evidence of Financial Support:

   - Job letters on letterhead paper.

   - Pay statements for past 2 months.

   - Current and previous year W-2's.

   - Bank letters on bank stationery for all accounts (showing
     title of account(s), date opened, current balance).

If you are supported by someone else, all the above must be
submitted with their affidavit of support (I-134) completely
executed and notarized.

If you have been in the U.S. more than 3 months, submit sworn
affidavits and supporting documentation (as above) showing how
you supported yourself or were supported since your arrival in
the U.S.

3. If you or your spouse has ever received any public assistance
(Welfare, Food Stamps, SSI, Medicaid, etc.), submit evidence from
the Department of Social Services that you are no longer
receiving assistance.   Also, submit verification from the
Department of Social Services that they are aware of your marital
status and the date you married.

4. If you have ever been arrested by anyone, anywhere, for any
reason, whether there was a dismissal, an exoneration, a quilty
plea or a conviction, you must submit complete documentary
evidence of the disposition of your case with your application.
This applies even if you are arrested between the date you file
your application and the date you are notified of action taken on
your case.

(OVER)

ER-737 NYC
02/93 3230

5.   Original or Certified copies of supporting documents must be submitted. A certified English translation must be submitted for every foreign language document.

6.   Form G-325A completely filled out.

7.   Color Photos & Fingerprint Charts (FD 258)-Although the instructions on the application require that you submit two(2) photographs and one (1) fingerprint chart, it is highly recommended and strongly suggested that you submit four (4) photographs and two (2) fingerprints charts when you file your application for adjustment of status. This will avoid any unnecessary delay in completing your case and additional trips to this office if your fingerprint chart is rejected by the FBI for any reason or the Texas Card Facility in Arlington, Texas, cannot issue an I-551 (Alien Registration Card) to you because the photograph has been damaged.

8.   Every applicant under 21 must be accompanied by a parent or legal guardian to the interview, if one is scheduled.

9. I-130 Visa Petition and appropriate supporting documents or notice of an approved relative visa petition
                                or
Notice of an approved I-140 Visa petition accompanied by original or certified copies of supporting documents and evidence that the principal alien will continue employment with the same individual or firm for whom he or she is lawfully employed as a nonimmigrant (e.g. Hs Ls Es) (Submit a copy of Nonimmigrant Visa from alien's passport).

NOTE: YOU MUST COMPLY WITH THESE INSTRUCTIONS AS WELL A THOSE ON THE I-485 APPLICATION ITSELF.

INSTRUCTIONS: USE TYPEWRITER. BE SURE ALL COPIES ARE LEGIBLE. Failure to answer fully all questions delays action.
Do Not Remove Carbons. If typewriter is not available, print heavily in block letters with ball-point pen.

U.S. Department of Justice

Immigration and Naturalization Service

FORM G-325A

BIOGRAPHIC INFORMATION

OMB No. 1115-0066

(Family name)	(First name)	(Middle name)	☐ MALE ☐ FEMALE	BIRTHDATE(Mo.-Day-Yr.)	NATIONALITY	FILE NUMBER A

ALL OTHER NAMES USED (Including names by previous marriages)		CITY AND COUNTRY OF BIRTH	SOCIAL SECURITY NO. (If any)

	FAMILY NAME	FIRST NAME	DATE, CITY AND COUNTRY OF BIRTH(If known)	CITY AND COUNTRY OF RESIDENCE
FATHER				
MOTHER(Maiden name)				

HUSBAND(If none, so state) OR WIFE	FAMILY NAME (For wife, give maiden name)	FIRST NAME	BIRTHDATE	CITY & COUNTRY OF BIRTH	DATE OF MARRIAGE	PLACE OF MARRIAGE

FORMER HUSBANDS OR WIVES(if none, so state)

FAMILY NAME (For wife, give maiden name)	FIRST NAME	BIRTHDATE	DATE & PLACE OF MARRIAGE	DATE AND PLACE OF TERMINATION OF MARRIAGE

APPLICANT'S RESIDENCE LAST FIVE YEARS. LIST PRESENT ADDRESS FIRST.

STREET AND NUMBER	CITY	PROVINCE OR STATE	COUNTRY	FROM MONTH	FROM YEAR	TO MONTH	TO YEAR
						PRESENT TIME	

APPLICANT'S LAST ADDRESS OUTSIDE THE UNITED STATES OF MORE THAN ONE YEAR

STREET AND NUMBER	CITY	PROVINCE OR STATE	COUNTRY	FROM MONTH	FROM YEAR	TO MONTH	TO YEAR

APPLICANT'S EMPLOYMENT LAST FIVE YEARS. (IF NONE, SO STATE.) LIST PRESENT EMPLOYMENT FIRST

FULL NAME AND ADDRESS OF EMPLOYER	OCCUPATION(SPECIFY)	FROM MONTH	FROM YEAR	TO MONTH	TO YEAR
				PRESENT TIME	

Show below last occupation abroad if not shown above. (Include all information requested above.)

THIS FORM IS SUBMITTED IN CONNECTION WITH APPLICATION FOR: ☐ NATURALIZATION ☐ STATUS AS PERMANENT RESIDENT ☐ OTHER (SPECIFY)	SIGNATURE OF APPLICANT	DATE

Are all copies legible? ☐ Yes	IF YOUR NATIVE ALPHABET IS IN OTHER THAN ROMAN LETTERS, WRITE YOUR NAME IN YOUR NATIVE ALPHABET IN THIS SPACE:

PENALTIES: SEVERE PENALTIES ARE PROVIDED BY LAW FOR KNOWINGLY AND WILLFULLY FALSIFYING OR CONCEALING A MATERIAL FACT.

APPLICANT: BE SURE TO PUT YOUR NAME AND ALIEN REGISTRATION NUMBER IN THE BOX OUTLINED BY HEAVY BORDER BELOW.

COMPLETE THIS BOX (Family name)	(Given name)	(Middle name)	(Alien registration number)

Form **9003** (January 1992)	Department of the Treasury—Internal Revenue Service ## Additional Questions to be Completed by All Applicants ## for Permanent Residence in the United States	OMB Clearance No. 1545-1065 Expires 8-31-94

This form must accompany your application for permanent residence in the United States

Privacy Act Notice: Your responses to the following questions will be provided to the Internal Revenue Service pursuant to Section 6039E of the Internal Revenue Code of 1986. Use of this information is limited to that needed for tax administration purposes. Failure to provide this information may result in a $500 penalty unless failure is due to reasonable cause.

On the date of issuance of the Alien Registration Receipt Card, the Immigration and Naturalization Service will send the following information to the Internal Revenue Service: your name, social security number, address, date of birth, alien identification number, occupation, class of admission, and answers to IRS Form 9003.

Name *(Last—Surname—Family)*   *(First—Given)*   *(Middle Initial)*

Taxpayer Identification Number ....

Enter your Social Security Number (SSN) if you have one. If you do not have an SSN but have used a Taxpayer Identification Number issued to you by the Internal Revenue Service, enter that number. Otherwise, write "NONE" in the space provided; i.e., " |_|_|_|_|_|N,O,N,E| ".

	Mark appropriate column	
	Yes	**No**
1. **Are you self-employed?** Mark "yes" if you own and actively operate a business in which you share in the profits other than as an investor.		
2. **Have you been in the United States for 183 days or more during any one of the three calendar years immediately preceding the current calendar year?** Mark "yes" if you spent 183 days or more (not necessarily consecutive) in the United States during any one of the three prior calendar years whether or not you worked in the United States.		
3. **During the last three years did you receive income from sources in the United States?** Mark "yes" if you received income paid by individuals or institutions located in the United States. Income includes, but is not limited to, compensation for services provided by you, interest, dividends, rents, and royalties.		
4. **Did you file a United States Individual Income Tax Return (Forms 1040, 1040A, 1040EZ or 1040NR) in any of the last three years?**		

If you answered yes to question 4, for which tax year was the last return filed? .... 19 __ __

Paperwork Reduction Act Notice—We ask for the information on this form to carry out the Internal Revenue laws of the United States. You are required to give us the information. We need it to ensure that you are complying with these laws and to allow us to figure and collect the right amount of tax.

The time needed to complete and file this form will vary depending on individual circumstances. The estimated average time is 5 minutes. If you have comments concerning the accuracy of this time estimate or suggestions for making this form more simple, we would be happy to hear from you. You can write to both the **Internal Revenue Service**, Washington, DC 20224. Attention: IRS Reports Clearance Officer, T:FP, and **Office of Management and Budget**. Paperwork Reduction Project (1545-1065) Washington, DC 20503. **DO NOT send this form to either of these offices. Instead, return it to the appropriate office of the Department of State or the Immigration and Naturalization Service.**

Remarks

Cat. No. 10126D

Form **9003** (Rev. 1-92)

U.S. Department of Justice
Immigration and Naturalization Service

Medical Examination of Aliens Seeking Adjustment of Status

(Please type or print clearly)
I certify that on the date shown I examined:

1. Name (Last in CAPS)	3. File number (A number)
	4. Sex ☐ Male ☐ Female
(First) (Middle Initial)	5. Date of birth (Month/Day/Year)
2. Address (Street number and name) (Apt. number)	6. Country of birth
(City) (State) (ZIP Code)	7. Date of examination (Month/Day/Year)

General Physical Examination: I examined specifically for evidence of the conditions listed below. My examination revealed;

☐ No apparent defect, disease, or disability.

☐ The conditions listed below were found (check all boxes that apply).

Class A Conditions

☐ Chancroid   ☐ Hansen's disease, infectious   ☐ Mental defect   ☐ Psychopathic personality
☐ Chronic alcoholism   ☐ HIV infection   ☐ Mental retardation   ☐ Sexual deviation
☐ Gonorrhea   ☐ Insanity   ☐ Narcotic drug addiction ☐ Syphilis, infectious
☐ Granuloma inguinale   ☐ Lymphogranuloma venereum   ☐ Previous occurrence of one ☐ Tuberculosis, active
                                                                or more attacks of insanity

Class B Conditions

☐ Hansen's disease, not infectious   ☐ Tuberculosis, not active

☐ Other physical defect, disease or disability (specify below).

Examination for Tuberculosis - Tuberculin Skin Test

☐ Reaction _____ mm   ☐ No reaction   ☐ Not done

Doctor's name (please print)   Date read

Examination for Tuberculosis - Chest X-Ray Report

☐ Abnormal   ☐ Normal   ☐ Not done

Doctor's name (please print)   Date read

Serologic Test for Syphilis

☐ Reactive Titer (confirmatory test performed)   ☐ Nonreactive

Test Type

Doctor's name (please print)   Date read

Serologic Test for HIV Antibody

☐ Positive (confirmed by Western biot)   ☐ Negative

Test Type

Doctor's name (please print)   Date read

Immunization Determination (DTP, OPV, MMR, Td-Refer to *PHS Guidelines* for recommendations.)

☐ Applicant is current for recommended age-specific immunizations.

☐ Applicant is not current for recommended age-specific immunizations and I have encouraged that appropriate immunizations be obtained.

REMARKS:

Civil Surgeon Referral for Follow-up of Medical Condition

☐ The alien named above has applied for adjustment of status. A medical examination conducted by me identified the conditions above which require resolution before medical clearance is granted or for which the alien may seek medical advice. Please provide follow-up services or refer the alien to an appropriate health care provider. The actions necessary for medical clearance are detailed on the reverse of this form.

Follow-up Information:

The alien named above has complied with the recommended health follow-up.

Doctor's name and address (please type or print clearly)   Doctor's signature   Date

---

Applicant Certification:

I certify that I understand the purpose of the medical examination, I authorize the required tests to be completed, and the information on this form refers to me.

Signature   Date

Civil Surgeon Certification:

My examination showed the applicant to have met the medical examination and health follow-up requirements for adjustment of status.

Doctor's name and address (please type or print clearly)   Doctor's signature   Date

---

Form I 693 (Rev. 09/01/87)

ORIGINAL: INS A-FILE

Instructions To Alien Applying for Adjustment of Status

A medical examination is necessary as part of your application for adjustment of status. Please communicate immediately with one of the physicians on the attached list to arrange for your medical examination, which must be completed before your status can be adjusted. The purpose of the medical examination is to determine if you have certain health conditions which may need further follow-up. The information requested is required in order for a proper evaluation to be made of your health status. The results of your examination will be provided to an Immigration officer and may be shared with health departments and other public health or cooperating medical authorities. All expenses in connection with this examination must be paid by you.

The examining physician may refer you to your personal physician or a local public health department and you must comply with some health follow-up or treatment recommendations for certain health conditions before your status will be adjusted.

This form should be presented to the examining physician. You must sign the form in the presence of the examining physician. *The law provides severe penalties for knowingly and willfully falsifying or concealing a material fact or using any false documents in connection with this medical examination. The medical examination must be completed in order for us to process your application.*

Medical Examination and Health Information

A medical examination is necessary as part of your application for adjustment of status. You should go for your medical examination as soon as possible. You will have to choose a doctor from a list you will be given. The list will have the names of doctors or clinics in your area that have been approved by the Immigration and Naturalization Service for this examination. You must pay for the examination. If you become a temporary legal resident and later apply to become a permanent resident, you may need to have another medical examination at that time.

The purpose of the medical examination is to find out if you have certain health conditions which may need further follow-up. The doctor will examine you for certain physical and mental health conditions. You will have to take off your clothes. If you need more tests because of a condition found during your medical examination, the doctor may send you to your own doctor or to the local public health department. For some conditions, before you can become a temporary or permanent resident, you will have to show that you have followed the doctor's advice to get more tests or take treatment.

If you have any records of immunizations (vaccinations), you should bring them to show to the doctor. This is especially important for pre-school and school-age children. The doctor will tell you if any more immunizations are needed, and where you can get them (usually at your local public health department). It is important for your health that you follow the doctor's advice and go to get any immunizations.

One of the conditions you will be tested for is tuberculosis. If you are 15 years of age or older, you will be required to have a chest X-ray examination. *Exception:* If you are pregnant or applying for adjustment of status under the Immigration Reform and Control Act of 1986, you may choose to have either a chest X-ray or a tuberculin skin test. If you choose the skin test you will have to return in 2 - 3 days to have it checked. If you do not have any reaction to the skin test you will not need any more tests for tuberculosis. If you do have any reaction to the skin test, you will also need to have a chest X-ray examination. If the doctor thinks you are infected with tuberculosis, you may have to go to the local health department and more tests may have to be done. The doctor will explain these to you.

If you are 14 years of age or younger, you will not need to have a test for tuberculosis unless a member of your immediate family has chest X-ray findings that may be tuberculosis. If you are in this age group and you do have to be tested for tuberculosis, you may choose either the chest X-ray or the skin test.

You must also have a blood test for syphilis if you are 15 years of age or older.

You will also be tested to see if you have the human immuno-deficiency virus (HIV) infection. This virus is the cause of AIDS. If you have this virus, it may damage your body's ability to fight off other disease. The blood test you will take will tell if you have been exposed to this virus.

Instructions To Physician Performing the Examination

Please medically examine for adjustment of status the individual presenting this form. The medical examination should be performed according to the U.S. Public Health Service "Guidelines for Medical Examination of Aliens in the United States" and Supplements, which have been provided to you separately.

If the applicant is free of medical defects listed in Section 212(a) of the Immigration and Nationality Act, endorse the form in the space provided. While in your presence, the applicant must also sign the form in the space provided. You should retain one copy for your files and return all other copies in a sealed envelope to the applicant for presentation at the immigration interview.

If the applicant has a health condition which requires follow-up as specified in the "Guidelines for Medical Examination of Aliens in the United States" and Supplements, complete the referral information on the pink copy of the medical examination form, and advise the applicant that appropriate follow-up must be obtained before medical clearance can be granted. Retain the blue copy of the form for your files and return all other copies to the applicant in a sealed envelope. The applicant should return to you when the necessary follow-up has been completed for your final verification and signature. *Do not* sign the form until the applicant has met health follow-up requirements. All medical documents, including chest X-ray films if a chest X-ray examination was performed, should be returned to the applicant upon final medical clearance.

Instructions To Physician Providing Health Follow-up

The individual presenting this form has been found to have a medical condition(s) requiring resolution before medical clearance for adjustment of status can be granted. Please evaluate the applicant for the condition(s) identified.

The requirements for clearance are outlined on the reverse of this page. When the individual has completed clearance requirements, please sign the form in the space provided and return the medical examination form to the applicant.

Form I-693 (Rev. 09/01/87) N

APPLICANT

LEAVE BLANK

TYPE OR PRINT ALL INFORMATION IN BLACK

| LAST NAME NAM | FIRST NAME | MIDDLE NAME |

FBI   LEAVE BLANK

SIGNATURE OF PERSON FINGERPRINTED

ALIASES AKA

| O R I | NYINSNY00 USINS NEW YORK, NY |

RESIDENCE OF PERSON FINGERPRINTED

DATE OF BIRTH DOB
Month   Day   Year

CITIZENSHIP CTZ

| SEX | RACE | HGT. | WGT. | EYES | HAIR | PLACE OF BIRTH POB |

DATE   SIGNATURE OF OFFICIAL TAKING FINGERPRINTS

YOUR NO. OCA

LEAVE BLANK

EMPLOYER AND ADDRESS

FBI NO. FBI

CLASS _____

ARMED FORCES NO. MNU

REASON FINGERPRINTED

SOCIAL SECURITY NO. SOC

REF. _____

MISCELLANEOUS NO. MNU

| 1. R. THUMB | 2. R. INDEX | 3. R. MIDDLE | 4. R. RING | 5. R. LITTLE |

| 6. L. THUMB | 7. L. INDEX | 8. L. MIDDLE | 9. L. RING | 10. L. LITTLE |

LEFT FOUR FINGERS TAKEN SIMULTANEOUSLY   L THUMB   R THUMB   RIGHT FOUR FINGERS TAKEN SIMULTANEOUSLY

FEDERAL BUREAU OF INVESTIGATION
UNITED STATES DEPARTMENT OF JUSTICE
WASHINGTON, D.C. 20537

APPLICANT

LEAVE THIS SPACE BLANK

TO OBTAIN CLASSIFIABLE FINGERPRINTS:

1. USE BLACK PRINTER'S INK.
2. DISTRIBUTE INK EVENLY ON INKING SLAB.
3. WASH AND DRY FINGERS THOROUGHLY.
4. ROLL FINGERS FROM NAIL TO NAIL, AND AVOID ALLOWING FINGERS TO SLIP.
5. BE SURE IMPRESSIONS ARE RECORDED IN CORRECT ORDER.
6. IF AN AMPUTATION OR DEFORMITY MAKES IT IMPOSSIBLE TO PRINT A FINGER, MAKE A NOTATION TO THAT EFFECT IN THE INDIVIDUAL FINGER BLOCK.
7. IF SOME PHYSICAL CONDITION MAKES IT IMPOSSIBLE TO OBTAIN PERFECT IMPRESSIONS, SUBMIT THE BEST THAT CAN BE OBTAINED WITH A MEMO STAPLED TO THE CARD EXPLAINING THE CIRCUMSTANCES.
8. EXAMINE THE COMPLETED PRINTS TO SEE IF THEY CAN BE CLASSIFIED, BEARING IN MIND THAT MOST FINGERPRINTS FALL INTO THE PATTERNS SHOWN ON THIS CARD (OTHER PATTERNS OCCUR INFREQUENTLY AND ARE NOT SHOWN HERE).

1. LOOP

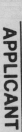

CENTER OF LOOP

DELTA

THE LINES BETWEEN CENTER OF LOOP AND DELTA MUST SHOW

2. WHORL

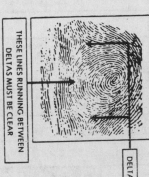

DELTAS

THESE LINES RUNNING BETWEEN DELTAS MUST BE CLEAR

3. ARCH

ARCHES HAVE NO DELTAS

FD-258 (REV. 12-29-82)

THIS CARD FOR USE BY:

1. LAW ENFORCEMENT AGENCIES IN FINGERPRINTING APPLICANTS FOR LAW ENFORCEMENT POSITIONS.*

2. OFFICIALS OF STATE AND LOCAL GOVERNMENTS FOR PURPOSES OF EMPLOYMENT, LICENSING, AND PERMITS, AS AUTHORIZED BY STATE STATUTES AND APPROVED BY THE ATTORNEY GENERAL OF THE UNITED STATES. LOCAL AND COUNTY ORDINANCES, UNLESS SPECIFICALLY BASED ON APPLICABLE STATE STATUTES DO NOT SATISFY THIS REQUIREMENT.*

3. U.S. GOVERNMENT AGENCIES AND OTHER ENTITIES REQUIRED BY FEDERAL LAW.**

4. OFFICIALS OF FEDERALLY CHARTERED OR INSURED BANK-ING INSTITUTIONS TO PROMOTE OR MAINTAIN THE SECURITY OF THOSE INSTITUTIONS.

INSTRUCTIONS:

*1. PRINTS MUST FIRST BE CHECKED THROUGH THE APPROPRIATE STATE IDENTIFICATION BUREAU, AND ONLY THOSE FINGERPRINTS FOR WHICH NO DISQUALIFYING RECORD HAS BEEN FOUND LOCALLY SHOULD BE SUBMITTED FOR FBI SEARCH.

2. PRIVACY ACT OF 1974 (P.L. 93-579) REQUIRES THAT FEDERAL, STATE, OR LOCAL AGENCIES INFORM INDIVIDUALS WHOSE SOCIAL SECURITY NUMBER IS REQUESTED WHETHER SUCH DISCLOSURE IS MANDATORY OR VOLUNTARY, BASIS OF AUTHORITY FOR SUCH SOLICITATION, AND USES WHICH WILL BE MADE OF IT.

*3. IDENTITY OF PRIVATE CONTRACTORS SHOULD BE SHOWN IN SPACE "EMPLOYER AND ADDRESS". THE CONTRIBUTOR IS THE NAME OF THE AGENCY SUBMITTING THE FINGERPRINT CARD TO THE FBI.

4. FBI NUMBER, IF KNOWN, SHOULD ALWAYS BE FURNISHED IN THE APPROPRIATE SPACE.

MISCELLANEOUS NO. - RECORD, OTHER ARMED FORCES NO.; PASSPORT NO. (PP); ALIEN REGISTRATION NO. (AR); PORT SECURITY CARD NO. (PS); SELECTIVE SERVICE NO. (SS); VETERANS ADMINISTRATION CLAIM NO. (VA).

☆ U.S.G.P.O. 1990-262-201/20000

U.S. Department of Justice
Immigration and Naturalization Service

OMB No. 1115-0145

Petition to Remove the Conditions on Residence

START HERE - Please Type or Print

Part 1. Information about you.

Family Name	Given Name	Middle Initial

Address - C/O:

Street Number and Name		Apt. #
City	State or Province	
Country	ZIP/Postal Code	

Date of Birth (month/day/year)	Country of Birth
Social Security #	A #

Conditional residence expires on (month/day/year)	

Mailing address if different from residence in C/O:

Street Number and Name		Apt #
City	State or Province	
Country	ZIP/Postal Code	

Part 2. Basis for petition (check one).

a. ☐ My conditional residence is based on my marriage to a U.S. citizen or permanent resident, and we are filing this petition together.

b. ☐ I am a child who entered as a conditional permanent resident and I am unable to be included in a Joint Petition to Remove the Conditional Basis of Alien's Permanent Residence (Form I-751) filed by my parent(s).

My conditional residence is based on my marriage to a U.S. citizen or permanent resident, but I am unable to file a joint petition and I request a waiver because: (check one)

c. ☐ My spouse is deceased.

d. ☐ I entered into the marriage in good faith, but the marriage was terminated though divorce/annulment.

e. ☐ I am a conditional resident spouse who entered in to the marriage in good faith, or I am a conditional resident child, who has been battered or subjected to extreme mental cruelty by my citizen or permanent resident spouse or parent.

f. ☐ The termination of my status and deportation from the United States would result in an extreme hardship.

Part 3. Additional information about you.

Other names used (including maiden name):	Telephone #
Date of Marriage	Place of Marriage

If your spouse is deceased, give the date of death (month/day/year)

Are you in deportation or exclusion proceedings? ☐ Yes ☐ No

Was a fee paid to anyone other than an attorney in connection with this petition? ☐ Yes ☐ No

Form I-751 (Rev. 12-4-91)   *Continued on back.*

FOR INS USE ONLY

Returned	Receipt
_____	
_____	
Resubmitted	
_____	
_____	
Reloc Sent	
_____	
_____	
Reloc Rec'd	
_____	
_____	
☐ Applicant Interviewed	

Remarks

Action

To Be Completed by Attorney or Representative, if any

☐ Fill in box if G-28 is attached to represent the applicant

VOLAG#

ATTY State License #

Part 3. Additional Information about you. (con't)

Since becoming a conditional resident, have you ever been arrested, cited, charged, indicted, convicted, fined or imprisoned for breaking or violating any law or ordinace (excluding traffic regulations), or committed any crime for which you were not arrested? ☐ Yes ☐ No

If you are married, is this a different marriage than the one through which conditional residence status was obtained? ☐ Yes ☐ No

Have you resided at any other address since you became a permanent resident? ☐ Yes ☐ No *(If yes, attach a list of all addresses and dates.)*

Is your spouse currently serving employed by the U. S. government and serving outside the U.S.? ☐ Yes ☐ No

Part 4. Information about the spouse or parent through whom you gained your conditional residence

Family Name	Given Name	Middle Initial	Phone Number ( )
Address			

Date of Birth *(month/day/year)*	Social Security #	A#

Part 5. Information about your children. *List all your children. Attach another sheet if necessary*

	Name	Date of Birth *(month/day/year)*	If in U.S., give A#, current immigration status and U.S. Address	Living with you?
1				☐ Yes ☐ No
2				☐ Yes ☐ No
3				☐ Yes ☐ No
4				☐ Yes ☐ No

Part 6. Complete if you are requesting a waiver of the joint filing petition requirement based on extreme mental cruelty.

Evaluator's ID Number:	State: ☐☐	Number: ☐☐☐☐☐☐☐	Expires on *(month/day/year)*	Occupation

Last Name	First Name	Address

Part 7. Signature. *Read the information on penalties in the instructions before completing this section. If you checked block "a" in Part 2 your spouse must also sign below.*

I certify, under penalty of perjury under the laws of the United States of America, that this petition, and the evidence submitted with it, is all true and correct. If conditional residence was based on a marriage, I further certify that the marriage was entered into in accordance with the laws of the place where the marriage took place, and was not for the purpose of procuring an immigration benefit. I also authorize the release of any information from my records which the Immigration and Naturalization Service needs to determine eligibility for the benefit being sought.

Signature	Print Name	Date
Signature of Spouse	Print Name	Date

Please note: If you do not completely fill out this form, or fail to submit any required documents listed in the instructions, then you cannot be found eligible for the requested benefit, and this petition may be denied.

Part 8. Signature of person preparing form if other than above.

I declare that I prepared this petition at the request of the above person and it is based on all information of which I have knowledge.

Signature	Print Name	Date
Firm Name and Address		

Form I-751 (Rev. 12-4-91)   * GPO : 1992 0 - 316-463

Purpose Of This Form.

This form is for a conditional resident who obtained such status through marriage to apply to remove the conditions on his or her residence.

Who May File.

If you were granted conditional resident status through marriage to a U.S. citizen or permanent resident, use this form to petition for the removal of those conditions. Your petition should be filed jointly by you and the spouse through whom you obtained conditional status if you are still married. However, you can apply for a waiver of this joint filing requirement on this form if:

- you entered into the marriage in good faith, but your spouse subsequently died;
- you entered into the marriage in good faith, but the marriage was later terminated due to divorce or annulment;
- you entered into the marriage in good faith, and remain married, but have been battered or subjected to extreme mental cruelty by your U.S. citizen or permanent resident spouse; or
- the termination of your status, and deportation, would result in extreme hardship.

You may include your conditional resident children in your petition, or they can file separately.

General Filing Instructions.

Please answer all questions by typing or clearly printing in black ink. Indicate that an item is not applicable with "N/A". If an answer is "none," write "none". If you need extra space to answer any item, attach a sheet of paper with your name and your alien registration number (A#), and indicate the number of the item to which the answer refers. You must file your petition with the required Initial Evidence. Your petition must be properly signed and accompanied by the correct fee. If you are under 14 years of age, your parent or guardian may sign the petition in your behalf.

Translations. Any foreign language document must be accompanied by a full English translation which the translator has certified as complete and correct, and by the translator's certification that he or she is competent to translate from the foreign language into English.

Copies. If these instructions state that a copy of a document may be filed with this petition, and you choose to send us the original, we may keep that original for our records.

Initial Evidence.

Alien Registration Card. You must file your petition with a copy of your alien registration card, and with a copy of the alien registration card of any of your conditional resident children you are including in your petition.

Evidence of the relationship. Submit copies of documents indicating that the marriage upon which you were granted conditional status was entered into in "good faith", and was not for the purpose of circumventing immigration laws. You should submit copies of as many documents as you wish to establish this fact and to demonstrate the circumstances of the relationship from the date of the marriage to date, and to demonstrate any circumstances surrounding the end of the relationship, if it has ended. The documents should cover as much of the period since your marriage as possible. Examples of such documents are:

- Birth certificate(s) of child(ren) born to the marriage.
- Lease or mortgage contracts showing joint occupancy and/or ownership of your communal residence.
- Financial records showing joint ownership of assets and joint responsibility for liabilities, such as joint savings and checking accounts, joint federal and state tax returns, insurance policies which show the other as the beneficiary, joint utility bills, joint installment or other loans.
- Other documents you consider relevant to establish that your marriage was not entered into in order to evade the immigration laws of the United States.

- Affidavits sworn to or affirmed by at least 2 people who have known both of you since your conditional residence was granted and have personal knowledge of your marriage and relationship. (Such persons may be required to testify before an immigration officer as to the information contained in the affidavit.) The original affidavit must be submitted, and it must also contain the following information regarding the person making the affidavit: his or her full name and address; date and place of birth; relationship to you or your spouse, if any; and full information and complete details explaining how the person acquired his or her knowledge. Affidavits must be supported by other types of evidence listed above.

If you are filing to waive the joint filing requirement due to the death of your spouse, also submit a copy of the death certificate with your petition.

If you are filing to waive the joint filing requirement because your marriage has been terminated, also submit a copy of the divorce decree or other document terminating or annulling the marriage with your petition.

If you are filing to waive the joint filing requirement because you and/or your conditional resident child were battered or subjected to extreme mental cruelty, also file your petition with the following.

- Evidence of the physical abuse, such as copies of reports or official records issued by police, judges, medical personnel, school officials, and representatives of social service agencies, and original affidavits as described under *Evidence of the Relationship*; or
- Evidence of the extreme mental cruelty, and an original evaluation by a professional recognized by the Service as an expert in the field. These experts include clinical social workers, psychologists and psychiatrists. A clinical social worker who is not licensed only because the State in which he or she practices does not provide for licensing is considered a licensed professional recognized by the Service if he or she is included by the National Association of Social Workers or is certified by the American Board of Examiners in Clinical Social Work. Each evaluation must contain the professional's full name, professional address and license number. It must also identify the licensing, certifying or registering authority.
- A copy of your divorce decree if your marriage was terminated by divorce on grounds of physical abuse or mental cruelty.

If you are filing for a waiver of the joint filing requirement because the termination of your status, and deportation would result in "extreme hardship", you must also file your petition with evidence your deportation would result in hardship significantly greater than the hardship encountered by other aliens who are deported from this country after extended stays. The evidence must relate only to those factors which arose since you became a conditional resident.

If you are a child filing separately from your parent, also file your petition with a full explanation as to why you are filing separately, along with copies of any supporting documentation.

When To File.

Filing jointly. If you are filing this petition jointly with your spouse, you must file it during the 90 days immediately before the second anniversary of the date you were accorded conditional resident status. This is the date your conditional residence expires. However, if you and your spouse are outside the United States on orders of the U.S. Government during the period in which the petition must be filed, you may file it within 90 days of your return to the U.S.

Filing with a request that the joint filing requirement be waived.
You may file this petition at any time after you are granted conditional resident status and before you are deported.

Effect Of Not Filing. If this petition is not filed, you will automatically lose your permanent resident status as of the second anniversary of the date on which you were granted this status. You will then become deportable from the United States. If your failure to file was through no fault of your own, you may file your petition late with a written explanation and request that INS excuse the late filing. Failure to file before the expiration date may be excused if you demonstrate when you file the application that the delay was due to extraordinary circumstances beyond your control and that the length of the delay was reasonable.

Effect of Filing.
Filing this petition extends your conditional residence for six months. You will receive a filing receipt which you should carry with your alien registration card (Form I-551). If you travel outside the U.S. during this period, you may present your card and the filing receipt to be readmitted.

Where To File.
If you live in Connecticut, Delaware, District of Columbia, Maine, Maryland, Massachusetts, New Hampshire, New Jersey, New York, Pennsylvania, Puerto Rico, Rhode Island, Vermont, Virgin Islands, Virginia, or West Virginia, mail your petition to: USINS Eastern Service Center, 75 Lower Welden Street, St. Albans, VT 05479-0001.

If you live in Alabama, Arkansas, Florida, Georgia, Kentucky, Louisiana, Mississippi, New Mexico, North Carolina, Oklahoma, South Carolina, Tennessee, or Texas, mail your petition to: USINS Southern Service Center, P.O. Box 152122, Dept. A, Irving, TX 75015-2122.

If you live in Arizona, California, Guam, Hawaii, or Nevada, mail your petition to: USINS Western Service Center, P.O. Box 30111, Laguna Niguel, CA 92607-0111.

If you live in elsewhere in the U.S., mail your petition to: USINS Northern Service Center, 100 Centennial Mall North, Room B-26, Lincoln, NE 68508.

Fee.
The fee for this petition is $75.00. The fee must be submitted in the exact amount. It cannot be refunded. **DO NOT MAIL CASH.**

All checks and money orders must be drawn on a bank or other institution located in the United States and must be payable in United States currency. The check or money order should be made payable to the Immigration and Naturalization Service, except that:
- If you live in Guam, and are filing this petition in Guam, make your check or money order payable to the "Treasurer, Guam".
- If you are living in the Virgin Islands, and are filing this application in the Virgin Islands, make your check or money order payable to the "Commissioner of Finance of the Virgin Islands".

Checks are accepted subject to collection. An uncollected check will render the application and any document issued invalid. A charge of $5.00 will be imposed if a check in payment of a fee is not honored by the bank on which it is drawn.

Processing Information.
Acceptance. Any petition that is not signed, or is not accompanied by the correct fee, will be rejected with a notice that the petition is deficient. You may correct the deficiency and resubmit the petition. A petition is not considered properly filed until accepted by the Service.

Initial processing. Once a petition has been accepted, it will be checked for completeness, including submission of the required initial evidence. If you do not completely fill out the form, or file it without required initial evidence, you will not establish a basis for eligibility, and we may deny your petition.

Requests for more information or interview. We may request more information or evidence, or we may request that you appear at an INS office for an interview. We may also request that you submit the originals of any copy. We will return these originals when they are no longer required.

Decision. You will be advised in writing of the decision on your petition.

Penalties.
If you knowingly and willfully falsify or conceal a material fact or submit a false document with this request, we will deny the benefit you are filing for, and may deny any other immigration benefit. In addition, you will face severe penalties provided by law, and may be subject to criminal prosecution.

Privacy Act Notice.
We ask for the information on this form, and associated evidence, to determine if you have established eligibility for the immigration benefit you are filing for. Our legal right to ask for this information is in 8 USC 1184, 1255 and 1258. Failure to provide this information, and any requested evidence, may delay a final decision or result in denial of your request.

All the information provided on this form, including addresses, are protected by the Privacy Act and the Freedom of Information Act. This information will not be released in any form whatsoever to a third party, other than another government agency, who requests it without a court order, or without your written consent, or, in the case of a child, the written consent of the parent or legal guardian who filed the form on the child's behalf.

Paperwork Reduction Act Notice.
We try to create forms and instructions that are accurate, can be easily understood, and which impose the least possible burden on you to provide us with information. Often this is difficult because some immigration laws are very complex. The estimated average time to complete and file this application is as follows: (1) 15 minutes to learn about the law and form; (2) 15 minutes to complete the form; and (3) 50 minutes to assemble and file the petition; for a total estimated average of 1 hour and 20 minutes per petition. If you have comments regarding the accuracy of this estimate, or suggestions for making this form simpler, you can write to both the Immigration and Naturalization Service, 425 I Street, N.W., Room 5304, Washington, D.C. 20536; and the Office of Management and Budget, Paperwork Reduction Project, OMB No. 1115-0145 Washington, D.C. 20503.

U.S. Department of Justice
Immigration and Naturalization Service

OMB #1115-0008
Application to File Declaration of Intention

START HERE - Please Type or Print

Part 1. Information about you.

Family Name	Given Name	Middle Initial

Address - In care of

Street Number and Name	Apt. #

City	State or Province

Country	ZIP/Postal Code

Date of Birth (Month/Day/Year)	Country of Birth

Social Security #	A #

Part 2. Processing Information.

Date you became a permanent resident (Month/Day/Year)

Since you were admitted to the United States for Permanent Residence have you been absent for a period of six months or longer? ☐ No ☐ Yes - Attach a list of departure/arrival dates of all absences

Part 3. Signature. Read the information on penalties in the instructions before completing this section. You must be in the United States when you file this application. (Also sign the second page).

I desire to declare my intention to become a citizen of the United States. I certify under penalty of perjury under the laws of the United States of America that this application, and the evidence submitted with it, is all true and correct. I authorize release of any information from my records which the Immigration and Naturalization Service needs to determine eligibility for the benefit I am seeking.

Signature	Date

Part 4. Signature of person preparing form if other than above. (sign below)

I declare that I prepared this application at the request of the above person and it is based on all information of which I have any knowledge.

Signature	Date

Print your Name

Firm Name

Firm Address

Form N-300 (Rev. 10/01/91)   *Continued on next page.*

Original to be retained by the Service -

Duplicate to be given to :

Family Name	Given Name	Middle Initial

Address   C/O

Street Number and Name		Apt. #
City	State or Province	
Country	ZIP/Postal Code	

Date of Birth (Month/Day/Year)	Country of Birth
Social Security #	A #

Affix
Photograph
Here

Not valid unless INS
Seal applied below

I am over the age of 18 years, have been lawfully admitted to the United States for permanent residence and am now residing in the United States pursuant to such admission.

I hereby declare my intention in good faith to become a citizen of the United States and I certify that the photographs affixed to the original and duplicate hereof are a likeness of me and were signed by me.

I do swear (affirm) that the statements I have made and the intentions I have expressed in this declaration of intention subscribed by me are true to the best of my knowledge and belief.

Signature of Applicant

Signature of Authorizing official

Purpose Of This Form.

This form is for a permanent resident to apply for a Declaration of Intention to become a citizen of the United States. A Declaration of Intention is not required for naturalization, but may be required by some States if you wish to engage in certain occupations or professions, or obtain various licenses.

Who May File.

If you are a lawful permanent resident over the age of 18, you may apply for a Declaration of Intention. You must be in the United States when you file this application.

Initial Evidence.

You must file your application with:

- A copy of your alien registration receipt card (I-151 or I-551) or other evidence that you are a permanent resident;
- Photos. You must submit 2 identical natural color photographs of yourself taken within 30 days of this application. The photos must have a white background, be unmounted, printed on thin paper and be glossy and unretouched. They should show a three-quarter frontal profile showing the right side of your face, with your right ear visible and with your head bare (unless you are wearing a headdress as required by a religious order of which you are a member). The photos should be no larger than 2 X 2 inches, with the distance from the top of the head to just below the chin about 1 and 1/4 inches. Lightly print your A# on the back of each photo with a pencil. Sign your full name in English on the front of each photograph in pen in such a manner as to not obscure your features.

Where To File.

File this application at the local Service office having jurisdiction over your place of residence.

Fee.

The fee for this petition is $70.00. The fee must be submitted in the exact amount.

It cannot be refunded. DO NOT MAIL CASH. All checks and money orders must be drawn on a bank or other institution located in the United States and must be payable in United States currency. The check or money order should be made payable to the Immigration and Naturalization Service, except that:

- If you live in Guam, and are filing this application in Guam, make your check or money order payable to the "Treasurer, Guam.
- If you live in the Virgin Islands, and are filing this application in the Virgin Islands, make your check or money order payable to the "Commissioner of Finance of the Virgin Islands."

Checks are accepted subject to collection. An uncollected check will render the application and any document issued invalid. A charge of $5.00 will be imposed if a check in payment of a fee is not honored by the bank on which it is drawn.

Processing Information.

Acceptance. Any application that is not signed or is not accompanied by the correct fee will be rejected with a notice that the application is deficient. You may correct the deficiency and resubmit the application. However, an application is not considered properly filed until accepted by the Service.

Initial processing. Once the application has been accepted, it will be checked for completeness, including submission of the required initial evidence. If you do not completely fill out the form, or file it without required initial evidence, you will not establish a basis for eligibility and we may deny your application.

Requests for more information. We may request more information or evidence, or we may request that you appear at an INS office for an interview. We may also request that you submit the originals of any copy. We will return these originals when they are no longer needed.

Decision. You will be notified in writing of the decision on your application. If your application is approved, the Declaration of Intention will be issued.

Penalties.

If you knowingly and willfully falsify or conceal a material fact or submit a false document with this request, we will deny the benefit you are filing for, and may deny any other immigration benefit. In addition, you will face severe penalties provided by law, and may be subject to criminal prosecution.

Privacy Act Notice.

We ask for the information on this form, and associated evidence, to determine if you have established eligibility for the immigration benefit you are filing for. Our legal right to ask for this information is in 8 USC 1445. We may provide this information to other government agencies. Failure to provide this information, and any requested evidence, may delay a final decision or result in denial of your request.

Paperwork Reduction Act Notice.

We try to create forms and instructions that are accurate, can be easily understood, and which impose the least possible burden on you to provide us with information. Often this is difficult because some immigration laws are very complex. The estimated average time to complete and file this petition is as follows: (1) 5 minutes to learn about the law and form; (2) 5 minutes to complete the form; and (3) 35 minutes to assemble and file the petition; for an total estimated average of 45 minutes per petition. If you have comments regarding the accuracy of this estimate, or suggestions for making this form simpler, you can write to both the Immigration and Naturalization Service, 425 I Street, N.W., Room 5304, Washington, D.C. 20536; and the Office of Management and Budget, Paperwork Reduction Project, OMB No. 1115-0008, Washington, D.C. 20503.

U.S. Department of Justice
Immigration and Naturalization Service

OMB #1115-0009
Application for Naturalization

START HERE - Please Type or Print

Part 1. Information about you.

Family Name	Given Name	Middle Initial

U.S. Mailing Address - Care of

Street Number and Name		Apt. #
City	County	
State	ZIP Code	

Date of Birth (month/day/year)	Country of Birth
Social Security #	A #

Part 2. Basis for Eligibility (check one).

a. ☐ I have been a permanent resident for at least five (5) years .

b. ☐ I have been a permanent resident for at least three (3) years and have been married to a United States Citizen for those three years.

c. ☐ I am a permanent resident child of United States citizen parent(s) .

d. ☐ I am applying on the basis of qualifying military service in the Armed Forces of the U.S. and have attached completed Forms N-426 and G-325B

e. ☐ Other. (Please specify section of law) _____

Part 3. Additional information about you.

Date you became a permanent resident (month/day/year)	Port admitted with an immigrant visa or INS Office where granted adjustment of status.

Citizenship

Name on alien registration card (if different than in Part 1)

Other names used since you became a permanent resident (including maiden name)

Sex ☐ Male ☐ Female	Height	Marital Status: ☐ Single ☐ Married	☐ Divorced ☐ Widowed

Can you speak, read and write English ? ☐No ☐Yes.

Absences from the U.S.:

Have you been absent from the U.S. since becoming a permanent resident? ☐ No ☐Yes.

If you answered **"Yes"** , complete the following. Begin with your most recent absence. If you need more room to explain the reason for an absence or to list more trips, continue on separate paper.

Date left U.S.	Date returned	Did absence last 6 months or more?	Destination	Reason for trip
		☐ Yes ☐ No		
		☐ Yes ☐ No		
		☐ Yes ☐ No		
		☐ Yes ☐ No		
		☐ Yes ☐ No		
		☐ Yes ☐ No		

Form N-400 (Rev. 07/17/91)N   ***Continued on back.***

Part 4. Information about your residences and employment.

A. List your addresses during the last five (5) years or since you became a permanent resident, whichever is less. Begin with your current address. If you need more space, continue on separate paper:

Street Number and Name, City, State, Country, and Zip Code	Dates (month/day/year)	
	From	To

B. List your employers during the last five (5) years. List your present or most recent employer first. If none, write "None". If you need more space, continue on separate paper.

Employer's Name	Employer's Address	Dates Employed (month/day/year)		Occupation/position
	Street Name and Number - City, State and ZIP Code	From	To	

Part 5. Information about your marital history.

A. Total number of times you have been married _____ . If you are now married, complete the following regarding your husband or wife.

Family name	Given name	Middle initial

Address

Date of birth (month/day/year)	Country of birth	Citizenship
Social Security#	A# (if applicable)	Immigration status (If not a U.S. citizen)

Naturalization (If applicable)
(month/day/year)   Place   (City, State)

If you have ever previously been married or if your current spouse has been previously married, please provide the following on separate paper: Name of prior spouse, date of marriage, date marriage ended, how marriage ended and immigration status of prior spouse.

Part 6. Information about your children.

B. Total Number of Children _____ Complete the following information for each of your children. If the child lives with you, state "with me" in the address column; otherwise give city/state/country of child's current residence. If deceased, write "deceased" in the address column. If you need more space, continue on separate paper.

Full name of child	Date of birth	Country of birth	Citizenship	A - Number	Address

Form N-400 (Rev 07/17/91)N   **Continued on next page**

Part 7. Additional eligibility factors.

Please answer each of the following questions. If your answer is **"Yes"**, explain on a separate paper.

1. Are you now, or have you ever been a member of, or in any way connected or associated with the Communist Party, or ever knowingly aided or supported the Communist Party directly, or indirectly through another organization, group or person, or ever advocated, taught, believed in, or knowingly supported or furthered the interests of communism? ☐ Yes ☐ No

2. During the period March 23, 1933 to May 8, 1945, did you serve in, or were you in any way affiliated with, either directly or indirectly, any military unit, paramilitary unit, police unit, self-defense unit, vigilante unit, citizen unit of the Nazi party or SS, government agency or office, extermination camp, concentration camp, prisoner of war camp, prison, labor camp, detention camp or transit camp, under the control or affiliated with:

    a. The Nazi Government of Germany? ☐ Yes ☐ No

    b. Any government in any area occupied by, allied with, or established with the assistance or cooperation of, the Nazi Government of Germany? ☐ Yes ☐ No

3. Have you at any time, anywhere, ever ordered, incited, assisted, or otherwise participated in the persecution of any person because of race, religion, national origin, or political opinion? ☐ Yes ☐ No

4. Have you ever left the United States to avoid being drafted into the U.S. Armed Forces? ☐ Yes ☐ No

5. Have you ever failed to comply with Selective Service laws? ☐ Yes ☐ No

    If you have registered under the Selective Service laws, complete the following information:

        Selective Service Number: _____ Date Registered: _____

    If you registered before 1978, also provide the following:

        Local Board Number: _____ Classification: _____

6. Did you ever apply for exemption from military service because of alienage, conscientious objections or other reasons? ☐ Yes ☐ No

7. Have you ever deserted from the military, air or naval forces of the United States? ☐ Yes ☐ No

8. Since becoming a permanent resident, have you ever failed to file a federal income tax return? ☐ Yes ☐ No

9. Since becoming a permanent resident, have you filed a federal income tax return as a nonresident or failed to file a federal return because you considered yourself to be a nonresident? ☐ Yes ☐ No

10. Are deportation proceedings pending against you, or have you ever been deported, or ordered deported, or have you ever applied for suspension of deportation? ☐ Yes ☐ No

11. Have you ever claimed in writing, or in any way, to be a United States citizen? ☐ Yes ☐ No

12. Have you ever:

    a. been a habitual drunkard? ☐ Yes ☐ No

    b. advocated or practiced polygamy? ☐ Yes ☐ No

    c. been a prostitute or procured anyone for prostitution? ☐ Yes ☐ No

    d. knowingly and for gain helped any alien to enter the U.S. illegally? ☐ Yes ☐ No

    e. been an illicit trafficker in narcotic drugs or marijuana? ☐ Yes ☐ No

    f. received income from illegal gambling? ☐ Yes ☐ No

    g. given false testimony for the purpose of obtaining any immigration benefit? ☐ Yes ☐ No

13. Have you ever been declared legally incompetent or have you ever been confined as a patient in a mental institution? ☐ Yes ☐ No

14. Were you born with, or have you acquired in same way, any title or order of nobility in any foreign State? ☐ Yes ☐ No

15. Have you ever:

    a. knowingly committed any crime for which you have not been arrested? ☐ Yes ☐ No

    b. been arrested, cited, charged, indicted, convicted, fined or imprisoned for breaking or violating any law or ordinance excluding traffic regulations? ☐ Yes ☐ No

(If you answer yes to 15, in your explanation give the following information for each incident or occurrence the **city**, **state**, and **country**, where the offense took place, the **date** and **nature** of the offense, and the **outcome** or **disposition** of the case).

Part 8. Allegiance to the U.S.

If your answer to any of the following questions is **"NO"**, attach a full explanation:

  1. Do you believe in the Constitution and form of government of the U.S.? ☐ Yes ☐ No

  2. Are you willing to take the full Oath of Allegiance to the U.S.? (see instructions) ☐ Yes ☐ No

  3. If the law requires it, are you willing to bear arms on behalf of the U.S.? ☐ Yes ☐ No

  4. If the law requires it, are you willing to perform noncombatant services in the Armed Forces of the U.S.? ☐ Yes ☐ No

  5. If the law requires it, are you willing to perform work of national importance under civilian direction? ☐ Yes ☐ No

Form N-400 (Rev 07/17/91)N

Part 9. Memberships and organizations.

A. List your present and past membership in or affiliation with every organization, association, fund, foundation, party, club, society, or similar group in the United States or in any other place. Include any military service in this part. If none, write "none". Include the name of organization, location, dates of membership and the nature of the organization. If additional space is needed, use separate paper.

_____

_____

_____

_____

Part 10. Complete only if you checked block " C " in Part 2.

How many of your parents are U.S. citizens? ☐ One   ☐ Both   (Give the following about one U.S. citizen parent:)

Family Name	Given Name	Middle Name

Address

Basis for citizenship:	Relationship to you (check one): ☐ natural parent ☐ adoptive parent
☐ Birth	
☐ Naturalization Cert. No.	☐ parent of child legitimated after birth

If adopted or legitimated after birth, give date of adoption or, legitimation: *(month/day/year)* _____

Does this parent have legal custody of you?   ☐ Yes   ☐ No

(Attach a copy of relating evidence to establish that you are the child of this U.S. citizen and evidence of this parent's citizenship.)

Part 11. Signature. *(Read the information on penalties in the instructions before completing this section).*

I certify or, if outside the United States, I swear or affirm, under penalty of perjury under the laws of the United States of America that this application, and the evidence submitted with it, is all true and correct. I authorize the release of any information from my records which the Immigration and Naturalization Service needs to determine eligibility for the benefit I am seeking.

Signature _____   **Date** _____

Please Note: *If you do not completely fill out this form, or fail to submit required documents listed in the instructions, you may not be found eligible for naturalization and this application may be denied.*

Part 12. Signature of person preparing form if other than above. *(Sign below)*

I declare that I prepared this application at the request of the above person and it is based on all information of which I have knowledge.

Signature _____   **Print Your Name** _____   **Date** _____

Firm Name and Address

DO NOT COMPLETE THE FOLLOWING UNTIL INSTRUCTED TO DO SO AT THE INTERVIEW

I swear that I know the contents of this application, and supplemental pages 1 through_____, that the corrections , numbered 1 through_____, were made at my request, and that this amended application, is true to the best of my knowledge and belief.

_____
(Complete and true signature of applicant)

Subscribed and sworn to before me by the applicant.

_____
(Examiner's Signature)   Date

Form N-400 (Rev 07/17/91)N

INSTRUCTIONS

Purpose of This Form.
This form is for use to apply to become a naturalized citizen of the United States.

Who May File.
You may apply for naturalization if:
- you have been a lawful permanent resident for five years;
- you have been a lawful permanent resident for three years, have been married to a United States citizen for those three years, and continue to be married to that U.S. citizen;
- you are the lawful permanent resident child of United States citizen parents; or
- you have qualifying military service.

Children under 18 may automatically become citizens when their parents naturalize. You may inquire at your local Service office for further information. If you do not meet the qualifications listed above but believe that you are eligible for naturalization, you may inquire at your local Service office for additional information.

General Instructions.
Please answer all questions by typing or clearly printing in black ink. Indicate that an item is not applicable with "N/A". If an answer is "none," write "none". If you need extra space to answer any item, attach a sheet of paper with your name and your alien registration number (A#), if any, and indicate the number of the item.

Every application must be properly signed and filed with the correct fee. If you are under 18 years of age, your parent or guardian must sign the application.

If you wish to be called for your examination at the same time as another person who is also applying for naturalization, make your request on a separate cover sheet. Be sure to give the name and alien registration number of that person.

Initial Evidence Requirements.
You must file your application with the following evidence:

A copy of your alien registration card.

Photographs. You must submit two color photographs of yourself taken within 30 days of this application. These photos must be glossy, unretouched and unmounted, and have a white background. Dimension of the face should be about 1 inch from chin to top of hair. Face should be 3/4 frontal view of right side with right ear visible. Using pencil or felt pen, lightly print name and A#, if any, on the back of each photo. This requirement may be waived by the Service if you can establish that you are confined because of age or physical infirmity.

Fingerprints. If you are between the ages of 14 and 75, you must sumit your fingerprints on Form FD-258. Fill out the form and write your Alien Registration Number in the space marked "Your No. OCA" or "Miscellaneous No. MNU". Take the chart and these instructions to a police station, sheriff's office or an office of this Service, or other reputable person or organization for fingerprinting. (You should contact the police or sheriff's office before going there since some of these offices do not take fingerprints for other government agencies.) You must sign the chart in the presence of the person taking your fingerprints and have that person sign his/her name, title, and the date in the space provided. Do not bend, fold, or crease the fingerprint chart.

U.S. Military Service. If you have ever served in the Armed Forces of the United States at any time, you must submit a completed Form G-325B. If your application is based on your military service you must also submit Form N-426, "Request for Certification of Military or Naval Service."

Application for Child. If this application is for a permanent resident child of U.S. citizen parents, you must also submit copies of the child's birth certificate, the parents' marriage certificate, and evidence of the parents' U.S. citizenship. If the parents are divorced, you must also submit the divorce decree and evidence that the citizen parent has legal custody of the child.

Where to File.
File this application at the local Service office having jurisdiction over your place of residence.

Fee.
The fee for this application is $90.00. The fee must be submitted in the exact amount. It cannot be refunded. DO NOT MAIL CASH.

All checks and money orders must be drawn on a bank or other institution located in the United States and must be payable in United States currency. The check or money order should be made payable to the Immigration and Naturalization Service, except that:
- If you live in Guam, and are filing this application in Guam, make your check or money order payable to the "Treasurer, Guam."
- If you live in the Virgin Islands, and are filing this application in the Virgin Islands, make your check or money order payable to the "Commissioner of Finance of the Virgin Islands."

Checks are accepted subject to collection. An uncollected check will render the application and any document issued invalid. A charge of $5.00 will be imposed if a check in payment of a fee is not honored by the bank on which it is drawn.

Processing Information.

Rejection. Any application that is not signed or is not accompanied by the proper fee will be rejected with a notice that the application is deficient. You may correct the deficiency and resubmit the application. However, an application is not considered properly filed until it is accepted by the Service.

Requests for more information. We may request more information or evidence. We may also request that you submit the originals of any copy. We will return these originals when they are no longer required.

Interview. After you file your application, you will be notified to appear at a Service office to be examined under oath or affirmation. This interview may not be waived. If you are an adult, you must show that you have a knowledge and understanding of the history, principles, and form of government of the United States. There is no exemption from this requirement.

You will also be examined on your ability to read, write, and speak English. If on the date of your examination you are more than 50 years of age and have been a lawful permanent resident for 20 years or more, or you are 55 years of age and have been a lawful permanent resident for at least 15 years, you will be exempt from the English language requirements of the law. If you are exempt, you may take the examination in any language you wish.

Oath of Allegiance. If your application is approved, you will be required to take the following oath of allegiance to the United States in order to become a citizen:

"I hereby declare, on oath, that I absolutely and entirely renounce and abjure all allegiance and fidelity to any foreign prince, potentate, state or sovereignty, of whom or which I have heretofore been a subject or citizen; that I will support and defend the Constitution and laws of the United States of America against all enemies, foreign and domestic; that I will bear true faith and allegiance to the same; that I will bear arms on behalf of the United States when required by the law; that I will perform noncombatant service in the armed forces of the United States when required by the law; that I will perform work of national importance under civilian direction when required by the law; and that I take this obligation freely without any mental reservation or purpose of evasion; so help me God."

If you cannot promise to bear arms or perform noncombatant service because of religious training and belief, you may omit those statements when taking the oath. "Religious training and belief" means a person's belief in relation to a Supreme Being involving duties superior to those arising from any human relation, but does not include essentially political, sociological, or philosophical views or merely a personal moral code.

Oath ceremony. You may choose to have the oath of allegiance administered in a ceremony conducted by the Service or request to be scheduled for an oath ceremony in a court that has jurisdiction over the applicant's place of residence. At the time of your examination you will be asked to elect either form of ceremony. You will become a citizen on the date of the oath ceremony and the Attorney General will issue a Certificate of Naturalization as evidence of United States citizenship.

If you wish to change your name as part of the naturalization process, you will have to take the oath in court.

Penalties.

If you knowingly and willfully falsify or conceal a material fact or submit a false document with this request, we will deny the benefit you are filing for, and may deny any other immigration benefit. In addition, you will face severe penalties provided by law, and may be subject to criminal prosecution.

Privacy Act Notice.

We ask for the information on this form, and associated evidence, to determine if you have established eligibility for the immigration benefit you are filing for. Our legal right to ask for this information is in 8 USC 1439, 1440, 1443, 1445, 1446, and 1452. We may provide this information to other government agencies. Failure to provide this information, and any requested evidence, may delay a final decision or result in denial of your request.

Paperwork Reduction Act Notice.

We try to create forms and instructions that are accurate, can be easily understood, and which impose the least possible burden on you to provide us with information. Often this is difficult because some immigration laws are very complex. Accordingly, the reporting burden for this collection of information is computed as follows: (1) learning about the law and form, 20 minutes; (2) completing the form, 25 minutes; and (3) assembling and filing the application (includes statutory required interview and travel time, after filing of application), 3 hours and 35 minutes, for an estimated average of 4 hours and 20 minutes per response. If you have comments regarding the accuracy of this estimate, or suggestions for making this form simpler, you can write to both the Immigration and Naturalization Service, 425 I Street, N.W., Room 5304, Washington, D.C. 20536; and the Office of Management and Budget, Paperwork Reduction Project, OMB No. 1115-0009, Washington, D.C. 20503.